BLUEBERRY GOD

The Education of a Finnish-American

Blueberry God

THE EDUCATION OF A FINNISH-AMERICAN

REINO NIKOLAI HANNULA

QUALITY HILL BOOKS
SAN LUIS OBISPO

ACKNOWLEDGEMENTS

I want to thank all the individuals who helped in the writing and publishing of this narrative. I appreciate the suggestions made by Amy Van Hazinga who read the original manuscript. Dr. John Lowry, my mathematics department colleague, gave me numerous ideas and encouragement after reading and editing the first draft of my narrative. My wife helped edit the final manuscript. I think her editing helped smooth the story. I also want to thank my brother Tarmo for his moral support to continue whenever I felt like scuttling the whole project, Elsa Linden for the information she provided me about the early days in Ash Street Hall, and Leon Winehill for his poem and his reminiscences of the first NRA strike.

May Coors, my colleague in the computer science department, designed both the title page and the book cover. I am deeply indebted for those two professional touches. *Isä's* granddaughter, Wendy Brouillet, is responsible for the sketches and the map of Gates Hill. Her sketch of Gates Pond is exactly as I remember it.

I am indebted to Holt, Rinehart and Winston for permission to quote from two of Robert Frost's poems—*Blueberries* and *Birches*. I thank Dr. Keijo Virtanen of the Institute of General History, University of Turku (Finland) for permission to use the Work Peoples College flyer.

I also thank Camera Ready Arts of San Luis Obispo for the excellent work in preparing my narrative for the printer. It was a great pleasure to work with the owners, Howard and Margaret Bond.

All of the opinions expressed in this narrative are mine. The assistance given by the individuals I have named does not imply that they agree with my point of view.

The Thrill That Comes Once in a Lifetime   BY WEBSTER

From *The New York Herald Tribune* (March 6, 1940)

The American Finns basked in the reflection of the prestige gained by their compatriots—the Finland Finns—who paid their war debt (World War I) and who stood up to the Soviet Union in the Winter War.

The Peasant Paavo

High among the moors of Saarijärvi,
On his frosty farm, lived peasant Paavo,
Diligently managing his farming,
But his fruits he from the Lord expected.
There he dwelt in peace with wife and children;
Earned for them their bread, a scanty living;
Dug his ditches, ploughed his fields and sowed them.

Springtime came, and from the sprouting corn-plot,
Half the crops went off with melting snow-drifts;
Summer came and then the pelting showers
Beat the ears to earth—just half the harvest;
Autumn came—the frost took the remainder.

Paavo's wife now tore her hair, lamenting:
"Paavo, Paavo, thou ill-fated husband!
Seize thy staff, the Lord hath us forsaken;
Begging bread is hard, but worse is dying!"
Paavo grasped his spouse's hand and uttered:
"The Lord is trying us and not forsaking.
Thou must mix with bark our bread together;
Ditches I will dig in double numbers;
From the Lord will I expect a blessing."

So she mixed with bark their bread together;
Ditches dug he then in double numbers;
Sold his flocks, and buying grain he sowed it.

Springtime came, and from the sprouting corn-fields
Nothing floated off with melting snow-drifts;
Summer came, and now the pelting showers
Beat the ears to earth—just half the harvest;
Autumn came—the frost took the remainder.

Paavo's wife now beat her breast, lamenting:
"Paavo, Paavo, thou ill-fated husband!
Let us die, the Lord hath us forsaken;
Death is hard, but ten times worse is living!"
Paavo grasped his spouse's hand and uttered:
"The Lord is trying us and not forsaking.
Twice as much bark thou must be mixing
With the bread; I'll dig as many ditches.
From the Lord do I expect a blessing."

Twice as much bark the wife now mixed
With the bread; he dug as many ditches;
Sold his kine, and buying corn he sowed it.

Spring-time came, and from the sprouting corn-field
Nothing floated off with melting snow-drifts;
Summer came and now the pelting showers
Beat no ears to earth in ripening corn-fields;
Autumn came—the frost no more destroying,
Left the golden crops to greet the reaper.

Peasant Paavo bowed the knee, and uttered:
"The Lord hath tried us only, not forsaken."
And his wife knelt down, and murmured with him:
"The Lord hath tried us only, not forsaken."
And with joy spoke she unto her husband:
"Paavo, Paavo, seize thy scythe, rejoicing;
It is time to live a life of gladness,
It is time to leave the bark for ever,
And to make our bread of pure corn only."
Paavo grasped his spouse's hand and uttered:
"O Woman, no one bears his trials so calmly
As the man who ne'er forsakes his brother;
Twice as much of bark with bread then mix thou,
For frost-bitten stands our neighbour's cornfield."

Johan Runeberg (1804-1877)

I fondly dedicate this book to all the first generation Finnish-Americans—without regard to their political and religious beliefs—who immigrated to the New World in 1880-1914. Thank you for the stimulating and unique culture you built.

CONTENTS

PREFACE

This book is divided into three parts; the main narrative, a Finnish glossary, and a section called *Notes, Views, and Vignettes*. The glossary is not a Finnish-English dictionary. It doesn't have to be since each Finnish word is translated at the point it is used. My glossary is intended to be a simple guide to the pronunciation of the Finnish words and names that appear in the narrative. I included the glossary because I felt that part of the fun of reading this book, especially if you are descended from one of the Finnish immigrants of 1880 to 1914, will be in learning how to pronounce such names as *Otto Huhtanen* and such words as *mustikka* and *kokko*.

The *Notes, Views, and Vignettes* is my innovative footnote section. It contains more than just footnotes, however. Since my frame of reference may be quite different than that of the average reader, I have given additional information about many concepts and incidents there. For example, if you are interested in the derivation of the term *Finglish*, look it up in the *Notes, Views, and Vignettes*. This section also has a recipe for blueberry soup and Finnish rye bread. There is even an explanation of why I cannot give a simple recipe for one of the Gardner (Massachusetts) Finnish-American favorite breads—the Polish *limppu* (sour-dough rye with caraway seeds).

You will notice that I don't use footnote symbols very often. I believe those little numbers tend to distract from a story. The references for most statements are in the *Notes, Views, and Vignettes*, however, referenced by keywords and page numbers. And they are even cross-referenced in a very easy to follow way—a form that is much easier to follow than the notation in a standard reference section. I think you will enjoy my narrative more if you use the *News, Views, and Vignettes* as a handy source of additional information.

APOLOGIA

I am a mathematician and computer scientist. At least I have a master's degree in mathematics from UCLA and I teach computer science at California Polytechnic State University in San Luis Obispo. I enrolled in UCLA to study mathematics in 1955 when I was 37 years old and I started my computer science education at the University of London in 1968. I have written two computer science textbooks, each dealing with an aspect of the IBM360/370 Operating System. I suppose it is, therefore, pertinent to ask what motivated me to go outside my field to write this narrative about the first generation Finnish-American community. I shall try to explain here what provoked me into doing that.

I am a history buff. One day, entirely by chance, I started to browse through a delightful-looking history of my hometown, Gardner. I recognized when I opened the book that it was a polite history, replete with detailed statistics including the names of the original Yankee settlers of Gardner. I expected, of course, some background material about the various ethnic groups that made up the greater portion of the town's population when I was a boy.

I thumbed through the book, very curious to find out how the author had handled the story of the Finnish-Americans since that is a "hot little potato." To a lesser extent, I was also curious how she had handled the labor movement in Gardner since I had, as a teenager, participated in organizing the still existing furniture workers union.

How had she and her Committee for Historical Research interpreted the facts? I was shocked. They hadn't. They had ignored the Finnish-Americans! These Gardner historians didn't bother to include the Finnish-American community in their history even though at least 10% of that city's population has had, from 1910 to the present, a Finnish background. Was it oversight? Or was that little potato too hot too handle?

Ash Street Hall, one of the most thriving ethnic community centers and the major nucleus of Finnish-American life in Gardner from 1913 to 1945, just never existed. *Into A.C.*, an Ash Street Hall organization which was the largest athletic club in Gardner from 1920 to 1938, never existed. The Ash Street Hall little theatre staged more productions from 1913 to 1945 than the combined efforts of all other little theatre groups in all of Gardner's history. In fact, the Ash Street Hall little theatre was one of the most active little theatres in the entire Commonwealth of Massachusetts. Had it really existed?

I tried to shrug it off but I felt as if I were throwing my identity away. I investigated further. I discovered that Finnish-American history nationwide is written, with some notable exceptions (See *Notes, Views, and Vignettes)*, to please the new middle-class second and third generation Finnish-Americans who don't want to be embarrased by their backgrounds. Maybe, I thought, the Gardner historian and her research committee omitted the Finnish-Americans from their narrative to spare the feelings of their Finnish friends.

Then I thought about my teenage surrogate Ash Street Hall parents: Oikemus, Annala, Puranen, Hanninen, Manninen, Walkonen, Aalto, Ahtio, Virta, Glad, Johnson, and all the others. They belong in Gardner's history. They contributed to its culture. They contributed to its labor movement. How could I let those indomitable men and women drop into oblivion without some effort on my part? I had to try to resurrect my friends of the 1930's. I had to write a story about my Finnish background as I remember it and to write about my old immigrant friends, the first generation Finnish-Americans, who, way ahead of their time, struggled to make the United States a more equitable society.

I hope you, dear reader, enjoy the story.

Chapter One

PROLOGUE

This is my history of the first generation Finnish-Americans who immigrated to our country in the years 1890-1914.* This is my story of the unique culture they built here. That culture impressed its ideals, its aspirations, and its mores deep within me; so deep that I can't shake them off no matter how hard I try. I am a hopeless "Finnophile" of the Finnish-American culture. That's sad in a way because that culture no longer exists. It's gone, gone forever. I wish, though, I could live through it once more. Maybe this book is a fulfillment of that wish. For one thing, I was surprised, when writing the first eight chapters, at my recall. The incidents were in my memory as if they had happened yesterday.

I recognize that anyone who writes a history has a responsibility to his or her audience to state his or her bias. That is part of the purpose of this first chapter. The other part is to introduce a character who might be called the "hero" of the Finnish epic poem *Kalevala*. My political and social attitudes are given in the first section of this chapter. My religious feelings are given in the second section. Bear in mind, as you read this chapter, that my present day attitudes and beliefs are not the same attitudes and beliefs I held as a boy. That's the reason for the subtitle of this book: *The Education of a Finnish-American*.

---

*The Finnish-Americans, those who emigrated from Finland to the United States, are called the first generation Finnish-Americans in this book. I and the other children of these immigrants are the second generation Finnish-Americans. This ordering of the hyphenated Americans—first promulgated by Louis Adamic in his book *From Many Lands*—is followed in my narrative.

MY BIAS

Some of this Finnish-American story has been told before but a great many of these histories leave me unsatisfied. Some of the writers distort the story. They tend to portray the American Finns of 1890-1920 as if they were living a comfortable middle-class existence in 1890. They are inclined to forget that the American Finn in the early part of this century was an unskilled laborer who was exploited almost beyond human endurance in that very cruel industrial age.

The first eight chapters tries to draw the picture of the Finnish-American environment of 1920-1936 in which I grew up. Some of my experiences are surely unique but I am certain that many a second generation Finnish-American youngster had the same doubts and the same aspirations as I had. But my folks ran a boarding-house. Isn't that different? I don't think so. Every Finnish-American community had a boardinghouse. There even was a Hannula boardinghouse in Astoria (Oregon). So I don't feel that my formative years were particularly different from that of hundreds of other Finnish-American kids.

The second half of my narrative covers Finnish-American history from 1906 to about 1920. I have tried to portray the American economic and political scene of 1900-1920 so that the Finnish-American attitudes of that time might be better understood. After all, the Finnish-American philosophy of that era was not much different from the philosophy of most progressive-minded dissenters who lived then. And, it should be borne in mind as you read my story, that there were a great many American dissenters at that time. There were far more dissenters then, in proportion to population, than there are today. The American Finn was in the main stream of American progressive thinking in the years from 1900 to 1920.

One thing I would like to set straight in this chapter. I love my country. I love the United States of America. I think our country gives, or tries to give, everyone an equal opportunity in the pursuit of happiness. I think we should all take a pledge to "defend and uphold the Constitution of the United States." I must confess one fact. Although I would rather live in the United States than anywhere else; I do have second and third choices. They are England and Finland, respectively.

The love I have for my country, however, does not blind me to

Ash Street Hall around 1918

the fact that the men in charge of industry and the government in the United States in 1890-1920 were often outlaws. The government officials were often the lackeys of the industrial barons. Many government officials violated their oaths of office much too often,* and without any qualms.

Our school history textbooks are inclined to picture all former American officials, be they Presidents, Congressmen, Senators, governors, or just plain sheriffs as heroes—as the "good guys", the men with the "white hats". One can easily get a false impression from the popular American histories of the first two decades of this century because (to many thoughtful Americans) the real heroes of that era were the dissenters—the populists, the single-taxers, the socialists, the wobblies, and other progressives—not the industrial barons and the government officials. These dissenters fought hard, lost most of their battles; but their struggle gave us the America we enjoy today. I'm proud that the first generation Finnish-American community was part of that great dissent. They contributed a bit, even if it was only a small bit, to make the American governments—local, state and federal—more responsive to human rights and human needs.

---

*Once, of course, is much too often.

The industrial barons and their government lackeys almost destroyed the American dream at the turn of the century. Our country might have suffered the fate of Brazil whose government, controlled by greedy, grasping entrepreneurs (the same type of men who controlled American industry 70 years ago), allows almost 1,000,000 abandoned children (under 10 years of age) to fend for themselves. These children, with no education, subsist on an animal level. They will never be brought into the mainstream of Brazilian life. That could have happened to our country.

What saved our country from Brazil's fate? What brought about the basic changes in our governments—local, state, and federal—so that they did begin to respond to human needs? These governments did, indeed, change. The change was slow and almost imperceptible until the Great Depression; then the pace quickened. I admit I didn't know what caused the shift in the basic philosophy in our country but I like to believe, it makes me feel good to believe, that it was the constant pressure and the effective educational work of the many dissenting groups. An appreciation of the Finnish-American contribution to this *Great Dissent* of 1900-1920 is the main purpose of this book.

The dominant influence in the Finnish-American communities from 1906 to 1920 was democratic socialism.* Is that surprising to you? It shouldn't be because the American democratic socialist movement, which will be discussed later in greater detail, was gaining adherents so rapidly in the first decade of this century that even many conservative political observers predicted woefully and wrongly that the Socialist Party would elect the White House occupant by 1920. Bear in mind, too, as you read this book that socialism, world-wide, was in its heyday.

I might be justified in saying that the Gardner (Massachusetts) Finnish socialist organization was a surrogate parent to me in my teens. Those Gardner Finnish-American socialists accepted me (and influenced me) in the 1930's even though I was born into what they called, quite sarcastically, a *pikkuporvari* (petty bourgeoisie) family. My religious education came from a strict fundamentalist church. I absorbed its beliefs literally and almost went insane to discard them. I think socialism and those Finnish

---

*Democratic socialism, the socialism of the Finnish-Americans in 1906 to 1920, is the only socialism this book talks about. The "democratic" qualifier is, therefore, dropped from here on.

4

socialists helped me over that hurdle. Hence I owe socialism and those first generation American Finns deep gratitude for helping me unload that tremendous burden of Christian fundamentalism. They helped set me free.

I don't recall now whether the "socialist bug" bit me first and then I discovered the socialist Finn hall on Ash street in Gardner *or* if I discovered the Finn hall first and then the "socialist bug," which may have been lying dormant in the walls, bit me. At any rate I did join the Ash Street Hall athletic club, always called by its Finnish name *Into* (*Spirit*, in the sense of being eager and ardent) when I was 12. At about 14, I—perhaps *we* is more correct—organized a circle of the Young Peoples Socialist League.

The *Into* Athletic Club was the largest sports group in the City of Gardner during the depression era. Our membership was well over 200. The club, incidentally, was run by its members—none over 20 years of age—without advice or counselling by the first generation Finns. They did subsidize us, however, by providing us with the hall facilities for a minimal fee.

We, the *Yipsels* (as the young socialists were called) were never able to garner more than three members. But just 10 years previously Gardner had a Yipsel circle with close to 100 members. These earlier Yipsels had a baseball team, a track team, and both a women's and men's basketball team. Many a third and fourth generation Gardner Finn may be shocked to learn that there is a Yipsel in his or her background. They shouldn't be too disturbed though. It's not much worse than having a populist or a cattle rustler in the family tree.

Many first generation Finns did bring their youngsters to our study meetings. The parents remembered their own enthusiastic conversion to socialism twenty years previously and hoped, I guess, that their children might imbibe and be inspired by the socialist elixir. Alas! These kids were usually 6 to 12 years of age and we were three teenage "intellectuals." Our discussions were way above their heads. They must have been extremely bored and restless as they listened to us. All of them, I suspect, convinced their parents to spare them the agony of attending our small study group. I must add here that I was—even though doubts continually arose in my mind—the only Yipsel in the United States who believed the Bible was literally true.

Many of the first generation Finns who frequented the hall (all

Marxists of the same mild Karl Kautsky persuasion, who believed socialism could be achieved by parliamentary means) took a liking to me, mostly because I "haunted" that hall, roaming around, asking questions, and making, one might say, a general nuisance of myself.

The hall had a little billiard room and a Finnish library that were open every night of the week (except Sunday) until about 10 P.M. These men, to show their confidence in me, put me in charge of the hall several times. My responsibilities included opening the hall at 5 P.M. and closing it around 10 P.M. I also ran the billiard room and collected all monies paid for playing pool and for the sale of tobacco, soft drinks, and an occasional piece of literature.

There was no cash register in the building. I was given a roll of sequentially numbered tickets, each marked "5¢". I tore off one ticket from the roll for each five cents I collected. The audit committee met with me on Saturday night. They determined how much money I had collected by subtracting the number in the first ticket in the original roll—a ticket they had kept—from the number of the first ticket on the remaining roll. That difference times .05 was the amount of money they expected from me.

I don't think this process had any great educational value for me but I did and do now appreciate their confidence in me. It was good for my soul. It also helped strengthen my "socialist ties". Those men, almost all of whom worked in the Gardner chair factories, were devoted to socialism. Oh, they were no longer, in the 1930's, the energetic, evangelistic socialists they had been a decade or so before but they still believed socialism was the next step forward in human society. They believed socialism was inevitable. They were realistic enough to recognize that they themselves would not live to see the day when socialism was the "order of the day".

Their major concern then, it seems to me as I look back, was how to keep their enormous hall from going into receivership. The number of first generation Finns was constantly dwindling. They had no pool from which to draw new members since immigration from Finland had slowed to a trickle just before the First World War. The activity at Ash Street Hall, although it wasn't noticeable to me at that time, was slowly winding down. I think my friends, those first generation Finnish socialists knew it was 10 P.M. for all Finnish organizations in the United States. Shortly the clock would strike midnight.

My studies and conversations in Ash Street Hall did not convince me of the validity of Marxism. Maybe I wasn't bright enough to understand the theory but I prefer to believe that it was because Marxism impressed me as a new type of religion. I do recall that once I told my buddies in the Yipsel study group (which, by the way, was eqivalent to a Bible study class) that *dialectical materialism* with its *thesis, antithesis,* and *synthesis* reminded me of the Father, Son, and the Holy Ghost. They thought I was being facetious but I wasn't. I confess I still have the same feeling about Marxism that I had then.

I am not a socialist today and the Socialist Party discussed in this book has been gone for many years but I have no quarrel with the socialist ideals of my youth. The precept: "Each should contribute according to his ability and each should receive according to his need" is a much nobler thought than "How much is there in it for me?" There must be a better incentive than the profit motive. No, I don't have a quarrel with the socialist ideals of my youth but I don't believe socialism is possible. Socialism, the socialism I believed in as a teenager, just like the society in Edward Bellamy's *Looking Backward,* will never be.

I don't believe there exists a class struggle today. There was a class struggle in the early decades of this century. Quite often that struggle broke out into open warfare. Wealth and industry might have more influence with the government today than the ordinary person does but the possessors of wealth and the managers of industry do not "own" the government as they did in the early 1900's. Certainly, there are exploited people today such as the migrant farm workers and those who work for minimum wages but these people, more often than not, have the government on their side, not against them.

This is my bias. I thought you should know it when you read my narrative. It will become obvious to you that Eugene Victor Debs is my great American hero. I hope you become interested enough in him to read his definitive biography *The Bending Cross,* by Ray Ginger.

VÄINÄMÖINEN

Are you acquainted with the Finnish epic poem *Kalevala?* If not, then this narrative will introduce you to a lovable Finnish pagan god *Väinämöinen* (pronounced almost as if it were spelled *Vannamoyen* with *oy* as in *boy*). A lot of Finns, especially those who are Christians, will deny *Väinämöinen* is a god. They'll tell you he's a folk hero, a Homeric hero like Achilles. I have no quarrel with their beliefs, by which I mean I don't want to try to change their attitudes. To each his own.

I believe *Väinämöinen* is. He exists. I mean I believe *Väinämöinen* is a god who exists. It doesn't bother me one whit to have *Väinämöinen* called a pagan god. And that term, to the best of my knowledge, doesn't bother *Väinämöinen* either. He's not a jealous god in the sense that the Christian God is a jealous God. Why should *Väinämöinen* be jealous? If God is God, what does He have to be jealous about?

The only reason a god has to be jealous is if there are other gods who get more attention than he does. But it would seem to me that if a god has accomplished a lot his confidence increases, and thus his jealousy should diminish if not disappear altogether. Maturity also helps. I think all gods, including *Väinämöinen* and the Christian God, gain confidence with the passage of time. Robert Ingersoll put it another way, "God improves as man progresses." And that's true, too. The Presbyterians, for example, cook hamburgers at their barbecues today, not human beings. I think that's an improvement, don't you? I think the improvement came because their God has gained a little more confidence with the passage of time and the general improvement of humankind.

A great many of my Finnish-American friends think I'm spoofing when I say I believe in *Väinämöinen*. There seems to be nothing I can do to convince them otherwise. "You're kidding!" and 'Stop pulling my leg," are the usual responses given me. I'm a little more polite than some of my friends are. I never, for instance, say "How ridiculous can you get?" when they tell me that the Father, the Son, and the Holy Ghost are a Trinity and a Unity at the same time. Some of my Lutheran friends also tell me they believe Martin Luther had daily conversations with the Devil and that once, he became so angry, that he threw an ink bottle at the Evil One. No, not once have I told them that, in my opinion, Luther must have been temporarily insane at the time.

I knew only one man, when I was a boy, who believed in *Väinämöinen*. Some years ago, when he was a very old man, I gave him a ride home. I told him that I, too, felt, at times, the presence of *Väinämöinen.*

"You know, Hermanni," I said, "I'm lucky in the big things in life. The little things average out. Sometimes my life gets so muddled that I expect nothing but an utter fiasco. The, suddenly, every piece in the mess fits into place. That's how you told us kids *Väinämöinen's* magic works.

"I remember you used to warn us that *Väinämöinen* messes things up so badly that it is extremely difficult to believe he's trying to help. Then when everything is really loused up—nothing could be in worse shape—things begin to unravel. The sun begins to shine! Every idiotic mishmash turns out to have a reason and to be very advantageous!"

Hermanni laughed out loud and with a noticeable twinkle in his eyes, said, "Aha!* So you found a little bit of the truth. Well, don't become too evangelistic about *Väinämöinen.* Oh, I suppose one or two more converts won't hurt. But I'm going to die soon and when that happens I expect to go to *Väinölä.*** I suspect eventually you'll find your way there, too. But, remember, I don't want my paradise to ever become overcrowded."

Now let me tell you about *Väinämöinen* so that some of the references in the narrative will have more meaning. Bear in mind that I'm not evangelizing. Anyway I agree with Thomas Paine who said a revelation is only good for the person who received it.

> ...Revelations, when applied to religion, means something communicated *immediately* from God to man.
>
> No one will deny or dispute the power of the Almighty to make such a communication, if he pleases. But admitting, for the sake of a case, that something has been revealed to a certain person, and not revealed to any other person, it is a revelation to that person only. When he tells it to a second person, a second to a third, a third to a fourth, and soon it ceases to be a revelation to all those persons. It is revelation to the first person only, and *hearsay* to every other, and consequently they are not obliged to believe it. (Paine's emphasis)

Actually it doesn't matter if you believe in *Väinämöinen* anyway. It doesn't matter what your religion is because if you, dear reader, have the tiniest drop of Finno-Ugric blood flowing in your veins, then you, dear reader, are *Väinämöinen's* responsibility. That's my

---

*Hermanni used the Finnish exclamation *Niin!* Aha! is the best translation I can think of in this case.

***Väinölä* is another name for *Kalevala, Väinämöinen's* home.

revelation. But don't expect too much. *Väinämöinen* is a god with limited powers. Do you understand what that means? I can explain that best by saying I feel a lot safer flying in a Finnair plane with a bunch of other Finns with me than when I am the only Finn in a Pan American plane.

Here's *Väinämöinen's* story. Remember I am not interested in converts. Keep in mind, though, as you read the story that it's difficult for a true believer, like myself, not to proselytize even without meaning to.

Väinämöinen was born of the air. He was never young. The Finnish phrase *"vaka vanha Väinämöinen"* is repeatedly used in the *Kalevala* to describe him. All English versions translate *"vaka vanha Väinämöinen"* into *Väinämöinen, old and steadfast.* I don't think that English phrase gives a good picture of *Väinämöinen's* nature. A better phrase is *Väinämöinen, old and lusty. Old* because he has never been young. *Lusty* because he was full of life, ever ready for an adventure, and animated by beautiful young women.

One of the incidents with a beautiful young woman named Aino had a sad ending. *Tragic,* I feel is to strong a word to describe Aino's fate but I concede *sad* might be too weak. Another incident, which involved the beautiful Maiden of *Pohjala* (The North) had a bizarre ending. That incident demonstrated that whatever powers *Väinämöinen* possessed, those powers were limited.

Väinämöinen, out on one of his escapades, tried to entice the beautiful Maiden of *Pohjala* into his carriage. She, interested only in heroes, wanted *Väinämöinen* to prove himself worthy of her. *Väinämöinen,* at her request, performed a series of magical tricks. The beautiful Maiden of *Pohjala* was impressed. She insisted on a final test. She promised to enter *Väinämöinen's* carriage if he would build her a magical boat.

What she really wanted was a *Sampo.* The quest for a *Sampo* is, by the way, the key to understanding the epic poem *Kalevala.* A *Sampo* is a magical mill. I view it as a mill on a boat. A *Sampo* is a magical mill because it not only grows, harvests, and grinds the grain but it also bakes the bread. What a prize a *Sampo* would have been to anyone living in Finland in those ancient days when hunger lurked on every doorstep.

The task in *Väinämöinen's* opinion was no big deal:

"*None in any land or country,*

Under all the vault of heaven,
Like myself can build a vessel,
Or so deftly can construct it. "

So *Väinämöinen* began his task. He sharpened his axe one day, two days, and on the third he gave the axe a mighty swing. The steel blade buried itself, not in the trunk of a tree, but deep in *Väinämöinen's* leg.

The "blood burst forth in streaming torrents". The blood covered every bit of ground, every hillock in Finland, Karelia and Esthonia. *Väinämöinen* tried but he couldn't stop the flow of blood. He had forgotten the magic words! Finally, after a long search which took him from village to village, he found a lowly peasant, a very old man, who remembered the magic formula. The flow of blood stopped immediately.

Since almost all Finnish-Americans are of peasant origin, I take it for granted that many of my compatriots are descendants of that old man who helped *Väinämöinen*. I hope I am a descendant, too, bcause that lowly peasant, that old man, put *Väinämöinen* in debt to the Finns forever and if there is a privileged class of Finno-Ugrics, then they are descendants of that old graybeard.

Väinämöinen has already performed some extraordinary feats in return for the assistance rendered him. He rid Finland of a catastrophic pestilence sent from *Pohjala* (The North), the land of evil. He also freed the sun and the moon when the forces of evil hid those precious orbits behind the Northern mountains.

Why *Pohjala* (The North)? Let me explain. The Hell of the Christian faith is hot because the Bible tells the story of a desert people. The Hell of *Kalevala* is cold. Heat is sacred! That is why the Finns believe "taking a sauna" will cure your illness. The heat will drive out the forces of evil. If, however, the sauna does not cure your illness, then you better see a doctor.

Väinämöinen heated a sauna in his efforts to drive out the pestilence. He splashed water on the *kiuas* (hot rocks) and used his magic to turn the steam into honey. The pestilence was, however, such a powerful curse that *Väinämöinen* had to implore a more powerful Finnish pagan god *Ukko* to help him. *Ukko*, a god powerful enough to have two names, is reluctant to interfere in the affairs of men and women but he responded to *Väinämöinen's* songs. Together *Ukko*, whose other name is *Jumala*, and *Väinämöinen* wiped out the plague.

Väinämöinen, old and lusty
He the great pimeval sorcerer
Thus at length dispelled the evils,
Raised their burdens from his people,
Drove away the plagues of evil.

And from death he saved his people
Thus saved Kalevala descendants.

I have often speculated that the Midsummers Night Celebration when the ancient Finn burned a huge bonfire (called *kokko* in Finnish) was in honor of the sun, especially in honor of *Väinämöinen's* freeing the sun from the forces of evil. Today that day is called *Juhannus* in honor of St. John the Baptist. You and I both know that St. John has no connection with Midsummers Day. The Lutheran Church offers a lame excuse: The reason Midsummers Day honors St. John is because John the Baptist's birthday is six months before Christmas. Do you, dear reader, believe the pagan ancient Finn who originated the Midsummers Day *kokko* (bonfire) ever heard of John the Baptist? I don't. And I don't believe the Lutheran Church of Finland can provide the slightest bit of evidence that John the Baptist was born on Midsummers Day.

I suspect the church found it easier to usurp a pagan holiday than try to ban it. In Mexico, the Catholic Church, faced with a host of pagan Mayan and Aztec feast days, merely declared those holidays to be Church festival days. Thus, the true believer could be faithful to the Catholic Church and still observe the holy days of his pagan religion. Was that done in Finland, too? The church did usurp the "polite" name, *Jumala*, of the *Kalevala* pagan god *Ukko* for their own God. I often wonder who listens when a Finn prays. Is it *Ukko* or the Holy Spirit?

Väinämöinen left Finland (but not the hearts of the Finnish people) because he was embarrassed and somewhat ashamed. He was ashamed of his reaction—jealousy—when he first met the baby Jesus. The wise old *Virolainen* (Esthonian) was hesitant about baptizing the infant Jesus because there was, as you will learn in Chapters 2 and 7, considerable misgivings with respect to the infant's birth. *Väinämöinen*, undoubtedly recognizing a rival in the infant Jesus, suggested getting rid of the baby boy. He offered several options. The infant Jesus startled the gathering who had come to pass judgment on Him, by accusing *Väinämöinen* of being unfair.

"O thou old and wretched creature,
Wretched old man, void of insight,
O how stupid is your judgment,
How contemptible thy sentence,
Thou hast grievous crimes committed,
Likewise deeds of greatest folly,
Yet to the swamps they did not lead thee,
Shattered not thy head on birch trees,

"And again thou was not carried,
And abandoned in the marshes,
When thyself in youthful folly,
Caused the young maidens to be sunk
In the depths beneath the billows."

The wise old *Virolainen* (Esthonian) hastily crossed himself when he heard the voice of the half-month old infant Jesus. Quickly he baptized Jesus as the King of all Carelia (Finland, Karelia, and Esthonia). *Väinämöinen*, hurt, angry, and ashamed, decided to leave Finland. He sang his last refrain.

"May time pass quickly o'er us,
One day come, another day go,
And again I shall be needed,
The Finn will look for me,
Waiting for me to fetch a new moon,
Free a new sun, construct another Sampo
When there is no moon, no sun,
Nor any other worldy joy."

Chapter Two

THE BLUEBERRY MYSTIQUE

Blueberries. That's what summer was all about when I was a kid. That berry managed to dominate most aspects of my pre-teen summers. I picked blueberries from early morning until late afternoon. I "packed" them into one-quart berry baskets in the summer twilight. And in the evening dusk I watched as the blueberry crates were loaded onto the Model-T truck that took them to the Boston wholesale market.

Blueberries even seemed to be the staple of my diet in these summer months. I ate them directly from the bushes as I picked. I ate them for breakfast, lunch and supper. Sometimes I ate them from a bowl with milk and sugar. More often, though, I had blueberry soup for breakfast and blueberry pie for lunch and supper. Delicious? Yes! But, oh, how I hated that blueberry when I was a kid.

The blueberry was very important to a great many Finnish-American families in those days. I didn't know why but I must confess that I did tell a tale to impress upon my young schoolmates the reasons for my blueberry-dominated summers. Some of my more gullible listeners, I'm afraid, accepted my tale at face value even though it was based on neither fact or legend. Let me relate that tale here.

The blueberry, I told my young schoolmates in the twenties, was once the sacred berry of the prehistoric Finn. Why? Well, once upon a time, shortly after the nomadic Finn settled on the land now called Finland—many years before the Christian influence reached that isolated Northern country, and long before the Russians and Swedes battled for dominance there—all the crops were destroyed by an early and devastatingly cold winter. Famine threatened as the long Northern winter slowly passed into spring.

But the blueberry, which grows wild in the Finnish wood, saved the day. The blueberry flourished that year as it had never done before nor since. Never before and never since has the blueberry ripened so early. And never before and never since has the Finnish blueberry grown so large, so blue, and—this is the real mystery—so full of the nutrients necessary to life. The blueberry of my tale sustained Finnish life and warded off the worst effects of a famine until the other crops could ripen and be harvested.

The Finn has built no blueberry monuments, has painted no blueberry icons, nor does he celebrate a sacred blueberry day. He doesn't have to. The Finn, I claimed, is blessed with an excellent ancestral memory and his debt to the blueberry is etched deeply in his brain. Even after the Christian awakening in Finland, and even after the schism in the church brought most of the Finnish people into the Lutheran fold, the Finn continued to pay homage to the blueberry by an annual pilgrimage to the blueberry pasture. And that pilgrimage, I pointed out, is not merely a one-day trek to observe a holy day. It lasts the entire summer.

Now, more than fifty years later, my little fairy tale haunts me. Does it have any basis in fact? Notice how the Finnish emigrants to America tend to settle in the areas where the wild blueberry flourishes—New England, Michigan, Minnesota, Wisconsin, Washington, and Oregon. Only a tiny trickle chose to live in the sunnier and warmer climates. Why?

Yes, my blueberry fairy tale may not be as far-fetched as it sounds. Finnish berries do have magical qualities. Marjatta (the Virgin Mary) became pregnant because she ate a berry. A cranberry according to some versions of the *Kalevala*, but my deepest instincts tell me that the berry was a big, bright-blue, blueberry. Only a blueberry could have enticed Marjatta!

From the hill there cried a berry,
From the heath there cried a blueberry,
"O thou maiden, come and pluck me,
Rosy-cheeked one, come and gather,
Come with breast of tin to pluck me.

Marjatta the petted damsel,
Went a very little distance,
Went to look upon the berry,
And the blueberry to gather,
With her skillful hands to pluck it,
With her beateous hands to pluck it.
On the hill she found the berry,
On the heath she found the blueberry;
'Twas a berry in appearance,
And it seemed to be a blueberry,
But from the ground too high for eating,
On a tree too weak for climbing.
From the heath a stick she lifted,
That she might pull down the berry;

Then into her mouth it glided,
And along her tongue it hastened,
From her tongue to throat it glided,
And it dropped into her stomach.
Marjatta the petted damsel,
After this had chance grew pregnant.

My fairy tale may be only a fairy tale but I did participate in the annual Finnish summer pilgrimage to the blueberry pasture from age six to age twelve. And if the Great Depression had not intervened, I might still be making that annual summer trek to the blueberry pasture.

GATES HILL

We were city people but *Isä's** heart belonged to the land and the blueberry. He purchased, in the fall of 1923 when I was five, approximately twenty-five acres of hay field and blueberry patches in the Gates Hill area of Hubbardston, Massachusetts. The only entrance to the acreage, about a quarter mile off the old Templeton Center-Hubbardston road, was a badly rutted country right-of-way which began just before the main road reached the top of Gates Hill.

In the spring of 1924 my family built, with the help of a "barn-

---

*Isä is the Finnish word for *father*. My father, who is called *Isä* in this narrative, was born in Alavieska, Finland. His name was John Heikki Hannula.

raising" picnic (called a *talkoo* in Finnish), a large one room structure on the land. This structure was often subdivided in some flimsy manner into smaller units so that there was a little sleeping privacy for the various families who were our guests. We called the new structure with its acreage *The Camp* when we spoke English with our peers among the second generation Finnish-Americans. When we spoke in *Finglish*** to the older generation we used the word *kämppä*.

There weren't enough blueberries on *Isä's* acreage for all the families that were invited to our camp so each summer *Isä* rented three wild blueberry pastures from Mr. Gates, a Hubbardston Yankee. The twenty-five acres purchased by *Isä* has also been part of Mr. Gates' landholding so these additional pastures were in close proximity to our camp.

We, the children, referred to two of these pastures in English by the names *Big Pasture* and *Little Pasture*. These English names were mere literal translations of their Finnish designations—*Iso Haka* and *Pikku Haka*, respectively. The third pasture was not a good blueberry patch. The trees had crowded out the blueberry bushes. I remember it as a somewhat spooky forest. It had, however, a more colorful name in English among us kids than it did in Finnish. The Finnish name was *Vuorentakana* (The Other Side of The Mountain). Our English name was *Behind The Chimney*. I think you will understand the derivation of that English name as I tell you more about Mr. Gates and Gates Hill.

Mr. Gates, the mystery man of my childhood*, was once a wealthy manufacturer. The First World War brought about his financial ruin because of his German ancestry and/or because of his investments in Germany. The cause of his financial ruin was never clear to me. At least I was never able to grasp why his German ancestry or his German investments should ruin him financially. When I asked, I was told that the same thing happened to the Bayer Aspirin Company. I never understood that either but I was afraid to press the older kids in my peer group for additional

---

**The Finnish language that developed in the United States and Canada is called *Finglish*. Finglish may vary from locality to locality. See *Notes, Views, and Vignettes* for additional information.

*The Mr. Gates of our childhood romanticizing may bear little resemblance to the actual Mr. Gates who owned Gates Hill.

Gates Hill

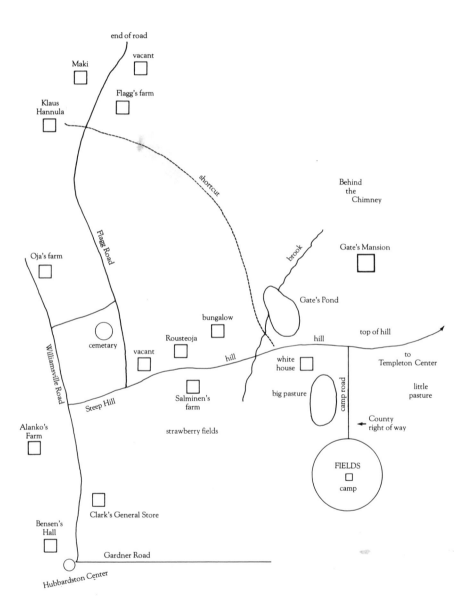

end of road

Maki

vacant

Flagg's farm

Klaus
Hannula

shortcut

Behind
the
Chimney

Flagg Road

brook

Gate's Mansion

Oja's farm

Gate's Pond

bungalow

top of hill

cemetary

Rousteoja

hill

vacant

hill

white
house

to
Templeton Center

Williamsville Road

Steep Hill

Salminen's
farm

big pasture

camp road

little
pasture

Alanko's
Farm

strawberry fields

County
right of way

FIELDS

camp

Clark's General Store

Bensen's
Hall

Gardner Road

Hubbardston Center

information because I had learned they became quite sarcastic and tended to belittle me when they could not supply the answers.

At that time we felt no contradiction in labeling our mystery man, Mr. Gates, both a Yankee and also a person of German descent. Actually, I suspect Mr. Gates came from an old New England Yankee family. I have never investigated nor do I intend to. If I do find out, I'm afraid that some of the romance of my childhood on Gates Hill will dissipate.

Mr. Gates owned most of the land in our section of Hubbardston. He owned, not only the blueberry pastures rented by *Isä*, but also all of the hay fields on both sides of the country road—the Templeton-Hubbardston Road—that ascends the high hill which overlooks Hubbardston. That hill was known to us and to everyone else of Finnish descent as *Gates Hill*.

Mr. Gates also owned a vacant but well-kept farm house about three-quarters of the way up the hill. This farm house had been used in Mr. Gates' heyday as the residence of the farm workers who were employed on his land. The house was painted white so we called it the *White House* or *Gates' White House*.

Directly across the country road from the White House was Gates Pond. This pond had been created by damming a small brook whose source was a spring near the top of the hill. But rainwater must have been the major contribution to the brook's flow since the amount of spill over the dam diminished to a trickle in a dry spell. We never named the brook, perhaps because it flowed entirely within a wooded area except for a short distance in the vicinity of the White House. The brook was dammed at an ideal spot because at this point, the rise of Gates Hill is reasonably level. This type of leveling in the contour of a hill I later learned is called a *bench*.

In those days Gates Pond had all of the conveniences of a large commercial outdoor swimming pool. There was a sandy beach where the water deepened gradually and a "regulation" diving board near the dam where the water's depth safely accomodated the youthful divers. I also remember a raft which was permanently anchored to a spot about twenty feet from the dam. The pond, along with a bungalow which was about two hundred yards south of the little beach, was owned at the time by the Nunn family of Gardner. The bungalow was visible from the little beach at the pond but it was hidden from the view from the White House and the Gates Hill Road by a small grove of birch and maple trees.

I didn't know very much about the Nunn's life style although I often saw them swimming or rowing a canoe in the pond. They never seemed to pay attention to us, but a surge of envy and admiration and fear would overwhelm me when I spotted their canoe. I was afraid they would "kick us out of the pond". But they just usually rowed across the pond, up the brook, and disappeared into the woods.

I would anxiously frolic with my companions as I anticipated their return. They will notice us, I thought, and forbid us to use their pond. But each time the Nunn's canoe returned from the brook, it would silently glide across the pond. The occupants, perhaps too busy rowing, never uttered a word of greeting or reproach.

The Nunns, bless them, never posted their land. My family and all the Finnish families in that farming area used the pond as if it were public property. We used the Nunn's diving board, their raft, and their beach. They never complained and they never asked us to leave.

Gates Mansion, the landmark from which we kids derived the name *Behind the Chimney*, was on the summit of Gates Hill. The mansion itself no longer existed. It had burned to the ground in the early 1900's. However, the ruins were so impressive to us kids in 1924 that we always referred to them as Gates Mansion. In our minds' eye the structure was still intact.

A tall chimney, so tall that it could be seen from Hubbardston Center—a distance of two or three miles—supposedly remained standing for several years after the fire. All that remained of the chimney in those days was the base and a few scattered bricks. The chimney had been blown down by a high wind early one spring. I said "supposedly remained standing" because I never saw the standing chimney and I never knew anyone who recalled seeing the chimney when it was standing.

The entrance to our third rented blueberry pasture was a lane which passed by Gates Mansion just behind the base of the chimney. Each time we passed the ruins, several of the kids would outline the fallen chimney in the stubble growth. I must admit I was never able to visualize the fallen chimney outlined for me in the ruins. Nor was I able to picture the standing chimney extrapolated from the rubble by some of my more knowledgeable and excited peers. But then I am not very good at spatial images. I can solve a problem in plane geometry in a matter of seconds but I find solid geometry resides in a world where the logic is closed to me.

We often discussed the origin of the fire that burnt the mansion to the ground. I believed the fire was caused by lightning because Gates Hill was always a spectacular place in the frequent electrical storms that occurred in the area. I recall once when a group of about ten of us, returning from a swim in Gates Pond, were caught in an open field near the summit of the hill by an unusually severe thunderstorm. The lightning flashed all around us and seemed to snap at our feet. The thunder was deafening. Terrified, we were incapable of any action. An older member of our group— I think it was my brother Toivo—insisted we lie prone on the ground. Most of us obeyed automatically but he was forced to push down some kids who were completely immobilized.

Toivo tried to assuage our fears as we lay on the ground by telling us that lightning struck the highest objects in any given area. He said that a cowboy in the Western plains always dismounted in a thunderstorm. Both rider and horse would lay flat on the ground until the storm passed. There was nothing to fear, he reassured, all we had to do was lie there until the storm dissipated.

There is another episode concerning an electrical storm which lends evidence to my belief that lightning caused the Gates Mansion fire. It occurred at our camp which I think had the same weather pattern as the summit of Gates Hill. The camp was only about a mile east of the summit and its elevation was at least three-fourths that of Gates summit.

One day the rain forced us out of the blueberry pastures into the shelter of the one-room camp building. We kept both doors wide open in order to capture any breeze that came along since the weather remained hot and humid in spite of the many intermittant thunder showers. We kids amused ourselves by bouncing up and down on the beds which were on one side of the one-room structure. The grown-ups busied themselves in their grown-up ways by the long picnic table in the southwest corner which served as our dining area.

Suddenly, during one of the thunderstorms, a lightning bolt entered the building. It seemed to stop midway in the path between the two open doors. The lightning, or thunderbolt hissed and crackled very loudly. It seemed to stay there, suspended in mid-air, an eternity. Then, apparently finding nothing amiss, the thunderbolt exited through the other door.

Hermani Valkonen stood up on a bench, pointed, and yelled wildly, *"Väinämöinen! Väinämöinen!"*

Everyone was completely awed! But the adults never made much of the incident. I think they were too dumbfounded immediately after the visit of the thunderbolt to say anything. Later, after some reflection, I suspect they decided to ignore the incident so that the fears of the children might be minimized.

It was the first time in my life that I heard the name *Väinämöinen*. No one, to my knowledge, has ever associated *Väinämöinen* with that thunderbolt since but I am today convinced that Hermani was correct. *Väinämöinen* did pay us a visit that day.

I am still amazed that not one of the more than twenty people inside the camp that day stood in the path of the thunderbolt which moved along the draft between the two open doors. The kids were constantly crossing the path to pick up a snack from the picnic tables. Even the adults moved about, often crossing the thunderbolt's path to complete some task. But the random dispersion of the camp's population when the thunderbolt passed through was just marvelous.

I never has much of a chance to express my opinions in our discussions about the cause of the Gates Mansion fire. I was much too young, with respect to the ages of the members of my peer group, to be given such an opportunity. And the truth is, although I can recall many conversations about the cause of the fire, the only opinion I can remember is a contrary opinion expressed by my brother Toivo, ten years my elder, who was the most active intellectual in our family in the twenties.

Toivo's thesis, simply expressed, stated that Mr. Gates, a wealthy and—most likely—an educated man, undoubtedly knew about Benjamin Franklin's invention of the lightning rod. He, Mr. Gates, would have insisted that lightning rods be installed to protect the mansion. Once installed, the lightning rods would have provided ample protection to the mansion from all lightning strikes.

This argument must have impressed although it didn't convince me because I remember a dream I had when I was in the third or fourth grade. Mr. Gates was lying on a big bunch of dollar bills and liberty-head dimes in front of a large fireplace. He was reading a book titled *Benjamin Franklin Invents The Lightning Rod*. There were no lights in the house and it was already dark outside, but the roaring fire provided him with sufficient light to read by. The floor of the extremely huge room was cluttered with all kinds of coins. There was a solid mahogany table in the center of the room on which rested hundreds of solid gold lightning rods. I entered the room to ask Mr. Gates a question. But as I approached him, I slipped on some of the scattered coins and woke up just before I fell down.

THE BLUEBERRY ECONOMY

Isä paid seventy-five dollars each summer for the right to pick the blueberries in *Little Pasture*, *Big Pasture*, and *Behind The Chimney*. I don't know how the negotiations were conducted to rent the pastures but I was present once when *Isä* paid the rent money to Mr. Gates. It was the first and in fact the only time I ever saw Mr. Gates.

One spring day, just after *Isä* and I had completed his fish peddling route in Hubbardston, he stopped his Model T truck in front of Mr. Gates' home on the Old Gardner Road in Hubbardston Center. *Isä* wanted me to wait in the truck but I was much to excited to obey him. Together we went to a side door where I rang the bell. A man, somewhat older than *Isä*, came out and closed the door behind him. A few words were spoken and *Isä* handed a check to the man who reentered the house. He returned a short time later to give us a receipt.

I was terribly disappointed because I had expected to see the inside of Mr. Gates' home which I knew must be fabulous in some extraordinary way. But I didn't even get a chance to peek inside since the door had been closed all the time. I expected to get inside Mr. Gates' house because almost every Finnish rural family served by *Isä* on his fish route invited him into their farmhouse for a cup of coffee when the business transaction was completed. *Isä* turned down most offers but he was the largest consumer of coffee that I ever saw.

"Why didn't he invite us in for coffee?" I asked (in Finnish) as we left the porch.

"He's not Finnish," *Isä* replied, "and besides, perhaps he doesn't even drink coffee."

None of us, including my family nor our invited guests at the camp, picked blueberries in these pastures free of charge. All of us paid *Isä* a nominal picking fee which we call the *rent*. Still *Isä* did not make a profit in his entrepreneur's role. Let me explain.

Each blueberry picker who sold his blueberries to the "blueberry man" paid *Isä* three cents a quart "rent" in the beginning of the season when the market price for blueberries was high. This rent dropped to two cents per quart when the blueberry market price dropped below fifteen cents a quart. Blueberries picked for personal use by guests were not subject to the rental charge. The rent was only attached to those berries that a picker sold to the blueberry man.

Isä collected the picking fee only until he was reimbursed for the seventy-five dollars he had advanced. My brother Tarmo, four years my elder, kept a running total of the number of quarts picked and the amount of money received from the blueberry pickers. When Tarmo's accounting showed that *Isä* had been reimbursed for his outlay, then Tarmo would announce the "No Rent" decree. From that day to the end of the season—which in the case of the immediate family lasted until one week after labor day—no one paid a picking fee. The entire price per quart paid by the blueberry man was given to each picker.

The term *blueberry man* is not a term I have coined to tell my story. It is the actual title used in the twenties and thirties to identify an individual who drove his truck to various Finnish farms in order to buy the blueberries that had been picked each day. The truck load of berries was then taken to the wholesale produce market in Boston. Blueberry man is the literal translation of the Finnish *mustikkamies*.

The blueberry man's arrival was the most exciting part of our day. The anticipation of being paid for our day's work generated the excitement. He usually arrived in his Model A truck at dusk. But sometimes it was already dark when he chugged his way slowly along the badly rutted county right-of-way to our camp. Those nights the job of transferring the ownership of the blueberries was accomplished by kerosene light since there was no electricity on Gates Hill in the 1920's.

There were, of course, many blueberry men in Worcester County. There was even a blueberry woman, Maija (Mary) Jaakoia in Gardner. All of the blueberry men (or women) that I knew about were first generation Finnish-Americans. Their sons accompanied them on their routes through the countryside. And because of the language barrier they also made their trip with them to the Boston wholesale market.

When I look back now I am surprised that any blueberry man bothered to pick up the berries at our camp. We were a good quarter of a mile off the main road which went up Gates Hill. The one lane right-of-way to camp, which was between two stone walls that separated some of Gates' hay fields, was so badly rutted that the speed of any vehicle traversing the right-of-way could not exceed five miles per hour. It was almost as fast to walk the distance as to ride and the walking was a good deal more pleasant. What a jostling the berries must have taken as the blueberry man's truck chugged along that bumpy way.

I don't think the blueberry men made a great deal of money. In the short span of five years we had three different blueberry men who bought the berries at our camp. And then the Finnish farmers' cooperative in Hubbardston discovered that transporting and selling blueberries in Boston was a service the co-op could provide its members. The co-op's entry into the blueberry business sounded the death knell for the blueberry man. The price we received for the berries when we sold them through the cooperative was considerably more than the blueberry man could afford to pay. We made more money but whatever romance existed in that blueberry culture seemed to end when the blueberry man stopped coming to the camp.

My favorite blueberry man, and the only one I can remember vividly, was a jolly, hefty man named Otto Haltunen. Otto was the antithesis of the common caricature which pictures the Finn as a somber, stolid creature. Otto found humor in every aspect of the human experience. He must have felt that life was meant to be laughed at because he was always merry and jolly. And when he laughed, the blueberry pickers—young and old—laughed with him.

The negotiations for the sale of the blueberries were conducted in the midst of good-natured bantering. But negotiations is not really the correct word since whatever price the blueberry man quoted was accepted without any bargaining. I do not recall that anyone ever refused to sell his blueberries because the offered price was too low. Oh, disappointment was expressed by the pickers if the blueberry man announced a precipitous drop in the wholesale blueberry price. In those cases, though, even the blueberry man commiserated with us. The general mood as the ownership of the blueberries changed hands was a friendly expectation on the part of the pickers—most of whom were young children. We were going to be paid for our day in the blueberry pasture.

Part of the job of picking blueberries is "packing" them. Our packing was done at noon—when we returned to camp for lunch—and in the late afternoon (sometimes in the twilight) in a makeshift shed which stood beneath the shade of some century old maple trees near the entrance to the camp. The packing and cleaning process consisted of slowly pouring the blueberries into quart baskets while removing the green berries, the leaves, and the assorted tiny twigs which had found their way into our blueberry pails as we picked and traversed through the woods. Perhaps *unripe* (Finnish: *raaka* or *kypsymäton*) is a better word than *green* since the blueberry's color changes from green to a purplish red and, finally in its mature state, to blue or black.

The cleaned blueberries were poured into one-quart baskets. The full baskets were placed into four-tier wooden crates—eight baskets to a tier. The biggest and bluest berries were placed on the top of each basket. The best baskets of blueberries went, of course, on the top tier of the blueberry crate.

In those days a blueberry basket was made of a very thin sheet of wood which was pressed into shape. A narrow strip of wood, called the rim, was stapled to all four sides to strengthen the basket. The corners of the basket often had to be plugged so that the blueberries would not dribble out. The volume of a basket could be reduced by pressing in on all four sides since the structure did not have the resilience to spring back into its original shape. Sometimes, therefore, a child when he or she found out that he or she was a few berries shy of a full quart—and too tired to dash off to a nearby blueberry patch to pick a few more—would pinch a basket to reduce its volume. Thus he or she had—with very little effort—rounded up his or her day's picking to a whole number.

Blueberries are delicate. If they are handled too much they tend to "sweat". The word *sweat* may not be the correct technical term for the phenomenon but we kids used *sweat* and the word *wet* in such phrases as "Your blueberries are *wet*" and "If you keep jostling those berries, they're going to *sweat*". Only the children

26

returned from the pasture with wet blueberries. It was, of course, the result of their restlessness and boredom. The younger a child, the more likely he or she would return to the packing shed with wet berries. How often I said to my mother, "Äiti, my blueberries are wet."

The wet blueberries were not thrown away, canned, nor made into blueberry pie for our home consumption. Those berries went to the bottom of the basket where their lack lustre appearance was well hidden by the big beautiful blueberries on the top. These inferior baskets of berries were placed on the bottom tier of the blueberry crate.

I don't think we fooled anyone. The blueberries from our camp, I suspect, found their way into the bakeries of the Boston area where they turned up in pies and blueberry muffins. I'm positive that the blueberries I picked were never sold in the produce department of the S.S. Pierce Company in Boston. I must admit, however, that when I was a kid—six to ten years of age—I did believe we received a better price for our blueberries because we hid the poor ones under the big, bright, beautiful blue blueberries. Caveat Emptor! Oh, I don't think the practice corrupted me. At least, not entirely. My outward appearance is bright and shiny, but for heaven's sake, don't peek inside.

THE YOUTHFUL BLUEBERRY PICKERS

The paraphernalia we kids carried into the pasture forced us to handle the berries too much. The adult pickers, more resistant to boredom, carried only two galvanized pails—either ten or twelve quart sizes—into the blueberry pastures. One of these pails was always attached to the waist so that both hands were free to pick. The other pail was stashed away in a convenient place in the woods. A good picker easily filled both pails before lunch and filled them again in the afternoon.

We kids carried an elaborate amount of equipment to help offset the boredom of picking. I usually changed one or two items of my paraphernalia every day but a typical assortment of containers consisted of four utensils such as a small kitchen measuring cup, and empty quart basket, a three quart pail, and a ten quart pail. The three quart pail was attached to my belt or, if I wore bib style overalls, the bib was looped through the aperture between the pail and the handle. The small kitchen utensil rested inside the three

quart pail. I stashed both the quart basket and the ten quart galvanized pail in some easy-to-remember spot in the woods. Since I "needed" the quart basket more often than the ten quart pail, these utensils were not put in the same place.

My picking procedure (Should I say ritual?) was to fill the measuring cup which was inside the three quart pail that was tied to my waist. When the cup was full, I poured the berries from it into the quart basket. When the basket was full, I poured the berries from the basket into the ten quart galvanized pail.

It was not always easy to remember the exact location where the quart basket or the large galvanized pail were stashed. A little time and effort was spent looking for the quart basket; if the basket was full, additional time was needed to find the ten quart galvanized pail. The searching, although sometimes frustrating, helped to relieve the boredom.

I did not start my personal ritual immediately on entering the blueberry pasture. First, for good luck, every kid was obligated to pick enough blueberries directly into his or her galvanized pail so that the bottom of the pail was not visible. When that stint was accomplished he or she would yell, "Hey! I've got a *bottomful!*" Since I was one of the youngest pickers I was never the first kid to yell "Bottomful." But I didn't start picking in earnest—start my own picking ritual—until my "good luck bottomful" was in my large galvanized pail.

Does the three quart pail attached to my waist seem superfluous to you? It was not. If in my meandering through the woods, I stumbled onto a *good bush*, I would put aside the kitchen measuring cup and "milk" the berries directly into the three quart pail. These berries, when the good bush was stripped of its fruit, were poured directly into the large ten quart pail. In that way, I lost track of the exact amount of berries I had picked.

Robert Frost in his poem *Blueberries** conveys the sentiments of a blueberry picker when he or she finds a "good bush."

> *"You ought to have seen what I saw on my way*
> *To the Village, through Patterson's pasture today:*
> *Blueberries as big as the end of your thumb,*
> *Real sky-blue, and heavy, and ready to drum*
> *In the Cavernous pail of the first one to come!*
> *And all ripe together, not some of them green*
> *And some of them ripe! You ought to have seen!"*

The adults moved methodically through a small area in the pasture. They picked every bush clean. That is, they did not leave any blueberry bush until they had stripped it of all ripe blueberries, being careful not to disturb the immature berries. These berries would be picked, when ripe, in a subsequent pass through the pasture.

The Poetry of Robert Frost, Holt, Rinehart and Winston, New York.

We kids wandered through the pasture looking for good bushes. We picked the best on each bush we passed and wandered on. We encountered each other rather frequently as we criss-crossed through the woods. And when we met the one inevitable question before the topic changed to more interesting matters was, "How many quarts have you picked?"

Early in each picking session, I was able to answer the question quite accurately by "I have almost a bottomful" or by "I have a little more than a bottomful." But later in the day, my answers were always guesses that tended to be optimistic because of my ritual of pouring berries from smaller containers into larger containers caused me to lose track of whatever amount I had picked.

"Surely," I would think before I replied, "There's six quarts in the pail because yesterday, when I had five quarts, the berries came this high in the pail. Besides, I must have dumped at least three full baskets into the pail, and that last good bush . . ."

"Six quarts!" I might shout back optimistically.

But at the packing shed I usually discovered that my pails contained one or two quarts less than I had so optimistically estimated. The other kids also overestimated their abilities as pickers. The disappointment, however, was only slight since the joy of having completed that day's work more than compensated for any diminished accomplishment.

Do not get the wrong impression. Don't think that we kids were not darn good pickers. We were. And I think I was one of the best. My personal record, for the number of quarts picked in a single day, is *sixteen*. I established that record when I was ten years old. Let me repeat that. I picked sixteen quarts of blueberries in a single day when I was only ten years old. And even though I picked blueberries for two summers after that record was established, I was unable to break it. That record will stand, of course, for the rest of my life, because I have no inclination to try to break it. In fact, I have no intention of ever picking a single blueberry again. My share of the Finnish debt to the blueberry was paid in full long, long ago. The burden belongs to someone else today.

My sister Vieno, six years my elder, was the best picker of the younger generation in our camp. Her record was thirty-two quarts picked in a single day. She set that record before she was fifteen years of age. I marvel at her accomplishment because, remember, we picked wild blueberries, by hand, from high bushes.

The title, Grand Master Blueberry Picker, of our generation and of all time should be bestowed, however, on my cousin Kanerva (Kenneth) Hannula who lived on a farm on Flagg Road in Hubbardston. He established a record that should be inscribed in the *Guiness Book of World Records*. Kenneth picked an unbelievable 64 quarts of high bush wild blueberries in a single day when he was only 13 years of age. No one—young or adult—will ever match that feat again.

There is an incident I must relate before I go on with my narrative which involves Vieno, most of the kids in camp, and a good bush that I found very early in the blueberry season.

I was six or seven when the incident occurred so it must have been the first or second summer that I picked. Blueberries were selling at a premium price on the wholesale market because ripe berries were very scarce in the pasture. Suddenly in my meanderings in the woods, I spied a tall bush which was completely loaded with clusters of big, ripe blueberries.

My sister Vieno, who was my favorite sibling in those days, was picking close by. I wanted to share my good fortune with her. But I was so excited that I could hardly contain myself.

"Vee!," I yelled, "Vee! Come here!"

That was the end of my good bush. An avalanche of kids stampeded in my direction in no time. The bush was stripped clean in seconds. I had tears in my eyes at the fate that had befallen me. I hadn't even been able to share my great prize with just Vieno.

"Never mind, Reino," Vieno consoled, "There are plenty of other good bushes. But remember, next time don't yell. Just come and get me. If you can't find me, pick it quietly yourself. But don't yell."

PAYDAY CAME EVERY EVENING

Our "payday" came every evening except Saturday when the blueberry man took a day off because the Boston wholesale produce market was closed on Sunday. We kids, however, didn't get Saturday off; the blueberries we picked that day were saved until the next regular visit of the blueberry man on Sunday evening.

We were paid for quantity, not quality. Even though we occasionally hid the *wet* blueberries in the bottom of the baskets in the bottom tiers of the crate, the overall quality of the berries picked in our camp was very good. But the blueberry man could not have cared less. He never inspected the quality. He never opened a single crate, not even to look at the blueberries on the top tier. He took all the berries available in our camp, paying the same price for every basket.

The computation to determine the total value of the blueberries was done by *Isä* on an empty blueberry crate. His calculations were checked by my brother Tarmo who was an excellent mathematician. The blueberry man did his arithmetic on one of the full crates he was taking with him. One of his sons, who accompanied him on his route, checked his figures. No sales slip of any kind changed hands. The writing on the crates, made from a light, soft wood, was very easy to read.

After the cash for the entire lot of berries had been paid to *Isä*, the blueberry man loaded the crates and empty baskets to replace the ones we had filled. Then he climbed into the cab of his truck and chugged it slowly over the one-lane country right-of-way back to the main road.

Now it was the pickers' turn to be paid. The children were paid first. My brother Tarmo, the assistant paymaster, using some method of random selection since we did not stand in line, asked each kid, "How many quarts did you pick today?"

Every kid's reply with respect to the number of quarts he claimed have picked was accepted at face value. No one ever questioned any kid about the number he stipulated in reply to Tarmo's question. Nor can I recall any type of reconciliation to balance *Isä's* account.

Tarmo calculated the amount of money due each kid and announced the figure to *Isä* who paid the child the specified sum. I'm sure everyone of us had done his own arithmetic long before Tarmo began his nightly task. I know I had. After all, it wasn't a very difficult problem: subtract the pasture rent (usually two cents a quart) from the blueberry man's price and multiply that difference by the number of quarts picked.

Change—money change—was never a problem at paytime. *Isä* always carried a lot of small coins with him because he needed it on his business route. And if he did run out, any kid in camp could provide a considerable amount of coins from his personal tin can bank in which he kept his blueberry earnings.

The favorite bank among the kids was an empty La Tourraine

coffee can. These cans were considered ideal banks because they had screw top covers. Almost every kid who picked regularly at the camp had one of these La Tourraine coffee can banks in which he stored his blueberry earnings during the summer months. Each kid's bank, accumulating more money each day, was partially filled with coins—pennies, nickels, dimes, quarters, and halves—along with a few bills of the smaller denomination. No attempt was made to convert the small currency into bills of a larger denomination.

Our La Tourraine coffee can banks were stored on the ceiling tie beams in the camp building. We could easily reach them by standing on a bed, a chair, or any box of sufficient height. They were never guarded although every bank was readily accessible to anyone at any time. We left them on the ceiling beams when we were picking blueberries. They were there when we went swimming. They were above our heads when we slept which was perhaps the only time the banks had any sort of a guard. But I was never conscious of missing any money from my La Tourraine bank nor do I know of any kid in our group who ever missed any money. In fact we never even thought about the possibility of losing money through theft. At least I didn't. It's very difficult to believe that fact, today, in this more sophisticated age.

I don't know what our average earning was each summer but I do know what I had left (not what I earned) at the end of the 1928 blueberry season because I noted the amount—$27.35—in my diary. But that figure, since I was the youngest picker at camp, must belong—statistically speaking—in the bottom of the fourth quartile in any frequency distribution of my peer group's earnings.

WORK HAS MANY REWARDS

We had complete control of the money we earned during the summer season. Although our camp was three miles from Hubbardston's center which, even if one stretched one's imagination, could not be considered a shopping metropolis, we did manage to find some delightful ways to spend at least a part of the money we earned.

Each morning *Isä* left our blueberry camp to attend his business ventures in Gardner. We kids had convinced him to let one of us accompany him to Gardner at least once a week. Whoever accompanied *Isä* on the designated day was our purchasing agent. An avalanche of orders descended upon him or her. Most of the orders directed the agent to purchase goodies in the F.W. Woolworth and J.J. Newberry candy departments on Parker Street.

Our purchasing agent never wrote down any of the candy orders. I'm not certain that the orders were filled as specified but they never had to face a dissatisfied clientele when the "booty" was distributed. I cannot describe how the purchasing agent went about fulfilling his role in the city as I was never allowed to perform the function. The older kids always preempted my turn. I was too young to insist on my turn and too old to complain to my parents.

The variety of candy in our camp in the evening of these shopping days must have brought happiness to the patron saint who oversees the confectionary manufacturers. Everyone had his or her own favorite that night. There were candy corn, licorice tidbits, orange slices, marshmallow peanuts, peanut brittle, peanut butter kisses, filled ribbon, sour balls, lemon drops, jelly beans, gum drops, candy coated chocolate, salt water taffy, and more. A great deal of trading took place as each tried the other's favorite. Very little candy was around the next day. Part of the reason for the lack of candy the next day was that no kid spent more than twenty-five cents on each shopping day. I'm sure that many wanted to spend more but the purchasing agent had a "logistics" problem. There was a limit on the amount of stuff he or she could carry for each of the ten or more kids in camp.

A second delightful way to spend our money was to buy jelly donuts, cream puffs, lemon pies, and custards from the Finnish bakery truck which visited our camp once a week. My sister Vieno, reminiscing in a letter about the camp, wrote, "...and if the bakerman's day fell on a rainy day, our La Tourraine coffee cans took a licking. Do you remember how each of us 'could' buy anything we wanted off the bakery truck? I am amazed how much Isä knew about human nature. We'd pick all the harder the next day."

The third way we kids had of spending our blueberry earnings— although it took some effort on our part—was to attend the Hubbardston movie night. Hubbardston was not then nor is it now a large enough community to support a movie theatre. But, in those days, once a week—on Friday night—movies were shown in the old Bensen Hall. I said it took some effort on our part because we

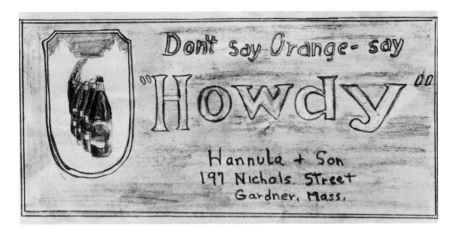

had to walk the three miles from camp to Hubbardston Center and, when the movie was over, we had to walk back up Gates Hill in the dark—and every Friday night, as I now recall, it was pitch black as we walked.

The admission to the theatre was only ten cents but once inside we were tempted by such goodies as soda pop, Eskimo Pies, and various brands of candy bars hawked by the other kids—Yankee kids, no doubt—who walked along the aisles with their wares during the intermissions in the show. The movie promoters, with true Yankee ingenuity, made sure there were several intermissions in the evening so that a maximum amount of hard-earned Finnish blueberry money might find its way into the Yankee coffers.

Yankee ingenuity laid other traps for us. To get to the Bensen Hall we had to pass Clark's General Store owned by Bill Clark who was keenly aware of our weaknesses. His collection of penny candies and dime novelties attracted our coins as a magnet attracts iron filings. Luckily, with typical Finnish foresight, we always left the bulk of our earnings safe in their La Tourraine coffee cans on the tie beams in camp.

The only soda pop available in the movie hall was *Isä's* carbonated drinks. In return for this exclusive *Isä* purchased advertising on the movie screen. The slide flashed on the screen read:

DON'T SAY ORANGE
SAY **HOWDY** AND GET A **REAL** ORANGEADE
Hannula & Son
197 Nichols Street
Gardner, Mass.

Let me quote again from my sister's reminiscences: "I remember walking to the movies in Hubbardston Center on Friday nights and when 'Howdy, the greatest orange drink' slide was flashed on the screen, our night was made. Everyone in the theatre clapped, shrieked, and stamped their feet....

"...I also remember how we could buy anything as long as we could carry it back to camp....

"...How scared we all were on that dark road of the wildcat which, the older boys said, stayed around Gates Pond at night! I remember how we all sang as loud as we could to bolster our courage as we walked past the pond and up the last mile of Gates Hill."

Chapter Three

THE BLUEBERRY PICKERS PLAY HOOKY

I do not want to give the impression that our parents were hard taskmasters. They weren't. In fact a child psychologist today might label them as overindulgent, permissive parents.

Still, we blueberry kids—and I am not talking just about the kids in my immediate family—were extremely goal oriented about our berry picking. But I cannot explain why. It seems to be that—despite a deep unconcious resentment—we considered blueberry picking the natural state of our lives. It was something we, as kids, didn't question any more than a kid today questions the existence of God.

My sister Lilja told me a few years ago, "...We went into the blueberry pasture as soon as the dew had dried. No one told us to go. We made ready in the early morning by gathering our utensils and, when the dew was gone, off into the pasture we went. It just never occurred to us to behave any differently...."

Still, we often played hooky to go swimming. The swimming urge usually hit us at lunch time in camp. We didn't keep our plans secret but neither did we talk about them in Finnish. The activity at the camp was charged with excitement as we kids, stimulated by the afternoon's prospects, made ourselves ready for the excursion. We put our swimming suits in underneath our blueberry picking clothes. I'm sure the older generation knew what was going on but they never raised any objections. And we never asked their permission.

After lunch, we went into the pasture in a jovial mood, making

Gates Pond

a lot more noise than usual. We picked a bottomful for good luck, stashed our pails and other paraphernalia under a convenient bush, and headed for Gates Pond. The last one in was a "rotten egg"!

We frolicked in the pond for about two hours. Then we lingered around the pond until our bathing suits dried before putting on our clothes over them. Sometimes, when we had overstayed our leave, we walked in our bathing suits, carrying our clothes until the swim suits had dried. Then we returned to the pasture, retrieved our picking paraphernalia and picked until the usual time to return to the packing shed.

There must have been a noticeable drop in the blueberry production on these "hooky" days but we kids never received any admonishment about our escapades. None of us felt the slightest twinge of guilt. I can't remember thinking about the matter in those days. It was just a part of life in a blueberry camp.

One summer we discovered one of our most enjoyable pasttimes—swinging birches. *Isä* was taken aback when he saw his first birches swing down. Did *Isä*, like the ancient pagan Finn, regard the birch trees as sacred? He may have because he, usually a very indulgent father, was visibly annoyed at us that night when he made the only prohibition ever issued by him.

We were not, *Isä* decreed, to swing on any birch which was in the proximity of the camp. The birch trees around the sauna were especially sacrosanct and were not to be violated in any manner. He didn't consider swinging birches a laudable activity but if we persisted in the game, then under no circumstances were we to swing a birch visible from the camp. Our swinging must be restricted to the birches in the woods.

I thought we invented the diversion we called "birch swinging" by accident. I never heard of anyone, except the kids at our camp, who engaged in this sport. Let me describe the game with the hope that everyone who reads this narrative is too old to take up the practice. *Isä* was right; it is very hard on the birch tree. Bear in mind that we, the original birch swingers of Gates Hill, were in the six- to fourteen-year old age bracket. Anyone much older (or heavier) than we were is likely to suffer a broken neck.

Birch swinging consists of the following steps:

1. Find a good supple birch tree.
2. Climb the chosen birch tree as high as your courage permits.
3. Grab hold of the birch tree as high as your hands can reach.
4. Swing your feet out and away from the branches they are resting on.

If the birch swinger is heavy enough—but not too heavy—the top of the birch, the part the swinger is hanging onto, will slowly descend to the ground, giving the swinger a smooth, graceful ride. Sometimes a little kid was not heavy enough to force the birch to descend all the way to the ground and the young swinger was left dangling ten to fifteen (and sometimes even more) feet from the ground. When this happened the kid had to make a rapid decision, "Am I close enough to the ground to let go or shall I call for help?" Assistance, if requested, was provided by a buddy who added his weight to that of the dangling swinger.

Sometimes, of course, the birch chosen was not very supple and the top of the tree would snap off when the kid swung his feet out. The trip down, in these instances, was very rapid; especially if the swinger did not pass through any branches of the broken birch and/or branches of other trees in close proximity.

A birch tree has considerable resilience. It does tend to regain its original stature if "swung" only once or twice. But if it is "swung" several times, then it tends to become slightly "hunch-backed"—part of the trunk will be higher than the tip of the tree. Probably the sight of these "hunchbacked" trees did not appeal to *Isä's* aesthetic sense. I don't believe, however, that he knew about the tips of the birches that were snapped off by the swingers. If he had, I suspect he would have issued an *ukase* forbidding all birch swinging by any member of our blueberry camp.

We did not, of course, invent the game of birch swinging. Robert Frost had swung them long before we did. As the follow-ing excerpts from his poem, *Birches**, indicates, Robert Frost didn't feel the swinging hurt the birches. I disagree.

> *When I see birches bend to left and right*
> *Across the lines of straighter darker trees,*
> *I like to think that some boy's been swinging them.*
> *But swinging doesn't bend them down to stay*
> *As ice storms do.*
>
> *. . . He always keeps his poise*
> *To the top branches, climbing carefully*
> *With the same pains you use to fill a cup*
> *Up to the brim, and even above the brim.*
> *Then he flung outward, feet first, with a swish,*
> *Kicking his way down through the air to the ground.*
> *So I was once myself a swinger of birches.*
> *And so I dream of going back to be.*

THE FINNISH SAUNA IN THE 1920'S

Everybody stayed out of the blueberry pasture on really hot humid days. The discomfort of the hot humid woods with the unusual activity of the insects—especially the horseflies that buzz-ed incessantly around one's head—was too much even for the most eager-beaver adult pickers. We kids took off for Gates Pond. The adults stayed in camp and heated the sauna.

**The Poetry of Robert Frost* (Holt, Rinehart and Winston, New York)

The Finnish word *sauna* had not as yet, in the years 1924 to 1934, entered the English language. We used the word steambath when we spoke in English about the sauna. Steambath, though, is not technically correct because there is no visible steam in a sauna. Oh, some steam—the Finns call it *löyly*—arises when water is splashed on the hot rocks, but that steam rapidly dissipates. The heat itself is dry and penetrating.

Isä built the sauna at our blueberry camp almost immediately after the "barn raising" had erected the big one-room structure we lived in. The sauna oven, called *pesä* in Finnish, was made of large stones found so readily in the old stone walls nearby. *Fire chamber* might be a better translation of *pesä* but we kids always used the word *oven*. I shall use both words interchangeably in this narrative.

The *kiuas*—a pile of small rocks on which water is thrown to produce the steam *(löylyä)*—rested on top of the oven. The fire chamber and the *kiuas* were built first. I mean the bath house, consisting of a hot room and a dressing room, was constructed around the fire chamber which, of course, was inside of the hot room of the completed sauna. There is no English equivalent for the Finnish word *kiuas*. Technically, only the pile of small rocks on top of the fire chamber is the *kiuas* but we kids, in the free parlance of our childhood, called the entire stone structure the *kiuas*. Our folks never seemed to think it was necessary to correct our misconception.

The sauna was heated by burning wood in the fire chamber. The smaller stones that formed the *kiuas* were heated to an extremely high temperature. The heat of the fire also caused the pine boards that lined the interior of the hot room to ooze resin. A chimney which went through part of the *kiuas* into the oven removed most but not all of the smoke. The smoke that escaped into the hot room combined with the oozing pine resin to permeate the sauna with a delicious odor.

The fire chamber of some Finnish country saunas do not have chimneys to remove the smoke. These saunas—called *savusaunas*, which might be translated into English as "smoke saunas"—are rare today even in Finland. I recall only two such baths in our rural area; one on my uncle Klaus' farm on Flagg Road and the other on the farm of *Isä's* best friend, John Porko of Pitcherville. (In 1968, I had the pleasure of finding a *savusauna* in Finland, about twenty miles north of Helsinki. The owner claimed the sauna was over 150 years old. He also told me that *savusaunas* were the original Finnish baths.)

All saunas with wood-burning stone fire chambers leak some smoke into the hot room even if the fire chamber had a chimney attached to it. Our sauna, therefore, like most rural saunas at that time, could not be used until the fire in the oven had been reduced to red hot embers. Still these saunas differed from the *savusaunas* (smoke saunas) described earlier in that the walls of the sauna were not covered with smoky soot. As a consequence, they didn't smell as good either.

My theory, when I was a kid, was that the larger the fire in the oven, the smaller the amount of smoke that escaped into the hot room. The exact reverse of my theory may be the actual fact, however, because I held onto my theory only to justify the size of the fire I built in the oven. Whenever I "fired" the sauna (and I was allowed to do so from age six on), I usually built a huge fire in the chamber. The bigger the fire the greater my enjoyment. The height of my pleasure came when the flames were visible between the stones that made up the *kiuas*. Whenever this phenomenon occurred, I would announce that there would be a minimum of *häkä* today.

There is no English word for *häkä** so we, when we spoke in English used the word *häkä* to refer to the obnoxious mixture of smoke and steam that often existed, to some extent, in a rural sauna then. The smoke generated during "heating of a sauna", even if it infiltrated the hot room, was not *häkä*. But that smoke, if allowed to remain in the hot room, would combine with *löyly* (steam) to form *häkä*. A bather might say, when his eyes began to smart and burn after splashing the hot rocks to create *löylyä* (steam), "Jeepers, there's a helluva lot of *häkä* in here!" A bather often used the same expression as an excuse to make a quick but graceful exit when the amount of *löyly* in the sauna exceeded the limits of his endurance.

One afternoon when it was my turn "to heat the steambath", I had a little difficulty in starting the fire. The smoke, which filled both the hot room and the dressing room, poured out the door. Finally the fire took off and the first licks of flame appeared above

---

*The Finnish-Americans of New England may have been the only people to use the word *häkä* in the manner I have pictured.

the *kiuas*. It must have been late in the afternoon because *Isä*, perhaps worried by the quantity of smoke that poured out of the bath house, peeked into the hot room. I was lying on the floor to avoid the smoke which saturated the upper portion of the room. The flames, however, were readily visible above the *kiuas* as I agitated the fire into greater activity.

"That smoke is going to make a lot of *häkä*," *Isä* said in Finnish. "When the *kiuas* is hot, throw some water on it. *(heitä löylyä)* The steam will drive the smoke out. Keep the fire going very hot until all the smoke is gone." And he left with not a word of disapproval about my tremendous fire in the oven. I was relieved to learn that he did not disapprove of my inclination to build spectacular fires.

Our sauna was heated almost every day (and when the weather was wet and cold it was kept hot all day long). One of the boys (usually I grabbed the job) fired the sauna but the boys, however, were the last to have their baths each day. Everyone—the young girls, the single women, married guests, and older single male guests—had priority over the boys for a very good reason. After the boys took their bath, there was very little heat left in the sauna.

We played what might be called the Finnish game of *löyly* machismo. Who was man enough to stay on the upper level of the hot room platform as water was continually splashed on the *kiuas* (hot stones)? Our sauna, like most saunas, had a multilevel platform. The higher the level, the higher the temperature. *Löyly* (the steam) does not increase, so I am told, the temperature in the sauna but the body certainly reacts as if the temperature has risen when water is splashed on the hot *kiuas*. For example, the flesh under one's fingernails will tingle when one is engulfed by *löyly*. The tingling will stop or at least diminish in intensity when the *löyly* dissipates. So, when the boys were in the sauna, water was continuously splashed on the *kiuas* to "separate the men from the boys". By the end of an half-hour or so there was little, if any, heat left. The sauna had to be reheated to accomodate any unexpected guests who arrived after the boys had finished their bath.

Although the first generation Finn emigrated from a Finland where mixed bathing was the custom, there was no mixed bathing (except in the case of married couples) at the blueberry camp. In the city, however, children of both sexes accompanied their parents to a commercial steambath until they were about twelve years of age. I used the word *steambath* instead of sauna because that is what they were called. Commercial saunas were called *Finnish steambaths* by their owners and the people who used them. Even today they are still called steambaths in Gardner, even though the word sauna now appears in the dictionary.

There were five commercial saunas in Gardner when I was a boy. Since *Isä* sold soft drinks to all these establishments, my family managed to take a sauna in each one at least four or five times a year. My favorite was the Pleasant Street Steambaths which was in The Patch—the Polish-American district of Gardner. This steambath was operated by its owner, Kalle Hamalainen.

The Pleasant Street Steambaths had four family hot rooms (saunas) and one large common hot room reserved exclusively for men. Each family sauna had two attached dressing rooms. A little bell attached to each dressing room door enabled the occupants to signal the owner when the family had finished its bath. The owner then ushered a waiting family into the adjoining dressing room, thus maximizing the use of the hot room.

The walls between the adjoining dressing rooms were certainly not soundproof. In fact, some of the walls did not even reach the ceiling. The conversations in both dressing rooms were conducted, for that reason, in very hushed tones and, at times, even in whispers. When we kids were five and six years old we played a game in which the object was to identify the occupants of the adjoining dressing room. We had clues, though, because there was usually a thirty-minute (or longer) wait for a hot room and our next room neighbors, whoever they be, had most likely sat and conversed with us in the waiting room.

The heat for all the hot rooms was generated by steam boilers in the basement of the building. The temperature in each sauna was as hot as the rural saunas but did not reach the almost 100° centigrade so common in Finland. *Löyly* was created by splashing water on the steam pipes and steam radiators in the hot room. There were no *kiuas*. The modern technique of applying heat—either gas or electric—to a small pile of stones (the *kiuas*) had not been developed. The walls of the hot rooms were finished in cement—not pine board—but the *vastas* with their birch leaves helped to give the steam room the characteristic odor of sauna.

Let me digress a little to explain the Finnish word *vasta* that I used in the last pararaph.

Leafy birch twigs were wrapped together to form the *vasta*, or *vihta* as some Finns called it. The first generation found the *vasta* absolutely indispensable in the sauna. The Finns used the *vasta* to "flagellate" (beat) themselves in the heat of the sauna. The "flagellation" is done with a hot *vasta*, a vasta that is heated by placing it on top of the *kiuas* when water is splashed on those stones to create *löylyä*. The claim is that the "flagellation" improves the circulation of the blood. Even though the older folks propagandized us continually about the health value of beating one's self in the sauna with a *vasta*, the practice never caught on with the younger generation.

My Finnish-English dictionary translates both *vasta* and *vihta* as "whisk". We kids preferred a better English word "switch" because the *vasta* made a switching noise as it was swished in the sauna. Actually the *vasta* does resemble an oversized whick broom which may account for the dictionary's translation of the term. The *vasta* consists of about ten to fifteen leafy birch twigs tied together at one end. This end became the handle. A cross section of the other end has the diameter of a small tennis racket since the leaves are still attached to the twigs there. If the *vastas* are made at the right time in the summer season, they tend to retain their leaves all winter. Kalle Hamalainen, the proprietor of the Pleasant Street Baths, always made his *vastas* in the early part of July.

In my memory's eye, Kalle Hamalainen is always sweating profusely as he hurriedly performs one of the following five chores:

1. He is running down the basement steps to shovel more coal into the boilers.
2. He is responding to a bell signal by entering the associated empty room.
3. He is ushering a family group into an empty dressing room.
4. He is accepting payment from and exchanging farewell pleasantries with a family who have completed their bath.
5. He is reaching into the ice cooler to fill and order for a "cold" soft drink.

Isä always ordered a family-size quart bottle of Howdy orangeade for our refreshment. This drink—ice cold in the sense that it was cooled by ice refrigeration—was served without ice cubes. It was, of course, manufactured, as were all soft drinks sold in the Gardner steambaths in those days, in our bottling plant on Nichols Street, just three blocks from the steambath.

When I was about six years old, I thought *Isä's* purchase of the soda pop—always Howdy orangeade—was a totally irrational act. And I told him so in good Finnish many times. In our backyard plant on Nichols Street, I pointed out, there was a great deal of soda in many flavors. All of it was free for us. Why pay for it here? (My arguments were always given in the hot room out of the proprietor's hearing. My Finnish, incidentally, at age six was much better than it is today. I would have difficulty presenting my case in Finnish today.)

Isä usually brushed aside my rhetoric without articulate comment. But one Saturday night—perhaps I had been especially vehement—he replied to my arguments in English, the only occasion that I can recall his using English in a conversation with me.

"Reino," he smiled while standing naked before the sauna platform, "I have a love affair with Howdy Orangeade."

Isä and *Äiti* divided the family chores; *Isä heitti löylyä* (splashed water on the hot radiator) while *Äiti* switched the kids with a hot sauna *vasta*. The switching proceeded from the youngest to the oldest. A thoroughly switched kid was expected to get off the platform, shower, and leave the steam room.

My own "flagellation" with the birch-leaf *vasta* was troublesome but one would expect, especially at my age level then, to "enjoy" the discomfort of one's siblings when they were "under the switch." But, no, I didn't enjoy that. The movement of the hot air caused by the swinging *vasta*, when a sibling was switched, was almost as oppressive to me as my own switching. *Äiti*, I recall, always gave the *vasta* a lusty swing when she switched us.

It was easy enough to get out of the way of the hot turbulent air when someone else was being switched. All one had to do was to get off the top level of the sauna platform which was the scene of the switching. But no one did. I can't speak for anyone else but I know my reason. It had nothing to do with Finnish sauna machismo. It was simply shyness about my nakedness in the midst of a mixed group. After all, they couldn't see so much if you didn't move around. Perhaps the Americanization process started early. Indeed it did! But *Isä* also contributed to my sense of modesty because he always covered his genitals with one hand as he moved around the sauna.

My shyness and reluctance to take a family sauna increased as I grew older. I continually pointed out to Äiti that I had been allowed to change my "Dutch cut" to an "adult" haircut at age six. If, I argued, I was old enough for a man's haircut at six, surely I was old enough at 10 to sauna with the men in the male common room. Finally after two years of hassling, I succeeded in detaching myself from the family sauna group.

The Finnish sauna was much more than just a delightful way to take a bath. It was a social institution. The invitation, often heard in my youth, *"Tulkaa meille saunomaan"* meant much more than its literal translation, "Come to our house for a sauna." It meant: "Come visit us, we'll fire the sauna, socialize, take a bath and drink coffee with *pulla."* (Pulla is a cardamom-spiced braided sweet bread. It was the absolutely necessary companion of coffee years ago.)

The invitation included the entire family. The guests were expected to bring their children. And, unlike the informal procedure at our blueberry camp, each guest family took their bath as a group with the exception of the older boys and older girls.

Coffee was served continually throughout the evening. A second or third (or fourth) cup of coffee was always pressed on a seemingly reluctant guest who always disclaimed *"Piisaa! Piisaa!* (Enough! Enough!)

"Pikku tippa lisää. Vaan pikku tippa lisää," (One little drop more. Just a little drop more.) the hostess would reply as she poured coffee into the guest's cup.

"Ei, ei, piisaa jo! En voi juoda tippaakaan lisää!" (no, no, I have had enough. I couldn't drink another drop.) the guest would exclaim as he watched his cup being filled to the brim.

Both the guest and the hostess knew, of course, that the flow of coffee would cease only when the guest turned his cup upside down on his saucer.

The older children—around nine or ten (the Finnish-American addiction to coffee started very early in life)—also received coffee but they had to request seconds. The younger kids, the age depended on the hostess' discretion, were served an "ersatz" coffee consisting of hot water, cream and sugar. Any complaining kid, and there were some very young kids who drank coffee at home, were told that real coffee would cause the kid's hair to turn black in later life. A quip was invariably delivered by some bald-headed man—if one was present—"I wish my folks had given me coffee when I was small."

The hosts usually provided a special cardamon-spiced Finnish *pulla* called *lauantaikaakku* on these sauna social evenings. *Lauantaikaakku* means "Saturday buns." We kids assumed that the name implied the buns were baked only on Saturday, but our reasoning was wrong because the buns were available fresh every day. Undoubtedly the name *lauantaikaakku* implied the buns were for extra special occasions such as a sauna social.

Sugar in tablet form, or lump sugar as we called it, was another staple of coffee time. The tablets were placed on the table next to the granulated sugar. The first generation Finn would pour the hot coffee from his cup into his saucer, put the lump of sugar into his mouth, and pick up the saucer in both hands. He would blow gently to cool the coffee in the saucer and then he drank the coffee from the saucer with a soft sucking sound.

Most of the sauna social invitations that my family received were from rural families since very few Gardner city Finns had private saunas in those days. If we received an invitation to a local sauna social in the middle of the week, we did not forego our usual Saturday night visit to a commercial steambath. We were even cleaner, though, in the blueberry season when we took a sauna almost every day.

A BLUEBERRY FREE SUMMER

I don't know why *Isä* and *Äiti* felt that age six was the appropriate time to start a child's blueberry picking career but I still recall quite vividly many incidents that occurred in my last free summer, my last summer of leisure. *Isä* rented for the summer— this was one year before he acquired the blueberry camp—a little red brick garage behind the White House which, recall, was across the country road from Gates Pond. The blueberry pasture we called *Iso Haka* (The Big Pasture) was readily accessible from this garage. The older members of my family and some guests picked in this pasture while I enjoyed my last free summer. Except for our sojourn in the garage for that summer, both the garage and the White House were vacant for at least two decades.

The small size of the garage limited the number of blueberry pickers to a much smaller figure than we had at our camp in the ensuing years. Considering the garage was not big enough to hold two autos, the count is still impressive. The list, not including the transients of whom two or three were usually present, contained: the five Haapanen kids with their mother, the five youngest kids in my family, Isä and Äiti, and a very elderly widowed Finnish immigrant named Mrs. Karhumaa.

The word *karhumaa* means land of the bears, so we kids called this elderly lady Mrs. Land-of-the-Bears. She was not a relative of my family but she spent the last years of her life in our home because she had no other place to go.

It was a wonderful summer for me. I was five—too young to pick blueberries. The lady from the Land-of-the-Bears—too old to pick —had the resposibility of overseeing my activities. She had, in addition to baby sitting my year-old brother Waino, another five-year old from a neighboring Finnish farm. Mrs. Karhumaa was much too old to keep track of us two energetic five-year olds so we wandered, without restraint, all over Gates Hill.

I can't remember my friend's name anymore but I'll call him Pekka. Pekka came from Mr. Salminen's farm about one-half mile down Gates Hill. It seems to me that all of Mr. Salminen's children were grown. Still Pekka couldn't have been Mr. Salminen's grandson because he spoke Finnish very fluently, a skill rarely possessed by a third generation Finnish-American. I have always envied Pekka's tremendous forensic ability, using the Finnish language, even though he was only five years old.

One day Pekka became quite uptight about a fresh blueberry splash on his lunch plate. The lady from the Land-of-the-Bears had served us some blueberry soup as the first course at lunch that day. She used a dinner plate as a liner for the soup bowl and, when she served, some of the soup spilled over onto the dinner plate. After we finished the soup, Mrs. Karhumaa removed the bowls and was about to place a sandwich on Pekka's dinner plate when he objected.

He requested, without complaining or whining, a clean plate. Mrs. Karhumaa refused to give him one, explaining that the blueberry splash was fresh and, therefore, couldn't harm him in the least. Then as he persisted, she said, very much in error, that he himself had splashed his dinner plate when he slurped his soup.

My five year old friend's reply, given in excellent Finnish, impressed me so much that I still remember it fifty-five years later. He argued:

1. It didn't matter who had dirtied the plate. The important fact was that the plate was dirty and he wasn't used to eating from a dirty plate.
2. If Mrs. Karhumaa had followed the usual practice of serving the sandwich before the blueberry soup, the splashing of the soup, no matter who did it, would be of no importance.

The lady from the Land-of-the-Bears refused to budge from her position. She refused to give him a fresh plate even when I offered to dash into the garage to fetch it. The impasse was finally broken when Pekka declared, "O.K. I'll eat the sandwich from your dirty plate but I won't return tomorrow. I'll stay on my own farm where I'll prepare my own lunch."

That statement caused the lady from the Land-of-the-Bears to chuckle. She exclaimed, "Well, now I can't have that happened to my reputation. What will everybody think? Pick up your sandwich and give me your plate. I'll wash it."

She took the plate and, still chuckling, went to the well where she pumped a little water over the blueberry splash. Pekka sat at the picnic table beaming over his victory.

Another event of which I still retain a very vivid recollection did not end as happily for me as the "blueberry splash tussle" did for Pekka. When the climax was reached in this incident, it was too late for me to present an oral defense of my behavior. Besides, even if there had been time, I doubt it would have made any difference. My forensic ability was in no way equal to that of my friend.

One day, because of an early morning mist, the blueberry pickers did not enter the pasture until noon. Pekka, because of the mist, remained at his own farm. While most of the kids waited around the garage for the late sun to dry the dew in the pasture, my sister Lilja, her girl friend Aili, and I went over to Gates Pond.

I was with the two girls because I had a terrible crush on Aili. Wherever Aili went I was not far behind, trying my utmost to get rid of Lilja. My crush on Aili may explain some of my adventures that day so perhaps I should describe its extent.

Äiti had a practice, when we kids were cranky in the evening, of giving us a sugar tablet saturated with a Finnish patent medicine named *Tuskan Surma* (Pain Reliever). I enjoyed that medicated sugar tablet and, further, I was fascinated by its name. I translated *Tuskan Surma* as "pain reliever" but I do believe its literal meaning is "pain killer." *Tuskan Surma* was not made in Finland. I called it a Finnish patent medicine because it had a Finnish name. Its alcoholic content was 20% by volume.

I bestowed that name—*Tuskan Surma*—on Aili. At least I called her *Tuskan Surma* when no one else was around. She must have accepted the name because she answered to it. Maybe she liked the sugar tablet saturated with *Tuskan Surma*, too.

Gates Pond, covered by a mist, was deserted that morning. Someone had left a makeshift raft near the dam. I found a long pole, jumped on the raft, and invited the girls (meaning, of course, only Aili) to join me in a ride across the pond.

Aili was willing and actually got on the raft but backed off when my sister Lilja pointed out that none of us swam well enough to reach shore should the raft sink in the middle of Gates Pond. I pooh-poohed the dangers and, with a great display of courage, pushed the raft from the dam. About halfway across the pond, I lost my grip on the long pole with which I pushed the raft. It stuck to something when I pushed so that I was momentarily knocked off balance when I tried to pull it up. The raft glided away from the stuck pole leaving me sitting quite dejected on the raft.

I was much too far from shore to try to swim since I was only a dog paddler, and a rather poor one at that. I was much too proud to ask the girls to get help. Suddenly as I sat forlornly on that raft, I felt a great urge to defecate. I looked around the pond. A little steam that rose from the water impaired my vision but it seemed no one was in sight. Lilja and Aili had disappeared, mostly likely they had returned to the garage. I was sure that the Nunns, even if present at their bungalow, couldn't see me. The urge was tremendous, so down went my trousers. I squatted on the edge of the raft and defecated into gates Pond. The raft slowly inched its way toward the dam as I sat—more than a little unhappy—on it. I gripped the ladder near the dam and pulled myself onto the cement wall. I returned to the garage and found, with a great sense of relief, that the family had gone into the pasture.

When *Äiti* returned from the blueberry pasture, I realized immediately, without a word being spoken, that she was quite annoyed with me. Lilja had tattled on me! I took off fast, running in the direction of the neglected apple orchard behind the White House barn. I had always assumed I was a pretty fast runner for my age. In fact, like most Finnish kids of that era, I pictured myself as a five year old Paavo Nurmi—the great Finnish Olympic runner of the 1920's.

Äiti caught me. Never had I seen her move so fast. I can remember my thoughts as I raced desperately to get away, "How can an old person run so fast?" (*Äiti* was only thirty-seven at the time.) I remember the rather severe spanking administered with a switch ripped from a nearby sapling but the severity of the spanking didn't bother me as much as my lack of understanding of the reason for my punishment. Why was I being punished? Was it because I polluted Gates Pond? Or was it because I took a raft out to a depth that was "over my head?" I hoped it was for the latter reason but—alas!—I never found out why.

One night, when I was visiting *Äiti* during her terminal illness in the early 1960's, I recalled the incident. Ah! This is a good time' I thought, to settle a matter that had been nagging me in my subconscious for years. So I proceeded to relate the story about the raft and other incidents to *Äiti* to refresh her memory about our summer in that garage.

However, before I had a chance to pose the question, *Äiti* looked up at me, smiled, and said, "You must be mistaken. I cannot recall that I ever used physical punishment on you. I didn't have to. You were such a *kiltti poika* (a good-natured, kind, obedient, well-behaved boy) that I hardly ever even had to reprimand you orally . . ."

I don't think we kids were conscious about our deep aversion to picking blueberries. Even today my siblings and I tend to be proud of our youthful proficiencies in the art of picking. I asked my sister Vieno, quite recently, "What was your record?"

She replied with a voice full of pride, positive that the record should be inscribed in some blueberry hall of fame, "I was the best picker in camp. I picked thirty-two quarts—that's a full crate—a day three times before I was thirteen. I usually averaged about twenty-five quarts per day in the peak of the season. That was about five to ten quarts more than most of the kids."

But we kids had a very great aversion to blueberry picking hidden deep in our unconscious. I recall the day it exploded into the open. It was in the middle of August, the last blueberry summer at our camp. We had gone into the pasture in the morning but about noon it rained a little so we stayed in camp after lunch. The weather was hot and muggy so we children put on our bathing suits in anticipation of a swim in Gates Pond.

Then, before we had a chance to head towards the pond, a Gates Hill electrical storm arose. The skies darkened as the thunder echoed thoughout the area. The lightning flashed as if someone were turning lights on and off. The temperature dropped precipitously as the skies continued to darken. And instead of rain, it began to hail! The hail came down so hard it stung us as we ran in the field in our bathing suit. We were heedless of our fears of the lightning as it flashed in the sky. We were outside because we knew the hail was going to damage the blueberry crop. At least we hoped it would. And to help our hope become a reality, we sang and yelled to encourage the hail:

Hail! Hail! Knock those blueberries off the bush!
Hail! Hail! Knock those blueberries off the bush!
Hail! Hail! Knock those goldarn blueberries off the bush!

Chapter Four

THE MISSION STREET CHURCH

The sixth year was a significant milestone in the life of any American child in the 1920's but in the tradition of our family it was a triply notable event. Consider:

a) One month after my sixth birthday I became full fledged blueberry picker with my own La Tourraine coffee-can bank. My initiation into the "Gates Hill Order of Blueberry Pickers" was delayed a month beyond my birthday only because the blueberries did not ripen until after the Fourth of July.

b) One week after Labor Day in this same sixth year of my life, I was enrolled in the first grade of the West Street School in Gardner. One week later than the other six year olds because *Isä* felt that an additonal week of blueberrying was more beneficial to us kids than the first week of school.

c) The very first Sunday after our return to the city from the blueberry camp that year (1924), I was physically coerced into attending the Sunday school at the Mission Street Church which was officially named *The Finnish Evangelical Congregational Church*. It was on *Äiti's** insistence—*Isä* remained neutral in my uneven struggle—that I was introduced to some Christian teachings of a fundamentalist Finnish church.

My introduction to the Christian religion always reminds me of a picture of Charlemagne in our high school history textbook.

---

*Äiti is the Finnish word for mother. My mother, who is called Äiti in this narrative, was born in Alajärvi, Finland. Her maiden name was Karolina Hannula.

The picture was a reproduction of a painting of Charlemagne in which the Emperor held a sword in one hand and a cross in the other. I recall, when our teacher, Mr. Littlefield, asked for a volunteer to explain the painting, my hand shot into the air. I knew exactly what the artist meant when he painted that picture because I had experienced a little "religious coercion" myself ten years earlier. Here is what happened.

Äiti gave my two sisters, Lilja and Vieno, explicit instructions to deliver my body to the Mission Street Church Sunday school. And they did. But I put up a great resistance which increased in determination the closer we got to the church. My two sisters, each holding me by one arm, were literally forced to carry me into the basement of the building.

Tears, very shortly, gave way to feelings of pleasure when, once inside the church, I spied a very beautiful girl, who was about my age, named Helmi Ranta. Helmi was of Finnish-Italian descent—her father, a Finnish immigrant and her mother, a second generation Italian-American. I may be romanticizing now, fifty years later, when I state she had inherited the best physical characteristics of both nationalities but I do know her presence in that Sunday school melted away all the resistance I had to attending the church.

From that day on I was in fairly regular attendance at the Mission Street Church Sunday school for the next eight years, hoping each Sunday that Helmi would be present. Helmi, in all that time, never paid the slightest attention to me. I suspect, in hindsight, that she came to Sunday school because she was attracted to the minister's older son, Wilbur. The Lord, there is no question, gathers his flock in wondrous ways!

Äiti, of course, was tremendously impressed by my sudden change in attitude. On Sundays, I arose early, washed, had breakfast, and waited impatiently—whenever I waited—for my laggard siblings to get ready. *Äiti* had forced me to go to Sunday school because she had faith that, in time—and she was willing to be very patient—the presence of the Holy Spirit would influence me but she regarded my abrupt change of attitude as a miracle. And from that time on, in her own not very subtle manner she often expressed her wish to me that one of her sons might become a minister of the Gospel. That prospect never appealed to me, although, in my youthful wisdom, I never told her so.

The Mission Street Church had an exceedingly small membership. The Sunday school attendance never exceeded fifteen. The church services, which were always held on Sunday evening, never attracted more than seven or eight adults. The Pastor, Reverend Kalle Nurmi,* always gave a full hour Finnish sermon in his booming ministerial voice regardless of the number of people present in the pews.

At the annual Christmas night service, which was actually a Christmas party for the Sunday school children, the attendance swelled to about thirty-five including the children, five of whom belonged to the pastor's family.

The program at the Christmas services always included recitals by the children in Finnish. In most cases, we children did not understand the somewhat sophisticated Finnish *runot* (poems) we quoted from memory. But that didn't matter to us since our mood the entire evening was one of anticipation. Santa Claus was coming!

At the conclusion of the pastor's closing prayer, Santa Claus always clambered noisily up the stairs from the church basement, shouting joyously, *"Ho! Ho! Ho! Hauskaa Joulua! Ho! Ho! Ho! Hauskaa Joulua! Hauskaa Joulua!"* (Merry Christmas!)

When he approached the children's pew in front of the altar, he put down his seemingly heavy sack of goodies—which consisted mainly of toys and games selected by the older Sunday school girls from the F.W. Woolworth and J.J. Newberry five and ten cent stores—and asked, *"Oletteko olleet hyviä poikia ja tyttöjä tana vuonna?"* (Have you been good boys and girls this year?)

We children, very excited now because, for many of us, that sack contained most of the toys we would receive as Christmas presents, always responded with ecstasy, *"Kyllä! Kyllä! Ollemme olleet oikein hyviä lapsia!"* (Yes! Certainly! We have been exceedingly good children!)

And then Santa Claus, helped by the older girls who read the gift tags for him, distributed the presents to us.

I attended this pageant, which is my fondest memory not only of the Mission Street Church but also of Christmas, until I was

---

*The pastor, whom I call *Pastori* Nurmi in this narrative, is a composite of all Finnish ministers—Lutheran and Congregational—with whom I came into contact.

about fifteen years of age. When my class was in its early teens, we greeted Santa Claus with the same fervor as we had when we were six or seven. Our enthusiasm in the later years was, however, mostly for the benefit of the two or three youngest Sunday school children.

I don't know why Äiti chose to leave the Lutheran Church, the national church of Finland, to join the tiny (in membership) Mission Street Church. There was a Finnish Lutheran Church in Gardner which belonged to the *Suomi Synod*, the national organization of the Finnish Lutheran churches in the United States and Canada. Did life styles have anything to do with her choice? I do believe that the Mission Street Church expected its members to be more restrictive in their life styles than that expected by the Lutheran Church. But my family's life style—which included card games, dancing, and going to the movies—was even more relaxed than that of the average member of the Lutheran Church.

I asked the former Helmi Matilainen, a childhood friend whose family belonged to the Finnish Lutheran Church, if she could shed any light on Äiti's religious attitudes. Helmi replied,

> "...the Finnish Congregational Church emphasized *Conversion* (which leads to *salvation*) as a definite act of grace, which was not, and is not even yet, made clear in the Lutheran Church...that is why after my childhood in the Lutheran Church, I realized my need of a Savior and why I made a definite decision to follow Christ. I was born again! ...your mother, I imagine attended the Mission Street Church for the same reason."

WHERE DID ALL THE LUTHERANS GO?

The Finnish Lutheran Church in Gardner, although it had a much larger congregation than the Mission Street Church, did not attract the vast majority of the Gardner Finns either. The total number of first and second generation Finnish-Americans in the greater Gardner area must have exceeded 3,000 in the 1920's. The membership in the Gardner Finnish Lutheran Church was 290 according to the 1923 yearbook of the Suomi Synod. The total number of Finnish Lutherans in the entire Commonwealth of Massachusetts was only 2,360 in the same year. The 1920 U.S. census shows that 14,510 residents of Massachusetts were born in Finland. This suggests, since the second generation Finnish-

Americans are not included in the above census but are included in the Lutheran Church membership lists that only 10% (or less) of the Massachusetts Finnish-Americans belonged to the Lutheran Church. Since about 93% of the Finns in Finland were still Lutherans in 1960, one might ask: "What happened to all those Lutherans?"

The Finns in Massachusetts were not an exception to a general rule. The overwhelming majority of the Finnish immigrants, no matter where they lived—California, Oregon, Wisconsin, Minnesota, Michigan, Maine, or Ohio—stopped going to the Lutheran Church, or any church for that matter. The first generation Finns divorced themselves from the church at a rate that has no parallel in the history of any other immigrant group.

When I was a teenager (and even when I was younger), I often played cards—pitch, rummy, *kova Norja* (hard Norway), *pehmeä Norja* (soft Norway)—with some of the first generation Finns who lived in our boardinghouse. These players used a quaint expression, *kirkkomies* (churchman), to designate any card in the deck that was accidentally turned around. The explanation given was that "the card is on its way to church".

The early Finnish pastors in America and Canada placed the blame for the immigrant's lack of interest in the Lutheran Church on the "spurious doctrines of socialism, communism, anarchy, and free love". I quote from one such observation.

> If the individual lives of the vast number of Finnish immigrants in Canada has frequently been one of anguish, sacrifice, and uncertainty, a similar conditions has characterized the efforts to establish a Lutheran Church in their midst. F.J. Pennanen states that the Finnish people have alway found their strength throughout the ages in their Lutheran faith. From this faith they have been able to define their norms and objectives and achieve inner strength and tenacity. Pennanen believes that, outwardly observed, it would seem that the Canadian Finnish people have become largely estranged from this foundation. "To many an observer it would appear that the immigrant Finn no longer cares for those things that formerly had been dearest and holiest." Pennanen adds: "The God-denying tenets of the Communism have had freedom for too many years and have poisoned young minds."

Dr. John I. Kolehmainen, discussing the widespread indifference of the immigrant Finn to the church in his pamphlet, *The Finns in America*, lists drunkenness as one of the major evils faced by the church. Then he makes a remarkable statement:

...A more dangerous enemy** made its appearance early in the 1900's. From Brantwood, Wisconsin, as elsewhere, came the dismal tidings: "The monster of socialism has stolen into our quiet community and is disturbing our peaceful sleep." Marxism, brought from Finland by refugee radicals during the *Russification Years*, (1890-1905) engulfed the immigrants "like dry skin absorbs hot fat." Noted a minister sadly, "Before long all Finnish settlements were powerfully influenced by these doctrines. Our heads were literally swimming."

I am willing to concede the arguments given in these short excerpts. The question I'd like to pose is: Was the transition from the Lutheran doctrine to other beliefs as easy as one might infer from these quoted passages? I marvel at that transition if that was the case since my "unloading" of the fundamentalist beliefs instilled in me as a child was extremely painful and difficult. And it took many years to accomplish. I think the "miracle" in our story is that so many did leave the Lutheran Church. Were the Finnish immigrants on 1890-1914 a very unusual species? Let's take a closer look at them.

Almost all of the Finnish immigrants were literate in the sense that they were able to read Finnish even though their formal education had been usually limited to a few years in the Finnish *kansakoulu* (public schools) which were run by the Lutheran Church. These immigrants, thanks to the Lutheran Church, had the lowest illiteracy rate of any national group who immigrated to America at the turn of the century. But very few, since most of them came from the poverty-stricken rural areas of Northern Finland, possessed skills in any trade. They, therefore, had to take the menial, lowly-paid work, usually the work most dangerous to life and limb.

The Finnish immigrants had great expectations when they arrived in the New World. They envisaged an opportunity to forge a new life for themselves and they were willing to work hard, very hard, to achieve that goal. What happened? These rural peasants, used to working outdoors, found themselves "catapulted into the starless night of the of the coal, copper, and iron ore mines... feudally run graveyards which knew few, if any, safety regulations." Most of the Finnish miners were hired to push tram cars loaded with ore. These miners, called trammers, labored ten to twelve hours a day for an average wage of $2.50. The biggest op-

---

**I can't imagine how anyone can believe that socialism is more dangerous than alcoholism. Would you rather have a socialist spouse or an alcoholic spouse?

portunity these men were able to glimpse was a miner's drill job which paid $3.20 for the same workday.

Their work life was dominated by the petty lackeys of the industrial barons. Straw bosses often demanded tips from the miner before he was placed on a shift. The mules in the mines were held in higher esteem than the workers. The mules, after all, cost money; Europe seemed to have an endless supply of peasants. The mining companies denied liability for injuries and deaths that occurred on the job. Even the officials in the communities the immigrants lived in "pledged their allegiance" to the mining company, not to the laws of the land. Life was no "bowl of cherries" for these early Finnish immigrants.

These Finnish-American laborers were in desperate need of a champion, a champion to provide them with "spiritual sustenance" and to lead them (or guide them) in an effort to gain more equitable treatment in their work. The ministers of the Lutheran Church were incapable (or were not desirous) of providing this type of spiritual and moral support to their constituents. The concept of a Social Gospel, widely accepted by the American churches in the 1900's, had not influenced many Finnish pastors. The Finnish immigrants had to look elsewhere for help. An exodus from the Lutheran Church began.

Once the immigrants recognized that church membership was now voluntary, the exodus snowballed into an avalanche. The translated works of the renown American agnostic, Robert Ingersoll, "spread like wildfire through the Finnish-American communities. *God and Devil*, for example, became very popular—a New York Finn sold 140 copies in a single day; *Heaven and Hell* circulated, at times openly, at times surreptitiously from house to house". The net result most Finnish-American were no longer Lutherans; they got their spiritual strength from other sources.

Maybe the unchurching of the Finnish immigrant started even before she or he left Finland. At least they must have developed a skeptical view of the Lutheran Church when they were children. *Isä* used to tell us kids a story—a story *Äiti* never refuted—which I called *The Lutheran Church Confiscates the Family Cow*. The church, *Isä* said, used to collect taxes (tithes) from each and every person in Finland. Once, *Isä* recalled, when his family was unable to raise the church taxes in money, the church took away the family cow. The cow, incidentally, was the only property and the only source of income possessed by the landless and poverty-stricken Heikki Hannula family.

THE WAY OUT IS NOT EASY

Whatever the doctrinal differences that may have existed between the Finnish Lutherans and Congregationalists, I'm sure that my minister Pastori Nurmi would have agreed, substituting, however, the word *Congregationalist* for *Lutheran*, with the Reverend Juho Nikander, the founder of Suomi College and the first president of the Lutheran Suomi Synod, when he, Rev. Nikander, wrote the following in the Finnish *Paimen Sanomia* (Shepherd's Tidings): (my emphasis)

> Doctrine is pure only when its chief guiding principle is the Holy Bible, the Lord's own Word...When someone says that a Lutheran reads the Bible correctly, by this he reveals the universal character of the Lutheran Church. It demands, you see, unconditional obedience to God's Word and the *imprisonment of the mind* in obedience of faith.

I was mighty lucky that I did not encounter such a statement when the first doubts about the infalliability of the Bible began to percolate in my mind. I don't think I would have made it because the way out is not easy. Even then I had help. *Väinämöinen*, that delightful, pagan Finnish god—who had been born of the air and who had never been young—came to my rescue when my emotional conflicts about the church and the Bible threatened to overwhelm me. (Do you recall the last refrain he sang before he left? It was given in Chapter 1.) I believe he came. Let me now develop the story of my inner turmoil and relate how *Väinämöinen* came to the rescue.

Pastori Nurmi of the Mission Street Church, a heavyset man whom I recall as being always dressed in ministerial garb, preached the doctrine of grace. The Kingdom of God was open only to those who accept God's Word as revealed in the Bible without reservation. Although that doctrine didn't particularly bother me in my preteens because I didn't understand its meaning; it must have slowly seeped into my unconscious. (Did it function there as a superego in my teens to keep me in line whenever doubts began to crop up?)

What did frighten me in my preteens was another doctrine emphasized to us children by its constant reiteration. That doctrine went somewhat as follows: "Man is sinful. Man is depraved. And because man is depraved, he must earn his bread by the sweat of his brow. The first humans, Adam and Eve, transgressed against the Lord. Man, because of that original sin, is condemned to a lifetime of labor. ..."

I understood that dogma even when I was eight. It explained the world I lived in. Every male adult I knew, with the exception of *Isä* and a few other Finnish businessmen, earned their livelihood by farming or by working in one of the numerous chair factories in the Gardner area. But even *Isä* had to lift extremely heavy fish barrels and do much of his fish peddling in subzero weather. Since I was so sinful, I, too, was condemned to work forever in a place such as the Heywood-Wakefield furniture factory whose buildings dominated downtown Gardner.

Work meant work with your back, your brawn, and your hands. Saw, dig, shovel, push, pull, carry, and chop. That's work. Even today I find it difficult to believe that I am working when I prepare a lecture, write a chapter for a book, or give a talk. *Work?* A sense of guilt surges forth. Most of the tasks I do I would do for free but they pay me! I just don't earn my livelihood by the sweat of my brow.

But woe unto me when I was a kid! My manual dexterity "intelligence quotient" gave me the jitters then because it was (and still is) way below the idiot's level. How bad was it? Well, the seventh and eighth grade boys in the Gardner elementary schools were required to attend a two-hour manual training class once a week. The first project assigned to us in the beginning of the seventh grade was a broomholder. The other boys, at least most of the other boys, progresses easily and happily to airplane models and fancy birdhouses. But I, on the last day of class in the eighth grade, almost two years later, was still diligently trying to plane a level edge for the broomholder. My complaint to our teacher was, "The edge never ends up square." I was sure that the Devil and his henchmen had a special place reserved for me.

The first small doubts—doubts that I suppressed because they scared the wits out of me—began to bubble up when I was about thirteen. Since it has some significance later, I should mention that I had, by that time, discovered a great treasure-house, the Uptown Library in Gardner, a luxurious place compared to the library downtown. This library was in an upper middle class residential area. It was actually "above the tracks" as one had to walk up a slight grade and cross the tracks of the Boston and Maine Railroad, which passed through the town just above the Heywood-Wakefield factory, to reach the library.

I should also mention, since I feel it was closely related to my budding religious doubts, that my social consciousness was awakened at about this same time. I remember the occasion vividly. Pastori Nurmi asked a Sunday school teacher, an older woman inclined to give long tedious prayers full of excruciating details of distress, to lead the school's closing prayer. I shuddered a little and tried to think of a mental game I could play to while away the time as she prayed. And as she prayed, it hit me!

The people who grew the things we eat and the people who made the things we use—the very people who lived by the sweat of their brows—were rewarded the least by our society. Those who ate bread by the sweat of their brows ate the worst. And they always had the poorest homes, too. Pastori Nurmi himself, I thought, does not earn his bread by the sweat of his brow. He invariably—on cold days or hot days—wore his huge black ministerial frock coat which made manual labor (although not sweating) impossible. Several Finnish ministers had been guests at our blueberry camp but never had any one of them entered the blueberry pasture to pick, not even a "bottomful" for good luck.

Pastori Nurmi was, of course, quite conscious of the social ferment taking place in the Great Depression. Even though I was only fourteen during the presidential campaign of 1932, I feel now that my background knowledge then of the issues in that campaign was broader than his. His knowledge, I feel now as I look back, was minimal. But then such information was not of great importance to him.

I recall an amusing incident that occurred when Pastori Nurmi took a straw vote of the Sunday school pupils in the presidential election of that year—1932. I strongly suspect the results, overwhelmingly for Herbert Hoover, would have been published in the local newspaper, the *Gardner Daily News*, except the balloting took a rather exceptional turn.

We students were not invited to prepare an endorsing statement for the candidate of our choice. Instead Pastori Nurmi gave a short synopsis of each candidate's qualifications for the presidency along with some pertinent biographical information. His favorite,

Pastori Nurmi admitted, before he began his review of the candidates, was Herbert Hoover. The highlights of these synopses as I recall them were:

1. Herbert Hoover was a great Christian, a Quaker, a man who believed in the Eighteenth Amendment to the Constitution and who, if reelected, would enforce the Volstead Act which forbid the existence of the sinful saloons that were so prevalent before America adopted prohibition.

2. Franklin D. Roosevelt was the candidate of the liquor interests. Roosevelt, if elected, would repeal the prohibition laws. The saloons, with all the evils associated with them, would be brought back. It would be tragedy for the country if the liquor interests succeeded in placing their candidate in the White House.

3. Norman Thomas was a good man even though he was a socialist. He was a former minister who believed that the government should find work for the unemployed. Norman Thomas, however, did not have a chance to be elected.

4. Earl Browder was a communist. He was a man who had been in jail several times. Actually, he did not deserve to be considered for the presidency because he was an anti-Christian.

Why did Pastori Nurmi include the minor party candidates in his resumé? He had to because the largest group of organized Finnish-Americans in Gardner was the Finnish socialists who supported Norman Thomas. And my family, although not members of the *osasto* (as this branch organization of the Finnish Socialist Federation was known among the Finns), also supported Norman Thomas. Besides my "VOTE SOCIALIST - NORMAN THOMAS FOR PRESIDENT" button was plainly visible to every Sunday school pupil.

There was also a sizeable group of Finnish-Americans who supported Earl Browder's candidacy but I suspect Earl Browder was included in the list of candidates by Pastori Nurmi in order to influence two Sunday school pupils who lived downstairs of a two-story apament house owned by a leading Finnish *vasemmistolainen* (left-wing) family. Since the father of these two pupils was a hopeless alcoholic, the family was often dependent on their communist-leaning landlord for economic assistance.

Most of the pupils voted for Herbert Hoover. Roosevelt did not receive a single vote. But Eino Nurmi, the pastor's youngest son who was about eight years old then, was intrigued by Earl Browder. Was it because Browder had been in jail? Anyway, Eino voted for Browder.

The pastor knew exactly how each of us had voted because our balloting was done by raising our right hand. Eino's vote must have distressed the minister because he said, "Perhaps everyone did not understand my explanation of each candidate's qualifications. Let me repeat them. Listen carefully. And think before you vote."

He repeated his resumé, emphasizing and commenting at length about Browder's sojourns in jail. Pastori Nurmi spoke in generalities about Browder's imprisonment. I'm sure he didn't know the specific reasons why Browder had been incarcerated. I squirmed in my seat, itching to point that Jesus, too, had been in jail but I didn't have the courage to interrupt.

The vote was retaken but the tally did not change. Eino insisted on supporting his jailbird, Earl Browder. And perhaps that is why our Sunday school straw vote was never published in the *Gardner Daily News.*

Sometime in the early 1930's, a short time after the 1932 presidential election, a young second generation Finnish-American from Hibbing (Minnesota), who was an enthusiastic member of, if not an organizer for, the Young Communist League, often argued with me about politics and religion. He often pointed out to me—in his attempts to shake my confidence in the Christian religion—that the Finnish Lutheran churches in the copper and iron mining districts of Minesota and Michigan had accepted money and land from the big mining companies such as Calumet and Helca. In return, my friend claimed, the pastors of these Finnish churches adopted an attitude favorable to the mining companies which was detrimental to the workers' interests when those mining companies were struck. These ministers maintained their bias even when many of their own Lutheran parishioners were strikers.

I, of course, didn't believe his story. I had, by the age of fifteen, become acquainted with sufficient labor history to realize that the copper, iron, coal, and railroad barons of the early twentieth century were not the least bit interested in the souls of their employees. Those industrial barons were only interested in two P's—Power and Profit. For how could they have been interested in their workers' souls when they didn't give a single hoot about the well-being of their workers' bodies? For the body, I believed as Pastori Nurmi taught us, was the temple of the soul, a temple provided by God for the soul's sojourn on this earth.

With braggadacio I used to tell my young communist friend that I would personally break every window in the Finnish Lutheran Church on West Street in Gardner if his allegations were true. Now, more than forty years later, while researching Finnish-American history for *Blueberry God*, I discovered that my young friend from Hibbing was correct. And I always thought he was merely spouting communist propaganda.

I quote from an essay written by Dr. Arthur E. Puotinen, a former instructor of religion at Central Michigan University in Mt. Pleasant. (The emphasis is mine and I have separated the text into three paragraphs in order to give more emphasis to each thought.)

> The Company (a mining company) stronghold in the mining region surfaced in other forms as well. Partly as a means of *seeking stability* and *social order,* companies donated *land* and *modest* sums of cash for the building of churches.
>
> Facing a few stewardship problems of financing on the basis of voluntary contributions rather than the tax subsidies from a state church, Finnish pastors and laymen accepted the gifts as a necessary mission enterprise. Thus, recipients of both company benevolence and also contributions of workers and their families who comprised a goodly portion of the church membership, local pastors appeared caught in the middle when strikes occurred.
>
> A steady mining industry seemed necessary for both the church and the families in the congregation. Those workers expecting prophetic proclamations from the clergymen in favor of unionization and collective bargaining were to be largely disappointed as pastors adopted a more conciliatory tone calling for cooperation and good will between labor and management.

I have a hunch that Dr. Puotinen is being "gentle" with the early Finnish church authorities. For, how can there be cooperation and good will between labor and management without collective bargaining? How can there be collective bargaining if the workers do not belong to a union?

My interest in politics and social questions helped me keep a lid on my continually percolating doubts. The greater the doubts, the greater my social awareness. The greater the doubts, the tighter the lid was pressed on. There was a safety valve though. I developed an overwhelming and, at times, irresistible urge to tap each telephone pole I passed three times. Was it one for the Father, one for the Son, and one for the Holy Ghost? Thank Heavens, I never saw Reverend Nikander's statement about "imprisoning the mind"! But I marvel at what appears to have been the easy and almost effortless transition of the first generation Finn out of the Lutheran Church. Was it really as easy as it seems to have been?

Although the concept of an all-powerful and vengeful God was instilled into me in the Mission Street Church; interestingly enough it was Pastori Nurmi himself who planted the first seeds of doubt in my mind. Pastori Nurmi, perhaps worried we might stray from the Biblical truths, often reconciled the apparent inconsistencies in the Bible. One Sunday he reconciled Genesis with the age of the earth as accepted by scientists.

The age of the earth from the time of Adam to the present was, according to the Holy Scripture, he said, not much more than 5,000 years. The geologists and other scientists claimed that the earth was more than two billion years old. How did a Christian reconcile this scientific hypothesis with the Genesis' account that the Lord created the earth in six days? This rather troublesome disparity was easily resolved if one realized that the six days God took to create the universe were not literal days. Each day in the Genesis may have been eons long, millions of years long, not the twenty-four hour day of our present time.

That shook me! Why, if God was all-powerful, could He not create the universe in exactly six of our present twenty-four hour days? And why, if He desired, could He not leave evidence to suggest that the earth was actually two billion years old? What a great way, it occurred to me, for a vengeful and jealous God to test the faith of the believers. Those, who believed in His Word as given in the Bible, in spite of all evidence to the contrary, were God's true believers, the ones to be saved. Those whose faith was weak, too weak to withstand the evidence brought forth by the scientists, were doomed to eternal punishment.

The beginning of the resolution of my personal religious crisis came one wintry night. Although I wasn't aware of it then, I now believe that it was *Väinämöinen*, the Finnish pagan tribal god, who stepped into the breach to halt the mental tortures that had lasted several years. I found myself extremely restless that snowy and cold evening, so I decided to visit the Uptown Library. Perhaps some female high school classmate might find her way there too. I trudged along the unplowed sidewalks to the library, somewhat dispirited and troubled. I avoided as many telephone poles as possible by taking "short cuts" through alleys and backyards.

I was the only patron in the library. I walked around the two large reading tables, glancing at the magazines which lay on them. Finally I picked up a magazine at random. An article in it caught my attention. I sat down and began to read. I was amazed. I cannot remember the name of the magazine, the article, nor the articles's author, but I do recall that the author quoted and essay on religion by John Stuart Mill in which Mill analyzes the concept of an all-powerful god. I quote:

> . . . For it is impossible that anyone who habitually thinks, and who is unable to blunt his inquiring intellect by sophistry, should be able without misgiving to go on ascribing absolute perfection to the author and ruler of so clumsily made and capriciously governed a creation as this planet and the life of its inhabitants. The adoration of such a being cannot be with the whole heart, unless the heart is first considerably sophisticated. The worship must either be greatly overclouded by doubt, and occasionally quite darkened by it, or the moral sentiments must sink to the low level of the ordinances of Nature: the worshipper must learn to think blind partiality, atrocious cruelty, and reckless injustice, not blemishes in an object of worship, since all these abound to excess in the commonest phenomena of Nature. It is true, the God who is worshipped is not, generally speaking, the God of Nature only, but also the God of some revelation; and the character of the revelation will greatly modify and, it may be, improve the moral influences of the religion. This is emphatically true of Christianity; since the Author of the Sermon on the Mount is assuredly a far more benignant Being than the Author of Nature. But unfortunately, the believer in the Christian revelation is obliged to believe that the same being is the author of both. This, unless he resolutely averts his mind from the subject, or practises the act of quieting his conscience by sophistry, involves him in moral perplexities without end; since the ways of his Deity in Nature are on many occasions totally at variance with the precepts, as he believes, of the same Deity in the Gospel. He who comes out with least moral damage from this embarrassment, is probably the one who never attempts to reconcile the two standards with one another, but confesses to himself that the purposes of Providence are mysterious, that its ways are not our ways, that its justice and goodness are not the justice and goodness which we can conceive and which it befits us to practice. When, however, this is the feeling of the believer, the worship of the Deity ceases to be the adoration of abstract moral perfection. It becomes the bowing down to a gigantic image of something not fit for us to imitate. It is the worship of power only. . . .

The author ended his article with a clarion call for the defiance of an all-powerful God in the name of justice, love, and compassion. That ending, and now I quote from memory, went as follows.

> ". . .If such an all-powerful God exists, one who condemns men to

eternal damnation for whatever reason, then I cannot sit by His side in Heaven. My place is with the eternally damned, sharing their fate, offering whatever solace I can to those who need my solace. It doesn't matter to me if the soul has been damned because the man it belongs to believed in a wrong religion, failed to worship the Almighty according to some prescribed rite, or even if the man committed the most despicable crime of all time. The punishment does not fit the crime. Eternal punishment is too severe. If an all-powerful revengeful God does exist, a God who condemns men to eternal damnation, then I have no choice, I am needed in the Inferno, therefore I must choose the Inferno. That is the meaning of *love* to me. ..."

Vänämöinen performed some of his magic to open a tiny door for me that night. A wave of relief surged through me as I read and reread the article. I marveled at the author's audacity to challenge the concept of an omnipotent God because of his feelings of love and compassion to his fellow man. The next day, after school, I hurried back to the library because I was anxious to copy some of the pertinent paragraphs but the magazine was gone. At least I couldn't find it and the librarians were unable to assist me because in my excitement the evening before, I had forgotten to note the magazine's name, the article's title, or its author. *Vänämöinen*, I became convinced years later, had played a magic trick to save me from my mental tortures. My compulsions did not suddenly go away. No, there were still many telephone poles in Gardner that received whatever message was transmitted by my knocking. But I was on the road to freedom.

Perhaps the most thrilling story that gave me additional courage to eradicate more of the old irrational fears was told me, to my best recollection, by a first generation Finnish socialist who was the volunteer janitor for Ash Street Hall. The janitor, Julius Ahtio, acted out the debate between Clarence Darrow and a fundamentalist minister before a packed audience in New York's Cooper Union.

Clarence Darrow, in his rebuttal, pulled out a pocket watch and placed it on the podium. Then he quietly told the audience he was going to perform a demonstration to aid his opponent who, it was obvious, needed a little help in arguing the affirmative side of the debate: Does God Exist?

"Oh, Lord," Darrow intoned, "If you exist, please send a bolt of lightning in the next sixty seconds to smite down this rank disbeliever, this blasphemous heretic, Clarence Darrow."

The entire audience was shushed. The silence was as complete as the sixty seconds ticked away. Darrow was the only confident person in the huge auditorium as he stood at the podium. Everyone, including his supporters, his adversaries, and his debating opponent, sat out the sixty seconds in a cold sweat.

Darrow's bold and dramatic presentation of the negative side in the Cooper Union debate opened the church door a little wider for me. My freedom, however, came in a conscientious objectors' camp. Let me explain.

Pastori Nurmi had a fondness for a parable which he often repeated in his informal talks to us in Sunday school. The parable was about a young boy who often had trouble falling asleep because he was disturbed by a knocking on his bedroom wall (or door?). One night the boy called his father and complained about the mysterious knocking.

His father told him it was the Lord knocking. He told his son to shout, whenever he heard the knocking, "Enter. Lord. I am ready to do Your bidding."

The parable was based, I think, on Revelation 3:20—"Behold, I stand at the door and knock. If any man hears my voice and opens the door, I will come unto him and will sup with him, and he with Me."

Maybe it's strange but, although I must have heard the entire parable at least a dozen times, I cannot remember how Pastori Nurmi ended the story. Then when I was in a conscientious objectors' camp during World War II surrounded by a group of men, almost all of whom had extremely strong beliefs—Quakers, Mennonites, Brethren, Molakans, Christadelphians, Theosophists, Swedborgians, single taxers, Lemurians, Presbyterians, Methodists, Baptists, anarchists, orthodox Jews, reformed Jews, Vendaists, Catholics, Jehovah's Witnesses, Russelites, Dukabors, Unitarians, Universalists, vegetarians, Seventh Day Adventists, socialists, DeLeonists, Tolstoyans, Bhuddists, fruitarians, and even one communist (who left when Russia was invaded by Nazi Germany)—and I suddenly knew the meaning of Revelation 3:20.

Do *not* believe anything so strongly, with such fervor that you can't hear the Lord when He knocks on your door. Do not let the truth drown in the intensity of your belief. Do not be so convinced you have found the only road that you cannot recognize the Lord when you meet Him. Remember if you meet Him, you will be going in the opposite direction, maybe the wrong direction.

Chapter Five

ISÄ WAS AN ENTREPRENEUR

Isä, at one time or another, ran a commercial sauna, owned a retail shoe store, sold groceries, peddled fish, or manufactured and sold soft drinks. I remember vividly the fish peddling and soda businesses but the other enterprises were before my time. *Isä* manufactured soft drinks, using a hand-operated carbonating machine, in a large building at the rear of 197 Nichols Street in Gardner. I am told that before 1917 he delivered his soft drinks by horse and wagon, going as far as North Rutland, about twenty miles away. When I arrived on the scene *Isä* had graduated to a model T truck.

The soda business, as we called it, was successful enough so that he had Alex Havumaki, a Pitcherville first generation Finnish-American, and my oldest brother Toivo working in the soda factory. When cooler weather arrived, *Isä* delegated the responsibility for the soda business to his two employees and he concentrated on selling fresh fish—haddock, salmon, and smelts—in Northern Worcester County communities of Hubbardston, Rutland, Templeton, South Royalston, Otter River, Ashburnham, and Gardner.

The fish, packed in ice in large wooden barrels was delivered by the American Railway Express from Russo & Sons of Boston. The barrels were so heavy that *Isä* was not able to handle them himself. Quite often I saw *Äiti* help him lift the wooden barrels and together they would dump the fish into the large galvanized trays that were in back of the model T truck he used on his fish route.

In the winter time, especially during the coldest weather, *Isä* would crawl behind the wood-burning kitchen stove and fall asleep after returning home on the completion of his route. We kids had to restrict our activities to the other rooms in the apartment until *Isä* was "thawed out." Then the entire family sat down to supper which, at least once a week, consisted of Maltex brand whole wheat cereal and Polish *limppu* (sour dough rye bread with caraway seeds).

The soda factory was started by *Isä* in partnership with my godfather, Aati Poikonen. The partnership owned the Nichols Street property on which the soda factory and the large tenement house in which we lived was located. The partnership also owned a farm on the western slope of Gates Hill.

Victor Starzynski, a former classmate, whose father baked the Polish *limppu* (rye bread) which was very popular with the Finnish people in Gardner, gave me a quart bottle which had the words HANNULA & POIKONEN 197-201 NICHOLS ST. GARDNER, MASS embossed on it. Victor found the bottle in the Polish-American picnic grounds where it may have lain for more than sixty years. That bottle is now one of my proud possessions but I often wonder, when I look at it, how many non-Finnish customers were able to say (pronouncing the names) to their grocer, "A quart bottle of Hannula and Poikonen's sarsaparilla soda, please."

The Hannula-Poikonen partnership was dissolved a few months after the armistice that ended World War I. Sugar was the cause. Sugar was very scarce during the war so the partnership, with the permission of the authorities, used saccharin as substitute for sugar in the soft drinks. The use of saccharin made the soda business very profitable because saccharin was much cheaper than sugar and the sweetener was the most expensive ingredient in the soft drinks.

When sugar became plentiful again, Aati Poikonen wanted to discontinue the use of saccharin. But *Isä* was extremely reluctant to change the profitable formula. He insisted that the firm continue to sweeten its soda pop with saccharin. Aati was equally adamant about reverting back to a sugar-based sweetener.

I don't know how explosive the argument became but *Isä* had an obstinate temperment (which, alas, I seemed to have inherited). He impulsively blurted out, "O.K. Let's break up if we can't agree." Aati accepted the suggestion. The winner of a single toss of a coin was to have his pick: the Nichols Street property and the soda factory or the farm on the western slope of Gates Hill. Aati won. He chose the farm.

Fate played a trick on those two men. Aati was an excellent businessman and *Isä* was attracted to the land. Aati sold the farm shortly after his winning toss and returned to Gardner where he opened a bakery which he ran successfully until his retirement. *Isä* changed the name of the bottling works to Hannula & Son. The highly profitable use of saccharin was stopped, at the insistence of the authorities, a few months after the dissolution of the partnership.

Hannula & Son continued *Isä's* policy of diversification. He put the company into the malt business. It was a natural expansion for him because he liked to make sure all his resources were being used. In this case, the resource was an old sauna in the basement of the building that housed the soda factory. *Isä* had a broad high platform built in the hot room. He then bought barley which he stored on the platform. The barley was wetted and the sauna was fired. The generated heat caused the moist barley to germinate.

I can remember, although it was not a weekly event, taking several baths in this basement sauna. The barley was stashed away on the highest platform, the family sat on the lower platforms. The barley, I presume, sweated as profusely as we did while *Isä heitti löylyä* (threw water on the hot rocks to generate steam).

When the barley was ready—had germinated sufficiently—*Isä* roasted it in a coffee bean roaster to remove all the extra moisture from the grain. The resulting malt—the barley became malt at some point in this process—was then packed into five-pound packages which *Isä* sold to the families on his fish-peddling route.

These customers brewed a Finnish near-beer called *kalja*, a non-alcoholic beverage, from the malt. I suppose *kalja* might have become alcoholic if the brew had been allowed to ferment long enough. If any Finnish *kalja* brewer did that he kept it a dark secret because alcoholic beverages were taboo in the social life of the first generation Finnish-Americans. I often saw *kalja* served at home social gatherings but I never saw a first generation Finnish-American host serve an alcoholic beverage to a guest. *Kalja* was even offered to the children who usually spurned it because of its bitter taste. *Isä*, of course, brewed his own *kalja*. And—because he believed it was good for us—he often served us kids a *kalja* eggnog (a whipped concoction of egg, *kalja,* and honey) just before bedtime. *Kalja* does have lots of protein but *Isä* didn't know that.

I have a feeling that each *kalja* brewer took considerable pride in the flavor of his near-beer. Almost without exception, they invited *Isä* to sample a batch they had brewed from their previous purchase of malt. Although I can't recall any praise or complaints about the quality of the malt, I do remember the comments of one Finnish farmer who had just replenished his supply of malt, "Would you like to sample my last batch of *Kalja?* It has a very unique flavor. I used some water from a new spring I found to make it."

ISÄ WAS A FREE THINKING LIBERAL

Almost all Finnish-American businessmen were conservative. Elis Sulkanen, in his history of the Finnish-American labor movement, states that the Finnish businessmen, without enlightenment about social and political issues, were generally more conservative than their native-born American counterparts. These Finnish businessmen, whose enterprises were often small and marginal, tended to identify with and adopt the attitude of the dominant industry in the locality in which they happened to live. Not *Isä.* *Isä* always, in success and in failure, identified with the workingman who earned his bread by the "sweat of his brow" in the chair factory, the woolen mill, granite quarry, or other industry.

Isä subscribed to and eagerly read the Finnish socialist daily newspaper *Raivaaja* (The Pioneer) and the left-wing *Eteenpäin* (Forward). When I was five or six, he also received an English language newspaper which always carried a picture of Eugene Victor Debs, the five-time Socialist Party presidential candidate and hero to a large segment of the first generation Finnish-Americans, on its front page.

Isä disapproved of organized religion. I never saw him inside of a church, not even for the confirmation of his own children. He felt that ministers would be tolerable if they preached a Social Gospel. They should involve themselves with their parishioners' earthly cares and woes as well as their spiritual needs. They didn't, *Isä* claimed, because they had never known hard physical labor, hunger, or the feeling of hopelessness that overwhelms a workingman who, after a week of backbreaking toil, finds his pay hardly enough to sustain his family with nothing left over to put aside for the purchase of his dream farm or house.

Isä died just before the end of World War II. He was buried, as he had wished, from home, not from a church. *Isä* also requested the family have a completely non-religious funeral because, he said, "I never went to church so I don't think it is fitting or proper that a minister should officiate at my funeral." *Äiti* reluctantly acceded to his wishes. Henry Puranen, a leader in the old Finnish socialist organization gave the farewell talk at the funeral.

I did not get a chance to visit *Isä* during his last two years which he spent in a tuberculosis sanitorium because I was stuck away in a conscientious objectors camp in California. I was told, however, that a *well-worn* Bible was always in handy reach on his bedside table. The implication is, of course, that he received consolation and inspiration thumbing through that *well-worn* Bible during his last days. Perhaps the Bible was there. If it was, it was there only to satisfy convention not to give solace. *Isä* would have smiled at the idea. I can hear him, "What if, at the last moment, I accidentally read Psalm 109?"

Isä, like thousands of other first generation Finns, had, after reading the Finnish-American labor press for twenty-five to thirty years, a well thought-out personal religious philosophy. Most of the unchurched first generation Finnish immigrants I knew in the 1930's had no doubts about their religious stance. Why should they? Their non-religious orientation was already over twenty-five years old. I regret, however, that I never asked any of them to relate their personal experiences on their road to "liberation".

Most of my contemporaries in the second generation never understood (and do not now understand) the philosophies of the first generation Finnish-American. The tremendous language gap that existed between the first and second generation Finnish-Americans hampered the older American Finns from passing abstract and subtle ideas to the younger generation. *Finglish* bridged the language gap in the work-a-day world but no Finglish words were invented to enable the older generation to explain the exciting ideas he or she had gained from reading the translated works of Ingersoll, Upton Sinclair, Jack London, or from the Finnish versions of Edward Bellamy's *Looking backward*, Robert Blatchford's *Not Guilty*, and John Spargo's *Socialism*.

Besides, the second generation was resistant to the progressive ideas and attitudes of the older generation. They, in general, refused to "buy" the ideals espoused by their elders. And no wonder. The younger generation faced tremendous pressure of their peers of all nationalities to accept conventional mores and establishment standards. And, in addition, the second generation was daily indoctrinated in the public schools by the obligatory participation in the Lord's prayer that began each school day. This rush to Americanization—which I think was a good thing— meant that most second generation Finnish-Americans grew to maturity with only a vague idea of their parents' philosophies. And they never gained any insight about the environment that begat those philosophies.

Even some of the well-educated second generation Finnish-Americans who became college teachers cannot accept the agnosticism of such a large segment of Finnish immigrants. One of these college teachers wrote, "It was not surprising that some readers (Finnish immigrants), only a *few steps removed* from rustic darkness, became *befuddled* by these *heady materials* (books by Ingersoll et al) which as a clergymen observed, they drank 'like dry wood swallowing hot tar'. 'They were not sufficiently *ripe* to read this kind of literature critically,' seconded another critic." (emphasis is mine)

That statement, in my opinion, is a bit of arrogant and condescending nonsense. Ingersoll was impressive. He knew the Bible more thoroughly than most of the ministers of his time. He attracted record audiences composed of all classes in American society at his lectures wherever he spoke. His fees, up to $4,000 a lecture, were enormous even by today's standards. Robert M. LaFollette, the famous Wisconsin Senator (surely many steps removed from rustic darkness) stated, "I never lost an opportunity to hear him (Ingersoll) speak. He had a tremendous influence upon me. He liberated my mind. Freedom is what he preaches. He wants the shackles off everywhere...."

If Ingersoll's works were not powerful, if his ideas and comments were easy to answer and refute, then his lecture notes would be required reading in our public schools and colleges today. The college students, certainly "some distance removed from rustic darkness", would study Ingersoll. The "heady material" would be critically evaluated, leaving the faith of both the students and the college professor reenforced or, at the least, completely undisturbed.

But Ingersoll's works gather dust in the libraries because he, Ingersoll, is not easy to refute even by those many miles from "rustic darkness". I concede that some who read Ingersoll go away unimpressed but others, as numerous members of the first generation Finnish-Americans could have testified, would never again find solace merely by reading the Bible. And they wouldn't need to. The high moral and ethical principles expounded by Ingersoll, as he argued against the superstitions of his time, should be sufficient for any man or woman who needs tenets to live by.

Surprise! Colonel Robert G. Ingersoll was a Republican. He was not responsible for the socialist ideology accepted by so many thousands of first generation Finnish-Americans. Ingersoll feared socialism might not be compatible with freedom. He recognized that the workingman of his time (around 1880) did not receive an equitable share of the country's economic production. He argued, however, that the working people had the numbers to correct this evil by the ballot box without changing the economic system.

Thus, we might say that thousands of first generation Finns were eclectics—a sign of sophisticated discrimination, not rural ignorance. They took their religious ideas from a Republican agnostic (but rejected his politics) and followed the political teachings of the socialist Eugene Victor Debs. Ingersoll, incidentally, was the most popular religious writer among the first generation Finns.

IS ISÄ IN HEAVEN?

Suppose a Lutheran God does actually rule the universe, readily bestowing eternal salvation to those who belong to one of the numerous Lutheran sects of His Church but quite reluctant to grant that salvation to any free thinking individual or any Christian of another denomination. If such a God allows the poor damned souls a chance to plea their cases in front of the Judgment Seat before being dropped into Hell, then I know how *Isä* handled his appeal.

Isä had the personal characteristics of the typical first generation Finn. He was extremely forthright. When he gave his attitude about any subject—personal or general—one knew exactly where *Isä* stood on the issue. He, like so many first generation Finns, tended to equate tactfulness with insincerity, diplomacy with guile. I can see *Isä* when his turn came to approach the Judgment Seat, cap in one hand, his left eye covered by his patch, "Lord, let me apologize. I was mistaken on earth but it was an honest mistake. All men and women make mistakes, as You very well know.

"How can I explain the stink I made about the family cow? Up Here it's easy to see that it was Your Way of impressing on my family and me about the Sin of Possession—being obsessed with earthly goods. But, down on earth it did seem to me that the Lutheran Church was being quite avaricious. *Now*, and I hope it is not too late, I no longer begrudge the Church for it.

"My only defense for what I am told is my greatest sin, that of denying Your existence, is easily explained and, I pray, readily forgiven. The Bible did not inspire me. Maybe Here, I'll gain a new insight into Its meaning,"

Do you think the Lutheran God threw *Isä* into Hell? If he did, *Isä* is enjoying his damned associates there. All the intellectuals he read in their Finnish translations—Ingersoll, Paine, Kautsky, Sinclair, Lenin, et al—are there. And for a change of pace, *Isä* is teaching them, teaching how to relax and enjoy the immense heat. The sauna has prepared Finns for a *hot* Hell. The hell of the ancient pagan Finn was a cold hell, a frozen hell. A cold Hell would have worried *Isä* just as much as it did the ancient Finn.

But *Isä* has not been severely punished, not even by a Lutheran God. The Lutheran God has, after all, an extremely strong Jewish background. And God, when he served only the Jews, gave the Jews 613 commandments to obey or to perform. The list included 365 proscriptions, or negative commandments (Don't work on the Sabbath) and 248 positive, or pious acts (good deeds). These positive acts are known as *Mitzvoth* (singular: *Mitzvah)* in Yiddish.

The Jewish philosopher, Maimonides, in his *Book of the Mitzvoth* said that the performance of only one *Mitzvah* (good deed) is sufficient for salvation provided the *Mitzvah* is done out of love for its own sake, not out of self-interest or to gain credit in the eyes of God. *Isä*, I'm happy to relate, performed innumerable *Mitzvoth*. And he performed all of them out of love for its own sake. He didn't do them to get into Heaven because he didn't believe in Heaven.

I have no worry about *Isä's* whereabouts. If there is life after death, then the process is a natural one and *Isä* participated in that process, as will everyone. If *Isä* was judged, there was no question about the verdict since his good deeds, his *Mitzvoth*, were legion. Let me mention a few.

Isä cosigned notes for his fellow Finns, mostly farmers, without any qualms. Rarely did these notes "bite" him. When a note did "bite" him, it was because the maker had died unexpectedly and the widow was in dire straits or because the maker had run into an unusual string of bad luck. In both these cases, he would have offered a helping hand anyway.

Isä was a total abstainer from alcoholic beverages but he had a soft spot in his heart for his farmer friends—his favorite people—who, after imbibing too much, found themselves in the local jail. *Isä* never refused to put up bail but in all such cases he insisted on driving his friend back to his farm to make sure there would not be another call from the same farmer on the same Saturday afternoon.

My recollections of these *Mitzvoth* that *Isä* performed in the early 1920's is rather vague. Most of the information I possess must have been imparted to me by my siblings since I was very young then. But I did directly observe *Isä's* great compassion for the "down and out" during the Great Depression when, after he had gone bankrupt, he and *Äiti* ran a restaurant *(ruokala)* at 255 Main Street.

There was a steady stream of transients (unemployed men looking for work) who came into the restaurant to request something to eat. *Isä* never turned anyone away. Each, without exception, was fed. Never, to my knowledge, did he ask any one of these unfortunate men "to prove their sincerity" by performing some work in the restaurant; even though there was, I know from personal knowledge, an awful lot of work in that restaurant.

Many times, though, the recipient of *Isä's* kindness insisted on working at some task to pay for his meal. So quite often, after high school classes were over, I washed dishes with a stranger and listened to tales about the great hardships faced by the displaced Americans in the Great Depression.

Roosa (Rose) Penttinen, a first generation Finnish-American who worked in our *ruokala* (restaurant) for many years, told me she recalled that *Isä* fed 17 transients on one terribly cold winter day. Roosa was eighty when she told me this so I pressed her on the point. She insisted that the number was correct, "I went to

Jussi (*Isä* was called Jussi by his close friends) and told him that I thought the restaurant was marked in some way. That's why so many people came in for a helping hand. But Jussi merely smiled, shrugged his shoulders as if to ask, 'What can I do about it?'"

Once, Roosa recalled, a boy about fifteen entered the *ruokala*. It was a cold, blustery, snowy day. The boy's shoes were almost completely disintegrated. *Isä* prepared the boy a plate of food, seated him at a table, and then—while the boy ate—scurried about to find him a decent pair of shoes. The boy left the *ruokala*, Roosa said, with a belly full of the best food you could buy in Gardner, a paper bag full of meat sandwiches, and a pair of good shoes on his feet.

THE GREAT DEPRESSION OVERTAKES ISÄ

Isä went bankrupt in 1931. Times were so good in 1928 he decided to expand his estate by building a two-story tenement building in the rear of 197 Nichols Street. Shortly afterwards, in 1929, just before the stock market collapsed, a fire gutted the interior of the three-story dwelling we called home. *Isä* decided to modernize the structure even though such renovation costs would be considerably greater than the settlement made by the insurance company for the loss. All four Finnish families who had apartments in the building "roughed it" in the gutted building (in the fall and early part of winter) while the renovations were being made.

The stock market crashed, signalling the advent of the Great Depression but I cannot recall that anyone in our environment paid the slightest heed to that harbinger of disaster. *Isä*, however, soon discovered that dollars were hard to come by as the effects of the depression widened. Dollars became precious! *Isä*, who had borrowed cheap dollars in the "good times", discovered that now, in the depression, he was expected to pay his mortgages and other debts with precious dollars. The value of *Isä's* property was so depressed that the proceeds from the sale of the real estate, if sold, would not have been sufficient to cover the mortgage.

Finally, after two years of mental anguish, *Isä* petitioned for voluntary bankruptcy. The petition was granted and *Isä*, at age 50, watched his life's work auctioned off. I saw tears in *Isä's* eyes that brisk autumn morning when we all stood on the front porch listening to the auctioneer ask for bids on the house. I maintained my composure only by a great display of bravado. There was only one bidder, the bank that held the mortgage.

It was downhill for *Isä* from that time. He took the debacle much too hard and only Finnish *sisu* kept him going. He never lost his compassion for those who were in worse straits than he was nor did he lose his deep interest in philosophical and political ideas but he did withdraw into himself. He did regain some of his old confidence, a few years later, when, at the depth of the depression, our family bought and moved into one of the finest homes in the city of Gardner. But he never again displayed the creative initiative, the tremendous energy, and the compelling drive which almost enabled him to grasp his fondest dream—financial success.

Äiti, in the middle 1920's, had talked *Isä* into buying a Finnish *ruokala* (restaurant) so that she might contribute to the family's then growing fortunes. *Isä* also acquired, a short time later, a second *ruokala*, a tiny establishment that was housed in the first floor apartment of one of the large tenement houses on Sherman Street. This *ruokala*, which was not licensed, served only the noon day meal to the Finnish workers who were employed in that area.

Isä managed to salvage both these restaurants and the blueberry camp from the auctioneer's hammer but the rest of the property was gone. We were finally evicted from our home in 1932. The other three Finnish families had preceded us out of the Nichols Street building by a few months. The elder Hyvonens had moved to another apartment on Nichols Street. The widow Riika Pullianen had died and her surviving daughter, Tynne, was assimilated into our family. The widow, Olga Haapanen, purchased the small Sherman Street *ruokala* from *Isä* and moved her family of four there to run that enterprise.

Several small Finish businessmen, who had cosigned *Isä* notes had been financially hurt by the bankruptcy. Neither *Isä* nor *Äiti* felt that the bankruptcy had ended their moral obligation to pay back these compatriots these losses. Both of them were troubled by these debts but, even though the restaurant had considerable "cash flow", there was little, if any, profit. So nothing could be done about these moral obligations until *Äiti* had a brilliant idea which resulted in a happy solution.

Mrs. John Piispanen, then a recent widow of one of the cosigners of *Isä's* notes, occasionally ate in the restaurant as my mother's guest. Then one day *Äiti's* brainstorm hit. She suggested that Mrs. Piispanen eat all her meals in the *ruokala* until the amount due her had been paid. It took almost an entire year—at $6.00 a week for 21 meals—before Mrs. Piispanen had eaten "the amount of money" her late husband had lost in the bankruptcy.

Both *Isä* and *Äiti* asked Mrs. Piispanen to continue taking her meals in the *ruokala* and to make a payment—weekly or monthly—not to *Isä* but to one of the other co-signers. In this way, after a passage of a few years, *Isä* and *Äiti* succeeded in paying off every Finnish creditor. The other creditors received only the amount the bankruptcy court awarded them. *Äiti* rationalized this with, "The *toiskieliset* (the non-Finns) were not individuals engaged in small businesses. They were large corporations."

I REMEMBER ISÄ

I remember *Isä* vividly in the last years (1934-1938) that I lived at home. He functioned adequately as the manager, cashier, purchasing agent, bookkeeper, errand boy, and general handyman in the *ruokala* (restaurant). He was already to assist wherever needed—peeling potatoes, cutting carrots, shredding cabbage, washing pots and pans, or making a hurried trip to a store for a needed item. But I don't think his heart was in his work. He was in *Äiti's* field and he knew it.

In the spring and summer *Isä* spent a good portion of his time at the blueberry camp growing potatoes and strawberries, now that picking blueberries was no longer commercially worthwhile. I had a definite impression in those days—watching him work in the potato and strawberry fields, preparing coffee over an open campfire, or heating the sauna for a quick bath before heading home—that he really belonged to the soil. But, now, reflectively looking back, I wonder if working on the land gave him solace from the nightmare of his business failure.

One day, at a time when people said the economy was "bottoming out" in the Great Depression, our *ruokala*, which usually served 40 to 48 cash customers with their noon meal (dinner in those days), had only eight customers. *Isä*, who with *Äiti* had been up since 5 A.M. to prepare breakfast and the noon meal, was visibly shaken. We were, at that time, at least two months behind in our rent and utility bills. *Isä* looked at the $3.20 gross income for the noon meal, shook his head in bewilderment, and decided to throw in the sponge.

He locked the front door, took whatever change there was in the till, and walked to the welfare office which was in the old Uptown City Hall to put the family "on relief". Welfare was a local matter in those difficult depression days. A family was said to be "on relief" when given financial assistance by the local welfare agency.

The head of the welfare agency, Martin C. Anderholm (or one of his deputies), offered *Isä* a slightly different option. "Keep your restaurant open," he said, "and we'll help you pay the overhead until the local factories get a little busier." *Isä* accepted the offer.

That night *Isä* chuckled out loud when he announced that the welfare department had placed the *ruokala* on relief. *Isä* always jokingly claimed that he came through the Great Depression with his "honor" unscathed, his family had not been on relief. The *ruokala* (restaurant) was too small to be eligible for the massive aid given Big Business by the Reconstruction Finance Corporation, he jokingly would continue, but then the *ruokala* didn't need it. A few injections of relief payments and all would be well again.

And he was right. A few months later the work in Gardner picked up and the *ruokala* was taken off the relief rolls. The *ruokala*, so close to death, survived for another twenty-eight years providing its customers with the best food in Gardner and providing *Isä* and especially *Äiti* with a great deal of work and very little profit.

Isä got a tremendous break in 1935. The family fortunes were at a very low ebb again even though we lived then in one of the most beautiful houses (with the restaurant in a picturesque downstairs room) in Gardner. The story of *Isä's* good luck demonstrates that lusty old *Väinämöinen*, the delightful old pagan Finnish god, watches over his own.

Isä's left eye was in an extremely serious condition. He had been able to distinguish only light from darkness with the eye for about a year. Now that eye became inflamed from an infection. It was painful and, most alarming, the infection threatened to extinguish the sight in his right eye. The opthalmologist said the left eye must be removed but we did not have enough money for the operation.

Isä's eye injury was the result of driving his model T truck on the rural roads of Hubbardston. Some of the roads he travelled on were so narrow, the brush so thick that he or his passenger (if he had one) were forced to push the brush away by hand as the truck slowly proceeded along. (I noticed, the last time I was in Hubbardston, that three of the roads *Isä* used to traverse were no longer passable.) One day, a branch he did not notice grazed his left eye. The eye became infected. The infection was stopped but slowly he lost the sight in that eye.

Isä's big break came when he was hired to work as a laborer, a ditchdigger, by the WPA. The eye doctor, whose name I know but shall not give—even though my family has always been grateful to him—found a happy solution.

"Tomorrow at work," he told *Isä*, "after you swing the pick, complain that something hit your eye. Come to my office and I'll take care of things from there on."

Isä was fitted for a glass eye but he preferred to wear a simple patch over the empty socket. *Väinämöinen's* magic works! Although *Isä* refused the glass eye, he was unable to refuse the workmen's compensation checks which began to arrive every two weeks. *Väinämöinen's* magic is not simple but it works! Those biweekly checks helped tide the family over one of the toughest spots we had ever been in.

I regret that the proprieties make it impossible for me to give the name of the Good Samaritan, the eye doctor, who had the brilliant but simple idea, even though he has long since gone to his reward. He was not of Finno-Ugric descent but our pagan god *Väinämöinen* is duty bound to watch over his descendants as carefully as he does us Finns. For, according to this pagan religion: A father's good deeds honor his sons for generations; Sins die with the sinner. I hope, however, that those descendants recognize when *Väinämöinen* is trying to help. It's not always easy to tell. *Väinämöinen's* magic has some extremely unusal and strange twists. His power, remember, is limited.

ISÄ LOSES HIS PREJUDICE

The rivalry between the organizations of the churched and unchurched Finns, a rivalry that had been very intense in the first two decades (1900-1920), diminished in the late 1920's. The immigrants mellowed as the years went by. They decided, I suppose, to live and let live. But even in the 1930's when I was a teenager, a churched Finn would have preferred to "drop dead" than be seen at any affair in the socialist hall. And the unchurched Finn, such as *Isä*, still kept his vow never to be seen in the vicinity of any Lutheran church. Both, however, shared a common prejudice; a prejudice against the Catholic Church.

The Lutheran (or Congregationalist) Finn was just as disturbed as the socialist Finn when one of his or her offspring married a Roman Catholic. The disturbance was even greater if the ceremony was a Catholic one. I don't know where this prejudice originated but I believe the Finnish prejudice in Gardner was a reflection of the deep prejudice against Catholics that permeated the entire Gardner Protestant community in the 1920's and early 1930's. The growth of this anti-Catholic sentiment may have been caused by the rapid growth of the French-Canadian population in Gardner (and in Massachusetts) at this time.

This prejudice against Catholics, whatever its reason, was very prevalent among the Gardner Protestants in the 1920's and 1930's.* This prejudicial atmosphere must have affected *Isä*, too. That surprises me, when I think about it, because he was seldom influenced by the popular sentiment. He took great pride in his "independent thinking". There was no doubt, however, that *Isä* had a deep-seated prejudice against French-Canadian Catholics. He admitted it and he finally overcame it. Here is the story of his triumph.

My brother Arvo, a bus driver for the Flanagan Bus Lines at that time, met, wooed, and won the affections of a student passenger named Rita Baker—a Catholic girl of French-Canadian and American Indian descent. Rita, well-liked by my family, was a frequent guest in the boardinghouse during the courtship. There was no particular hullabaloo when the couple announced their intention to get married. *Isä*, however, had a delayed reaction. He expressed his feelings on Arvo's wedding day.

Arvo, who idolized *Isä*, reminisced, "*Isä* came up to my room on the third floor where I was dressing for my wedding. He wished me all the happiness in the world. Then, in that blunt way he had, he told me that he wasn't going to come to any Catholic wedding ceremony. And he went on, 'You've made your bed,

---

*The prejudice against the Catholics broke out into the open in the early 1920's. The Ku Klux Klan began to burn their crosses on the hilltops that surround Gardner with apparent impunity. No one, to the best of my knowledge, was ever arrested in this futile attempt to terrorize the Catholic population. Luckily, the KKK episode was short-lived.

now you'll have to sleep in it.'

"That shook me a little," Arvo went on. "I didn't know what to say to him. Before I could collect my thoughts he had left the room. You know how he was, easily embarrassed by any sentiment. Funny, I never expected him to come to the wedding. You know, he no longer went anywhere."

Isä's prejudice may have permeated through the entire family. The most devastating indication of this prejudice is revealed by a family portrait that was taken in 1939. I cannot recall anything about that portrait even though we all posed for it in the library of our home on Elm Street.

Rita remembers the events surrounding that picture very well because Rita is missing from that portrait. Every member of the family, from far and near, is in that picture except Rita. Even Rita's first born, Douglas, then about a year old, is there—sitting on *Isä's* lap. Rita remembers. She told me, "I was working as a bookkeeper at LeMay's. The family told me to get Douglas prettied up for the portrait before I went back to work after supper. I did and then went back to the furniture store. The photographer arrived while I was at work, took the family portrait, and left. I was told the photographer couldn't wait until I had returned from my job!"

That photograph almost destroyed the marriage of Arvo and Rita. It continued only because Catholics married "for keeps" in those days. The marriage lasted for thirty-seven years, ending only when Arvo died of lung cancer in the summer of 1976. Arvo, incidentally, died as a member of the Roman Catholic Church. His baptism, which I accidentally attended, occurred only a few weeks before his death although he had been a faithful participant in church activities for twenty years.

The Protestant citizens of Gardner, my family, and especially *Isä* mellowed as the years went by. *Isä* may have mellowed faster than anyone else. Five years after this family photograph was snapped, in 1944 to be exact, *Isä* was a patient in the Worcester County Tuberculosis Sanitarium about twenty-eight miles from Gardner. He received a weekend furlough about once a month to visit his family. The war was on and everyone claimed to be busy, so Rita (who may have been the busiest of all) had the job of driving *Isä* to and from the hospital on his furloughs.

Isä's English was not good enough for elaborate conversations but one Sunday evening *Isä* broke the silence, 'Rita, something I tell you."

"Sure, *Isä*, tell me," Rita replied.

"My English not too good to say much. But understand me. I no go home again."

"What do you mean, *Isä?*" Rita asked, a little alarmed. "Weren't you happy this weekend? Didn't you have a good time? All your grandchildren were at home!"

"Sure, sure! Very good time. But, Rita, I no go home again. My time come. You understand?"

"Oh, come on, *Isä!* You look great! You're going to get well again. You looked just great this weekend. I've never seen you look better!"

"No, no. My last visit. I no go home again. Not sad. But I want you to know. I no like you when you marry Arvo. You Catholic. I no like Arvo marry Frenchwomen. But I tell you now, you better than my kids."

Chapter Six

THE RUOKALA WAS A BOARDINGHOUSE

The restaurant was a boardinghouse. I translated the Finnish word *ruokala* into *restaurant* in the last chapter, even though the correct translation is *boardinghouse*, because our *ruokala* was both a restaurant and a boardinghouse for several years. Some customers patronized the *ruokala* as if it were a family-style restaurant. They ate and paid for a single meal, usually the noon meal which we called dinner. These patrons were the cash customers without whom the *ruokala*, when the business was on Main Street, could not have survived.

Another group of men ate three meals a day and paid their board bill by the week. Usually the payment was not in advance. These workers didn't pay in advance because when they started to eat their meals in our *ruokala*, they had just gotten a job and they were flat broke. For many reasons, including alcohol and the very low wages paid in the Gardner factories, they were never able to save enough money to pay in advance. But the main reason was that Isä and Äiti were much too easy going in their business relationships. *Äiti* never believed that anyone would take advantage of her. This meant, of course, that when one of the boarders left the area or was laid off, he owed at least one week's board bill.

A third group of workers not only ate three meals a day in the boardinghouse but they also rented a room or, to be exact, a share of a room. The demand for rooms in *Äiti's* boardinghouse was so great that every room except *Isä's* and *Äiti's* has at least two beds in it. One of my brothers and I shared a room with two boarders. In the eighteen years I lived at home I never had a room all to myself.

Many of these permanent boarders were very close to the family. Some were as concerned about *Isä's* and *Äiti's* financial problems as any member of the immediate family. When the boardinghouse had to move, they not only moved with it, they helped with the moving. They moved out of the "nest" only to get married, to take a better job in another community, or because they were drafted into the armed forces in World War II.

Äiti's boardinghouse, incidentally, contributed the first two young men from the Gardner area to fight against Hitler and Mussolini. Oiva West, a second generation Finnish-American, and John Forsberg, a recently arrived Swedish immigrant, joined the Abraham Lincoln Brigade to fight to preserve the Spanish Republic in 1937. I had the great honor of driving them to Boston to catch the boat to their destiny.

Äiti's boardinghouse was not an unusual phenomenon in a Finnish-American community. The early Finnish immigrants often organized a cooperative boardinghouse in the communities where they were employed. A common name for these *ruokalas*, especially in the Middle West and Western mining and lumber towns, was *poikatalo* (bachelor home) even though the establishment was owned and operated by both men and women immigrants. The most famous of these boardinghouses was the *Elanto Company* of Nashwauk (Minnesota) which was organized so that the immigrants could not only have a "place to eat Finnish food but also a meeting place so that they might freely discuss topics of mutual interest." At least two of these Finnish cooperative boardinghouses sent delegates to the founding convention of the Central Cooperative Wholesale, the most successful Finnish enterprise in the United States.

These cooperative boardinghouses also served an obvious third purpose. They provided a place for the single man and woman to socialize. *Isä* and *Äiti* met in such a *poikatalo* in Fitchburg (Massachusetts). A number of other first generation Finnish couples that I knew in the Gardner area also met in a cooperative boardinghouse, fell in love, and were married.

Thus, these cooperative establishments had within themselves the seeds of their own destruction. As more and more of the couples paired off, there was less and less need for the continuation of the business. In Gardner, the Finnish immigrant boardinghouse, called the *Osuusruokala* (Cooperative Boardinghouse), was sold to a private party sometime before 1920. *Isä* and *Äiti* bought the business in 1927. The only visual reminder of *Äiti's ruokala's* historic past was the large clock which still had OSUUS-RUOKALA imprinted in the window which covered the face.

The *ruokala*, when *Isä* and *Äiti* bought it, was located in a building on a corner of Willow and Main Streets. The building was so old and musty that the restaurant premises were difficult to keep clean. *Isä* and *Äiti*, therefore, made arrangements to rent the three story *Yoffa* Building at 255 Main Street, a block away. The first floor of the Yoffa Building, which had a display window facing the street, was at least 30 by 60 feet—plenty of room to contain the kitchen, pantry, and still leave a dining area large enough to hold six tables, each of which could seat eight diners.

Before the Yoffa Building became available, however, *Isä* received an eviction notice to vacate the Nichols Street property. We made, therefore, an emergency move to a small three bedroom house at 47 Pelley Street. Five skilled cabinet makers from Grand Rapids (Michigan), who had recently arrived in Gardner to take new jobs at Heywood-Wakefield, moved in with us. Two young socialist organizers, who were devoting their time and energy to the 1932 Norman Thomas presidential campaign, also moved in with us.

There were sixteen people who lived in that small three bedroom house for about three months. Eight of us slept on the floor in the living room, the others were scattered in various "nooks and crannies" of the house. Only my parents and my sister, Lilja, had their own private rooms.

I don't know why the five experienced and skilled cabinet-makers chose to live there in all that turmoil. There were plenty of vacant cheap rooms in depression-ridden Gardner at that time. They, all first generation Finnish-Americans, apparently wanted to be "first in line" for a room in the Yoffa Building. The socialist organizers, two young idealists who were supported by the Socialist Party at only a subsistence level, didn't have much choice. They had free board in the *ruokala* and a free place to sleep in a friendly, even if overcrowded, atmosphere.

The Yoffa Building finally became available. Even though *Isä* and *Äiti* converted the two seven-room apartments on the upper floors into thirteen bedrooms and a common room—where there was usually a discussion or a rummy game in progress—the demand for rooms was so great that the luxury of a private room remained a perogative reserved for my parents and my sister Lilja. The boarders and the family mingled as one big clan. *Äiti* was the matriarch of the boardinghouse. Everyone, regardless of national background, called her *Äiti*. And everyone, of course, tried to please her.

THE BEST FOOD IN GARDNER

The dining room in the Yoffa Building fronted on Main Street. The entrance separated two huge plate glass windows, each of which had the words DINING ROOM lettered on it. The lettering had been done by an itinerant sign painter in return for a week's board.

During the best times about 50 to 60 workingmen ate their noon meal here. The cash customers paid 40¢ for dinner. Breakfast and supper were each 10 cents less. Twenty-one meals cost, if paid weekly, only $6.00.

All meals were served family style. Each diner helped himself to whatever was placed on the table but no diner had to worry about how much his neighbor took from the serving platter because the food was continually replenished at each table until everyone was satiated. A customer was allowed to eat all he wanted to. There was no limit on any of the food placed on the table. The variety and the quantity of food put on each table staggers me today. Am I remembering correctly? I am!

There were usually two kinds of meat, one especially prepared for the day and the other, leftover from the previous day. Finnish-Americans were meat-and-potatoes eaters, so, of course, potatoes and gravy were served every day. The potatoes were mashed or boiled in their jackets. Small new potatoes, freshly dug from *Isä's* potato patch, were served as a special treat quite often in the middle of the summer. Two hot vegetables—fresh when available—were served with the meat and potato entrees.

Five kinds of bread—Polish *limppu* (rye) from Starzynski's bakery, Finnish *reikäleipä* (a round rye bread with a hole punched in the center; *reikäleipä* literally means "a bread with a hole in it"), American white, hard tack, and *Äiti's* homemade—were always available.

The beverages, all one could drink, consisted of milk, buttermilk, coffee, or tea. Both milk and buttermilk were in pitchers on the table. Coffee or tea, neither popular at mealtime with the Finnish workers, was served on request. The buttermilk, naturally fermented—called *pitkää piimää* in Finnish—was not very popular with the younger generation.

Hot soup was always available from a serving bowl on the table. Although once in a while it was merely tomato soup, usually the soup served would be called an entree in any restaurant today. My favorites were Finnish style whole yellow pea soup with ham, fresh kidney stew and the Friday fish chowder. *Äiti's* boardinghouse rarely served a green salad but a platter of tomatoes and cucumbers, in season, was always placed on the dining table.

Do you have room for more? The boarder topped off his meal with a piece of homemade fresh apple pie (with cheese) or homemade blueberry pie. Since the pie tin was on the table a customer could help himself to a second piece. Or even a third piece if he found an empty spot in his stomach! Sometimes the dessert was a cold fruit soup—blueberry, strawberry, or cranberry—poured over Finnish style rice pudding. During the New England strawberry season the dessert was always strawberry shortcake with whipped cream. The strawberries were raised by *Isä* of course.

My favorite dessert? The greatest taste treat was the tart cranberry soup eaten with a piece of buttered Starzynski's Polish *limppu*. The tart cranberry soup stimulated the taste buds so much that one could count the caraway seeds in the *limppu* with one's tongue. I know how to make the cranberry soup; but where, oh where, can I find the Polish *limppu*.

ÄITI WAS THE BOARDINGHOUSE

Äiti was the source of strength for the hustle and bustle at 255 Main Street. *Isä* helped but *Äiti* was the boardinghouse. Two efficient hard-working first generation Finnish-American women helped *Äiti* with the countless tasks but *Äiti's* work never seemed to end.

Äiti rose at 5 A.M. to start cooking the breakfast and the noonday meal. While cooking and baking she oversaw every aspect of the business. Nothing escaped her individual attention. She even inspected the upstairs bedrooms after the woman who made the beds went home. She straightened out the bed clothes a little here and a little there, an action which exasperated me no end because

I thought the rooms cleaned and the beds made to unsurpassable standards. The rooms were in perfect shape, I told her. My complaints about her unnecessary chores went completely unheeded.

At 2:30 P.M. Äiti took a nap but she came back at 4 P.M. to prepare supper, a lighter, less formal meal than dinner. After supper she cleaned the kitchen, often scrubbing the floor on her hands and knees until everything sparkled. Her workday ended at around 8 P.M. Sunday was a little easier for her. Somehow she managed to find time, even though she had no outside help, to worship at the Mission Street Church which, because of its small membership, held its only church service in the evening.

Äiti did all the cooking and baking. She did it without using recipes and without measuring the ingredients. Everything, it seemed to me, was just thrown, helter-skelter, into a big pot; the pot placed on a gas burner and the ingredients beaten, stirred, and tasted. Äiti was a taster. The heating, the stirring (with a pinch of this and that), and the tasting continued until the concoction was "done". The result was the best food anyone could buy in Gardner at a price so low that I can't understand how our boardinghouse remained solvent—especially when I consider the large number of free loaders who ate that excellent food.

As I reflect back now I realize Äiti thrived in the restaurant business. She was a tremendous bundle of energy and good health. She had more energy than anyone I have ever known. But in my high school years, especially when the boardinghouse was in the Yoffa Building, I felt guilty, extremely guilty, that my mother had to work so hard. The lucky families, I thought, were the ones whose fathers had a 7 to 4 shift in a chair factory.

Äiti, in a way, is responsible for the existence of the United Furniture Workers union. Let me explain. Except for some first generation Finnish-Americans, there was no one in Gardner at that time who had any experience with the American labor movement. My oldest brother Toivo, however, an extremely erudite person whose voluminous background knowledge and interests ranged from the plight of the whooping cranes to Newton's invention of calculus, was thoroughly familiar with the history of the American labor movement. The young labor activists began, therefore, to turn to Toivo for intellectual stimulus and for practical guidance in their organizational efforts. Soon the boardinghouse became a beehive of labor activity during the so-called

NRA (National Recovery Act) strikes that broke out in the Gardner area in 1934-1936.

The boardinghouse became a hectic place during a strike. The judges in the district had a propensity to grant "anti-picketing" injunctions at the request of the employers no matter how trivial the pretext. The strategy meetings in the boardinghouse at these times lasted until early in the morning. Toivo always maintained the fledgling union had a Hobson's choice. If the injunction was obeyed, then the union might as well "close-up-shop". The union could not survive because the factory workers were not going to pay dues and follow a group of men who were afraid to fight injustice, even if the odds were overwhelmingly against them.

On the other hand, if the union defied the injunction (as Eugene V. Debs' American Railway Union did in 1894) *and* the government enforced the court order (which President Cleveland did against Debs); then the union was also finished. The union was *kaput* because its leaders would go to jail. Toivo usually suggested, and the particpants in these strategy meetings concurred, that an injunction be declared "illegal" (which they usually were) and be disregarded.

The anti-picketing injunction granted the employers in the long O.W. Siebert factory strike in 1934 stands out in my memory. The union leaders made themselves "very scarce" when they were cited for contempt of court for disobeying the court order. I recall two policemen barging into my third floor bedroom (illegally) as I was reading a textbook. One of them peeked under both beds and the other examined the inside of the clothes closet very carefully. They never said a word to me. I was happy about that because I was much too frightened to have replied.

I said *Äiti* was, in a sense, responsible for the existence of the furniture workers union because the boardinghouse provided these early Gardner labor activists with both a physical refuge and a spiritual home. And the boardinghouse couldn't have existed without *Äiti's* tremendous energy and her remarkable ability to make short shrift of the multitudinous menial tasks that had to be done. Toivo may have attracted the young labor activists there but *Äiti's* complete willingness to accept each person she met as a child of God made them feel welcome. There is no question in my mind that the union would not have been organized as easily nor as soon if *Äiti* and *Äiti's* boardinghouse had not existed. Neither the union nor the labor activists of that time have ever recognized *Äiti's* contribution to their success.

JOHN BROOKS WHEELWRIGHT, A NEW ENGLAND POET

John Brooks Wheelwright, an avantgarde wealthy socialist poet from Boston, became a frequent visitor to *Äiti's* boardinghouse during these days of labor unrest in Gardner. Wheelwright, as we called him, had a pedigree which linked him with some distinguished people in the early history of Massachusetts. His ancestors included Governor John Brooks (1817-1822) and the earliest champion of religious freedom in the Bay Colony, Reverend John Wheelwright.

In my mind's eye, John Brooks Wheelwright is always wearing a racoon coat. There is a photograph in the 1940 issue of *Modern Biography* which pictures him exactly as I remember him. His racoon coat, a magnificent fur coat, with collar up, seemed always to be wrapped around him. He wore that racoon coat on the slightest provocation, the slightest hint of inclement weather.

Äiti told me that one time he arrived in a chauffeured automobile, which made quite an impression on the diners in the boardinghouse. John's arrival in that chauffeured auto may have been, however, part of a protest against a labor injunction, an incident that I will relate later. Still he was certainly wealthy enough to have been driven around by a chauffeur.

John Brooks Wheelwright supposedly came to Gardner because he wanted to help the socialist local in its efforts to organize a union for the restless and lowly paid Gardner factory workers. But I suspect the real reason was that he enjoyed the atmosphere in the boardinghouse. I think he derived great pleasure from eating and associating with the workers from the factories, most of whom were first generation immigrants from Europe.

For some reason, he found great pleasure in helping *Isä* in the potato and strawberry fields in our camp. *Isä* said Wheelwright didn't accomplish a great deal of work because he had a tendency to wander off into the woods. Once he took it upon himself to prepare the coffee for the afternoon break. Once was enough. The coffee was so strong, *Isä* claimed, that the lump sugar wouldn't sink, it floated on top of the coffee.

"Turkish coffee," Wheelwright called it. But *Isä* was never convinced that anyone in the world could appreciate such strong coffee.

Wheelwright was involved in an amusing incident that occurred during the labor turmoil in this area. The Gardner socialist local was helping a group of striking woolen yarn workers in Fitchburg, a neighboring city. The company had obtained the usual court injunction which forbade picketing anywhere in the vicinity of the plant. The members of the Gardner socialist local were very reluctant to go to jail in a neighboring city because they had so much labor activity in Gardner. Still, unless something was done, the yarn workers were going to lose their strike by default.

Someone had a brilliant idea. Let John Brooks Wheelwright test the legality of the injunction. Let Wheelwright do the picketing in his racoon coat. Wheelwright was called and the arrangements were made. He was driven to the factory in a chauffeur-driven automobile. The automobile, I know, was owned by Wheelwright. The chauffeur may have been a family employee.

Early one morning the lone policeman on duty at the factory entrance watched a chauffeured car stop nearby. The chauffeur opened the back door of the limousine and helped a tall, gangly gentleman in a handsome racoon coat get out. The policeman, who, incidentally, was a second generation Finn, watched apprehensively as John Brooks Wheelwright began slowly walking back and forth in front of the factory entrance.

The policeman finally approached Wheelwright, "Hey, you can't do that. There's an injunction against picketing here."

"I am aware of that," Wheelwright replied, "but I think the injunction is in violation of the Constitution."

"I'll have to arrest you if you don't stop." the policeman said.

"Oh, you can't do that!"

"Whadaya mean I can't do that?"

"Well, you're a little late. My mother allows me to be arrested twice a year and I've already been arrested twice this year."

Wise guy! Huh!" the policeman said as he came closer to Wheelwright, taking a pencil and pad from his pocket. "What's your name?"

"John Brooks Wheelwright."*

---

*Everyone, Wheelwright claimed, had difficulty in writing down his last name. That's because it's unnatural to follow the *l* (in an Anglo-Saxon name) with a *w*. This policeman was no exception. He took a long time to get the name straight.

"What's your address?"

"Back Bay, Boston."**

"What's your occupation?"

"I'm a poet."

The policeman looked at Wheelwright in disbelief, hesitated, and then blurted out, "Jesus Christ! I thought they were all dead!"

John Brooks Wheelwright introduced five of us Fitchburg and Gardner young socialists to the world outside our small factory communities. He came by one day and offered to pay our expenses to a Socialist Party conference in Bound Brook (New Jersey) if we could supply the car and do the driving. One of us owned an old jalopy, so we left for New Jersey via New York City. I can't remember anything about the conference except for a few snatches of an anti-communist parody and the sight, my first, of the grand old man of the Socialist Party, Norman Thomas. But I do recall almost everything that happened on the trip down to Bound Brook.

Wheelwright recited some of his poems, enlightened us about socialist doctrine, and told us about his ancestor, Rev. John Wheelwright, who was also a poet and who was banished from the Massachusetts Bay Colony for defending religious freedom. He also told us some anecdotes, which I have forgotten, about his acquaintance (or friend) John Reed, the author of *Ten Days That Shook The World*. I forgot those anecdotes because, not knowing who John Reed was, I didn't pay attention to the narration.

We stopped in some little town in Connecticut for lunch. John ordered clam chowder. It was Manhattan style! Wheelwright went into a tizzy! He called the manager and berated him as if the restaurant had committed a cardinal sin, "Manhattan style clam chowder in a Connecticut restaurant so close to Boston! Soon," John declaimed, "the goddamned imitation clam chowder would be served in the restaurants around Boston common. Someone," and he pointed his long finger at the abashed manager, "someone must hold the line or New England will lose its character. New

---

**Snob appeal. Even socialists have weaknesses. I think Wheelwright expected a reaction from the policeman but he didn't get it. The policeman didn't know (and neither did I, then, for that matter) that Back Bay is the home of the Cabots and Lodges. And, you know, the Cabots only talked to the Lodges and the Lodges only talked to God.

England will be gone."

Still we parted from the restaurant with good feelings. The employees may have been nonplussed at John's unusual behavior, but we were friends with them. It wasn't the size of the tip that impressed them either. It was John Brooks Wheelwright. They had never met an agitator like him before. He had enlisted all of them, at least temporarily, in the struggle to keep Manhattan style clam chowder west of Greenwich, Connecticut.

In New York Wheelwright brought us to a fancy hotel in Times Square, the Waldorf Astoria, I think. We had dinner in the hotel restaurant, a plush place, where I carefully watched Wheelwright and the other experienced diners—lest I make a *faux pas*—before I made a single move.

We slept in one room on two large double beds and a cot. Wheelwright himself went to sleep at the Harvard Club. Just before he left us in our room he said, "Be happy! Comes the revolution, each of you will have a room for himself! Sleep well."

PIKKU AHO AND ISO AHO

Äiti's boardinghouse had two Otto Aho's—a Mutt and Jeff pair—in residence for more than two years. Although there existed only about five years difference in their ages, the tall Otto Aho was a second generation Finnish-American born in Minnesota and the short Otto Aho was an immigrant. We differentiated between them by calling one *Pikku Aho* (small Aho) and the other *Iso Aho* (big Aho).

Iso Aho, the tall one, was also tagged with a second nickname because no matter what the conversation was about, *Iso Aho* had been there "first and the fastest". He had worked in the richest copper mines, he had cut the largest redwoods, he had dug coal from the deepest mines, and he had even followed the wheat harvest as a migratory worker. And he flourished an old IWW card to prove it. Maybe he was telling the truth but his stories didn't sit well with his audience. Whenever he wasn't present—and *Äiti* was not in earshot—*Iso Aho* was called *Bullshit Aho* in plain English. I guess nobody believed him.

Pikku Aho, the short one, was a born loser. He worked diligently in one factory after another in the most menial jobs for the lowest pay. He was the last to be hired and the first to be laid off. But that didn't bother him because he has only one motivation in life—an idée fixe. He was obsessed with the *Aho Plan to Save the Lives of Sailors in Sunken Submarines.*

He claimed to have invented a device which could be somehow attached to a submarine so that if the submarine was disabled, then the device would release lighted buoys which would enable the rescue planes and ships to locate the sunken vessel.

Pikku Aho had a set of diagrams—"patent plans", he called them—which he carried around for over fifteen years as he moved from one Finnish-American community to another. He kept these diagrams in a flat metallic attache case which, when he lived in *Äiti's* boardinghouse, was stashed underneath his bed. The case was locked but the bedroom door, as all bedroom doors in the boardinghouse, was unlocked.

Pikku Aho was, I think, in the clutches of a greedy patent attorney. *Pikku Aho* worked diligently whenever he could find employment, and except for an occasional weekend of drinking, he saved his earnings which he sent to the patent attorney who was, supposedly, trying to obtain a U.S. patent for him. *Pikku Aho* was convinced the invention would make him wealthy but he insisted his motivation was humanitarian. The device would save lives.

Pikku Aho became interested in Mrs. Piispanen who, at that time, was still eating away *Isä's* debt to his fellow immigrants. Mrs. Piispanen must have been an extremely lonely woman at that time because *Pikku Aho* began to court her and, by golly, he won her. They were married and *Pikku Aho* moved out of *Äiti's* boardinghouse but not for long.

Pikku Aho had taken the pledge in order to win Mrs. Piispanen's hand. He had to because Mrs. Piispanen was a very ardent member of both the Finnish Lutheran Church and the Finnish Temperance Society named *Rauhan Aarre* (A Treasure of Peace). Dear Abby wasn't published then, but even I, still wet behind my ears, could have told Mrs. Piispanen, "John Barleycorn is a tough and jealous competitor. Not many people are able to quench their craving for the devil's brew. Be sure, doubly sure, and then check again that he's reformed before you marry him. Be prepared, even if all signs say go, that he'll drink again after being married. The probability is high, close to 90%, that he'll start drinking again. Beware!" But I guess such a lonely woman wouldn't have listened to Dear Abby, much less a teen-age kid.

Pikku Aho "fell off the wagon" one cold, snowy, and icy Saturday about three months after the marriage ceremony. He had arrived at his new home in a state called *humalassa* by the older Finns. I found him at 2 A.M. Sunday morning (when I was coming home from a dance) wandering in an alley near *Äiti's* boardinghouse. He was dressed only in his shorts. Still very inebriated, he stumbled along the icy ruts in his bare feet—not sure which direction to go. While I led him to the boardinghouse he continually repeated, *"Kyllä oli kamala akanilma!"* (What a terrible temper that old woman has!)

Pikku Aho was quite embarrassed by his plight, however. A few days later, after his belongings had been returned by his bride, he left Gardner with the *Aho Plan to Save the Lives of Sailors in Sunken Submarines* for another Finnish-American community. I never saw him again. I do hope fortune smiled on him, at least a little, before his final day.

FOOTPRINTS ON THE CEILING

Chet Nordstrom is the star of the incident I recall as the *Footprints on the Ceiling*. Chet was my favorite second generation Finn-Swede.* He was one of only three Finn-Swedes I knew well even though there must have been about a hundred Swedish-speaking Finnish immigrant families in Gardner.

Chet Nordstrom shared a bedroom with my brother Tarmo, myself, and another boarder whose name has slipped into oblivion. The room, which was mostly mine since the others used it only to sleep in and as a place to keep their clothes, was on the third floor to the immediate left of the staircase.

Chet, an upholsterer in a small furniture factory in the "Little Canada" section of Gardner, was a steady worker. I can't recall that he ever missed a single day's work if it was available, but he did, I felt, imbibe a little too much alcohol on weekends. Although he usually started to "relax" immediately after he had received his weekly pay envelope, he always came to the boardinghouse to eat, to bathe, to pay his board bill, and to dress up before

---

*A Finn-Swede is a Swedish-speaking person who was born in Finland. The terms Swede-Finn and Finn-Swede were used interchangeably in those days; the Finns used the term Finn-Swede and Swedish speaking immigrants (and their descendants) said Swede-Finn. I think Swede-Finn is the correct term but I shall use the same term I used as a boy.

starting the really serious business of his weekend.

One Friday evening, just before supper, when I was reading on my bed, I heard the outside door open and I soon recognized Chet's footsteps as he slowly clambered up the stairs. "Oh, Hell!" I thought, wondering whether to make myself scarce, "He's got himself an early start."

I went back to my reading although a vague feeling of unrest— worry—enveloped me. Intoxicated people in those days didn't bother me very much unless they were boisterous, violent, or demanding. Chet was never any of these but an anxiety began to irk me! Did he still have enough money to pay his board bill? *Isä* needed that $9.00 much more than any dealer in booze.

Finally Chet reached the third floor. I half-expected him to open the door to the hall, turn left, open the bedroom door and say, "Hi, Reino. How's the kid? Is that a good book?"

But, no! He was clambering up the stairs again. He was headed for the attic. I thought hard and listened carefully. Was he going to hide something in the attic? A half-pint, perhaps. He knew *Äiti* would blow her stack if she saw any liquor in the boardinghouse. The attic, I remembered, had no floor. Just the slats which held the ceiling plaster were attached to the beams. Chet paused at the landing halfway between the third floor and the attic.

"Christ!" I thought, "He really has a load on."

Chet began to climb again. I moved fast. I bounced out of bed, ran up to the landing, grabbed Chet by the arm, and escorted him to the bedroom.

"Hi, Reino," he said in the bedroom, "I thought you'd be reading. How are you anyway? Have you a date this weekend?"

I answered. He undressed, put on his bathrobe, went to the bathroom where he drew himself a bath, came back to the bedroom and put on his best clothes. Then he handed me $9.00 for *Isä* saying he didn't have time to go downstairs to eat and was off for his important weekend engagements.

The same thing happened a few more times but I was now alerted. I made it a point to be in my room at about the time Chet came home on Friday. I knew something had changed in Chet's life but I didn't have the slightest inkling of what it could be. I suggested to *Isä* that Chet be given a room on the second floor, away from the stairs, but since I didn't explain why, *Isä* let it pass.

Well, the inevitable finally happened. Chet didn't show up at his usual time. I fell asleep while reading. When I woke up it was early morning. I looked up at the ceiling. My heart jumped a beat. There was a pair of legs sticking through the ceiling plaster. My vigil had failed.

I woke my brother who was flabbergasted to see a pair of legs sticking out of the ceiling. Together we gingerly helped Chet, who was as astonished as we were, out of his predicament. We were careful not to do any additional damage to the ceiling.

Chet was very busy the entire weekend repairing the damaged ceiling while my brother and I kept *Isä* and *Äiti* away from the hustle and bustle of the third floor. I think it must have been the first weekend in many years that Chet stayed bone dry. Later I discovered what may have altered his behavior pattern. He was thinking of getting married. The shock of finding himself in the attic decided the issue for him. He didn't get married until almost ten years later.

A PALINDROME FOR A NAME

My next character has a place in this narrative only because of his name. Several times, usually after a local census, a sharp reporter would spot our boarder's name on some list and write a news item pointing out that this particular Finn who lived at 255 Main Street (and later: at 402 Elm Street) had the most *euphonious* name in Gardner, if not in the whole Commonwealth of Massachusetts.

I was still young enough to enjoy basking in the reflection of the small recognition gained by our boarder. The news item, however, didn't make much of an impression on my euphoniously named friend. He usually didn't even grunt when I translated the article into Finglish for him. Once, however, he did say, *"Niin! Niin!"* which I thought then might be best translated into the slang expression, "So what else is new?"*

Our euphoniously named boarder was a cheerful man and smiled a lot but otherwise he was the model of the common stereotype of a Finn. He didn't speak very often. When he spoke he didn't speak very much. I would do his memory an injustice, however, to say he reminded me of Edwin Markham's poem, *The Man with the Hoe*. Still his life seemed to consist of working, eating, and sleep-

---

*The boarder, I have been told recently, may have been actually quite excited and saying, "Go on! Read me more!" But I didn't know that then.

ing—with a few drinks too many on the weekend. I don't think he touched a drop of alcohol, not even beer, during the work week. He may have had, of course, a secret life of which I was not aware.

He made an unusual request during the O.W. Siebert strike in 1934. The strike, which lasted for more than six weeks, gave him too much leisure time. He asked if the union officials would make an exception of him. He didn't want to be a scab, he said, but it wouldn't hurt the union's cause for one man to got to work. He wanted the union to win but he just didn't know what to do with himself. The time was too heavy on his hands.

Later I discovered that our boarder's claim to fame should not have been based on a euphonious name. He had a *palindrome* for a name. A name is euphonious depending on one's taste in such matters but a palindrome is not a matter of judgment. It exists or it doesn't exist. I guess the sharp reporters weren't aware of palindromes in those days. Well, maybe his name is euphonious too, but I'll let you, dear reader, decide that. His name is very definitely a palindrome.

A palindrome is a word, a verse, or a sentence which is spelled backwards and forwards in exactly the same way. The English word *radar* is a palindrome. The first sentence spoken by a man to a woman was a palindrome.

"Madam, I'm Adam," was Adam's greeting when he spotted Eve.

"Eve was not outdone. She simply replied, "Eve."

The Finnish language has the longest known palindromic word ever discovered—*saippuakivikauppias* (lye merchant). Palindrome enthusiasts of every nationality are searching their native tongue for a palindromic word longer than *saippuakivikauppias.* They even go to such dubious practices as to manufacture artificial words in their desperate attempt to snatch the honor away from the Finnish language. May their endeavors be in vain!

Proper names that are spelled the same backwards and forwards are considered the most elegant palindromes. They are rare. Most of the ones known and printed are made up. I didn't make up our boarder's name—it was Otto Motto.

Did Otto's parents give him that name or did some emigration official—a palindrome enthusiast—who in processing Otto's papers, shorten some incomprehensible (to him) Finnish last name to Motto? One last question: Do you think the palindrome *Otto Motto* is euphonious, too?

Chapter Seven

THE BOARDINGHOUSE'S FINAL MOVE

I don't think that the involvement of *Äiti's* boardinghouse in the Siebert strike had anything to do with our eviction from 255 Main Street. The bank that owned the property sold it to a Lithuanian social and political organization whose members wanted to use the huge ground floor as their clubroom. Nevertheless the eviction notice threw me into a psychological panic.

Things had been going on an even keel once again in our family affairs. The cash flow in the boardinghouse was considerable although very little of that remained with *Isä* and *Äiti*. Their cash reserves were actually very low. I prayed a lot in those days in spite of my religious doubts. And, By *Väinämöinen!* A wealthy socialist came to the rescue! The eviction notice turned out to be a blessing.

Alfred Baker Lewis, the state Chairman of the Massachusetts Socialist Party, was a wealthy man very knowledgable about real estate. He believed that *Isä* and *Äiti* would find it difficult to relocate the boardinghouse, at least on the same scale, because of the strike and the socialist activity that had revolved around the establishment. He told *Isä* to find a good property where the boardinghouse might be continued on a smaller scale and he would personally help finance its purchase.

The search was on. And it wasn't easy. The attitudes of a wealthy sophisticated man experienced with the subtleties of purchasing real estate—even though he was a socialist—and the members of an immigrant family living barely above the poverty level are very divergent. Alfred Baker Lewis turned down every piece of property we brought to his attention.

"Keep looking." was his favorite phrase. *Isä* began to doubt that "Comrade Lewis" as he dubbed Mr. Lewis, really meant what he said. Finally, after stalling the bank month after month, we had no choice. Voluntarily or involuntarily, we had to move. I dreamt of beds, tables, chairs, dishes, and pots and pans piled in a great big heap in front of the Yoffa Building. A stern-faced judge with a gavel in his hand, flanked on both sides by innumerable faceless policemen, each with a poised nightstick, stood guard in front of the dining room forbidding my entrance into the boardinghouse.

In desperation we moved to a vacant, ill-kept three story building on Knowlton Street. All six tenements in the building had been vacant for years and even then, in the midst of the depression, nobody wanted to live there. I could remember how, when in a destructive mood, we had broken windows in the building as we passed on our way home from elementary school. We rented only two of the six apartments but the landlord kindly let us store all of the accumulated boardinghouse odds and ends in one of the empty apartments. We lost many of the permament boarders and all of the walk-in business.

I was a worrywart but *Äiti*, bolstered by her deep faith, commanded, "Don't be afraid. Don't worry. Our faith is being tested. Be strong and have faith. Remember Jesus is with us."

The Knowlton Street property was offered to *Isä* quite cheap but he didn't have enough money for the down payment. Alfred Baker Lewis wouldn't listen to *Isä's* arguments about how easily he could renovate the old building. "Keep looking!" he said, "Find a property you will be proud to live in, a home where you would be happy to stay for the rest of your lives."

Alfred Baker Lewis was right. There was a house in Gardner that suited *Isä* and *Äiti* to a T. A home they were proud as peacocks to own. It was a place where the boardinghouse continued to provide—though on a much smaller scale, thank *Väinämöinen!* —the best food in Gardner for almost 30 more years.

ÄITI'S HOUSE

The Sawyer house at 402 Elm Street was built around 1880 or 1890. The Home Owners Loan Corporation (HOLC)—a government organization set up in the depression to provide aid to needy middle class home owners—sold the house to *Isä* and *Äiti* for a down payment equal to the real estate agent's commission. They were able to borrow this money from the Workers Credit Union in Fitchburg. All Alfred Baker Lewis had to do was to cosign the note.

I think a newly graduated medical doctor had the 402 Elm Street house built in the 1880's as a wedding gift for his bride. The house was finished with an elegance that is not matched by the houses constructed today. The wood grain throughout the house, for example, gave the appearance of oak but was actually something called "softwood" which I understand is rare today. The carpenters had taken great care to match the grains in each room. The trim, finished with a light oak stain and varnished, still looked new on my last visit, twenty-eight years later—eighty years after the house was built—even though *Äiti* never did more than clean and polish it.

The four-gabled house had seventeen rooms (or more, depending how one counted) on three floors. A huge oak front door opened into a vestibule which had a clothes closet and a built-in hat and coat rack. A second huge door in the vestibule opened into the living room where a putty-colored fireplace caught one's eye. A large bay window with a full-length window seat took up most of the living room front wall. The view from the window covered the entire Union Station (depot) which must have been exciting in 1890-1900 but which had little appeal in the automobile society of the 1930's.

A double width oak open staircase led from the living room to the second floor. Above the landing in the turnway was a huge window frame that had about 50 small stained glass frames. A door on the left of the fireplace opened into the dining room and on the right a sliding door separated the living room from the library.

The library had built-in bookcases with glass doors. There was even a corner cabinet with a let-down secretary. The library and the dining room were separated by double sliding doors so high that when the doors were pushed all the way back the rooms seemed to merge into one. The library had its own vestibule which led to a side entrance and to three rooms where the doctor had practiced medicine.

The dining room had two adjacent doors that led indirectly to the kitchen. One of these doors opened to a large butler pantry.

106

The pantry had an unusual combination icebox-refrigerator, the only one I have ever seen. The contraption was built so that the ice man did not have to enter the house to make his delivery. The other dining room door opened into a small hall where the staircase to the second floor and the staircase to the full New England style basement were located.

The second and third floors put *Äiti's* boardinghouse into business again. The second floor had six rooms—two large rooms with fireplaces, two medium size rooms, a sewing nook, and an unheated closed sunporch. The unheated third floor had four fairly large rooms (each with a slanting ceiling waiting to give the unwary a bump) and a small windowless but completely furnished storeroom. All the rooms were easily rented. Otto Motto, our palindromic named Finn, fell in love with the unheated sunporch and lived there—winter and summer—for twenty years. Even the windowless storeroom was rented in an emergency whenever rooms for whatever reason were scarce in Gardner.

The bathroom facilities in the house were completely inadequate but that didn't matter since *Isä* immediately began to build a sauna about fifty yards behind the house where a small copse of trees met our property line. In fact he completed the fire chamber with its *kiuas* and was working on the sauna building itself before my brothers and I had finished moving the household goods from Knowlton Street. The sauna was heated at least three times a week. Thus, *Äiti's* boardinghouse had the cleanest workingmen in Gardner in spite of the limited bathroom facilities in the house itself.

ÄITI WAS BORN IN A SAUNA*

Äiti was born in the family sauna in Luoma-Aho on May 16, 1888.

---

*Even Jesus was born in a sauna. According to the Kalevala, Marjatta (the Virgin Mary) had difficulty finding a sauna in which to give birth to Jesus. Nobody, not even her father and mother, believed her story about the magical qualities of the big blue blueberry she had eaten. Ruotus, the head of the village where Marjatta lived, was asked if a sauna was available for Marjatta. His "wicked" wife replied,

> Vacant Saunas are rare in village,
> None at mouth of reed-fringed streamlet.
> There's a bath upon the clearing,
> And a stable in the pinewood,
> Where the whore may bear her children.

Yes, *Äiti* was born in a sauna, not an unusual place for a Finn born in the nineteenth century. In fact it was the best place available in those days. The sauna heat helped to relax the new mother's muscles. And since a sauna platform may have up to four levels—the higher the level, the higher the temperature—the mother-to-be could choose the most comfortable level on which to give birth.

Äiti was a very young immigrant—not quite sixteen, a little younger than the average Finnish immigrant of that era—when she left her home with her older brother Hemminki. *Äiti* said she left because one hot day, dusty and tired from threshing wheat (or barley), she decided the future in Finland was too bleak for her. All work and no play she said with a big smile. (Hemminki, incidentally, was one of the 25% of the Finnish immigrants who, finding the New World did not meet their expectations, returned to Finland.)

Äiti didn't have to change her name when she married. Her maiden name was Hannula too. Was that unusual? Yes and no. Hannula is certainly not as common a Finnish name as *Smith* is an English name but Luoma-Aho has at least fifteen Hannula families who live on *Hannulan Tie* (Hannula's Road) which runs around a lake called *Oja*. According to my first cousin Reino Hannula (who has exactly the same name as I do and who lives in the maternal ancestral farmhouse), none of these Lake Oja Hannulas are related to my family. Nor, he says, is any Lake Oja Hannula family related to any other Lake Oja Hannula family. I suspect the name Hannula was adopted by each family around 1900.

Yes, although there are lots of Hannulas in Finland, I get the impression that their grandfathers or great grandfathers weren't born with that name. While driving from Turku to Alajärvi, on our first day in Finland several years ago, my wife Alice spotted a big HANNULA painted on a barn. The sign was deep in the woods, some distance from the highway we were on. Curious, I searched and found a narrow lane that led to the sign.

The lane ended at a well-kept farm. I was a little apprehensive when I got out of the Volkswagen because everything was so quiet. (Rural Finland, by the way, is the quietest place I know.) No barking dogs to greet us, no chickens running around, and not a single person in sight. I walked rather briskly to the farmhouse and knocked on the door. A voice bade me enter. I did.

The most ancient woman I have ever seen was cleaning fish at a kitchen sink. In my best Finglish, I told her my name was Hannula. Perhaps, I suggested, we were related.

"Oh, no!" she exclaimed in a voice that said she had heard this story before, "My husband took the Hannula name more than 50 years ago when we first moved here from up North. Besides, we have no relations in America."

Why the name changing? The answer lies in Finnish history. It begins with the fact that Finland was dominated by Sweden for over 500 years, with intermittant challenges by the Russian Bear. The soldiers (the men who did the actual fighting and dying) used by the Swedes to meet the Russian challenges were Finns of course. And the Russians used the Finns also to fight the Swedes whenever they had the upper hand in these struggles for the control of Finland.

The Swedish government, incidentally, used the Finns on a wider capacity than merely defending Finland against Russian encroachment. The history books may say Swedes but the fact is that at least 50% of the soldiers in Gustav Adolphus' army, the army that overran much of Europe in the seventeenth century, were Finnish speaking Finns. The Finnish peasants were expendable cannon fodder.

During the 500 years of Swedish rule, Finnish was the language of the poor; the peasant and the working class that did the work in Finland. The government was run in Swedish. Written Finnish was an anomaly. It was quite rare. It has been said that at the worst point in the decline of the Finnish language only five people could write Finnish—and all five were Swedes.

Then in 1808 Czar Alexander I of Russia invaded Finland without a formal declaration of war. The invasion caught the Swedish government by surprise. The Russian Bear routed the Finnish soldiers commanded by Swedish officers in the battles that followed. The final defeat came at the Battle of Viapori where the Finnish soldiers, deserted by their Swedish officers, fought "to the last man". (Note: The castle at Viapori is now called *Suomenlinna*.)

The Battle of Viapori was the Finnish Battle of the Alamo. The dormant Finnish patriotic movement was inspired by the courage of the Finnish soldiers in the battle. Patriotic Finns rallied around a new slogan: "We are no longer Swedes, we didn't want to become Russians, so let us be Finns."

Czar Alexander I surprised the Finns! He did not incorporate the conquered territory into his empire. Instead he made Finland into a self-governing duchy. He even added the province of Karlelia, snatched from Sweden by a previous war, to the duchy. The Finns had their own schools, courts, church, and army. They had self-rule in every sphere of life except foreign policy. The language used to rule Finland, however, was Swedish so the greatest beneficiaries of Russia's benevolence was derived by the former Swedish ruling establishment.

The patriotic movement which stressed the use of Finnish in government, business, and literature began to exert greater and greater influence with the populace. Patriotic Finns—called Fennomans—began to change their Swedish and, in a few cases, Russian surnames to Finnish. The patriotic fervor became so intense that even names on the wooden grave markers were said to have been changed in some localities. It was not, however, considered unpatriotic to keep Latin names such as Sibelius, Topelius, Zillicus, etc. On May 12, 1906, the centenary of the birth of Johann Snellman, the leading Fennoman of the nineteenth century, sixteen thousand families changed their Swedish names into Finnish names.

Aiti's fraternal grandfather's name was Lindstrom. Her father changed that to *Hannulabacka* which, I understand, is Hannula Hill in Swedish. A few years later it was shortened to *Hannula*. When I first learned that my maternal great-grandfather's name was Lindstrom, my heart skipped a beat. Perhaps I was, after all, a Swede. Hot dog! Then something stirred in my mind and my hopes were dashed to pieces by a recollection.*

My wife and I were in Quebec, near the Vermont border, late one Sunday afternoon. We stopped for gas. The attendant, a middle-aged man, asked when he gave my change, *"Puthutko suomea?"* (Do you speak Finnish?)

"A little," I replied in my best Finglish, "But," I added, "How did you know I was a Finn?"

"Nenästä tiedän että olet suomalainen." I can tell by your nose

---

*Please don't take me seriously. I have no desire to "pass the color line." I'm proud to be a Finn. And I don't even consider myself a Scandinavian-American. The Scandinavian-Americans were completely different from the Finnish-Americans. After you finish this book I think you will agree.

that you're a Finn.)

FINNISH-AMERICAN WOMEN

Was *Äiti* a typical first generation Finnish-American woman? Yes, in most respects. She was, as I previously indicated, a tremendous bundle of energy and good health as were most of the other first generation Finnish women. The Finnish farm wife (of whom I know more about than the city wife) worked side by side with her husband on the New England rocky land to make their farm a paying proposition.

Most of the farm wives I knew did more work than their husbands because, after working in the field all day, they did the housework while their husbands rested. I say this, not to disparage the husbands, who always put in a good day, but to indicate that the first generation Finnish male was not a liberated man. He didn't help with the housework.

Äiti was somewhat of an anomaly though in that she persisted in going to church even though *Isä* scorned all organized religion. Almost all other first generation couples were compatible in their religious and political attitudes—the most important attitudes in the Finnish-American community then. Either both went to church, both went to the socialist Ash Street Hall, both went to the temperance society activities in the Finnish-owned Miller's Opera House, both went to the left-wing Casino Hall, or both did not take part in any organized political, social, or religious activity.

The only other Finnish woman I knew whose interests diverged from those of her husband was Aune Ryynanen. Aune's religion was the communist line. Olavi, her husband, had only one motivating force: to develop his farm in Hubbardston. He wasn't the slightest bit interested in the communist line or any other point of view—political or religious—but he didn't interfere with Aune's activities.

Aune was a persistent campaigner for the Communist Party. I recall in 1936 or 1937 when I was on the Gardner Cooperative Committee that Aune came regularly to our monthly meetings. Aune, who refused to trade in the consumers cooperative store because it was "run by the socialists", attended the meetings to request that the cooperative join the United Front Against War and Fascism, a communist-dominated organization. It didn't matter to Aune that our committee had no authority except to listen to suggestions how the cooperative might better serve the needs of Gardner consumers and to plan educational activity in order to attract more consumers to the cooperative movement.

Aune had a right to be present because our meetings were open to the public. She was given the floor at the appropriate times and the older Finns on the committee let her talk—even though her remarks were not apropos to our purpose—without listening to her. I tried to follow her arguments but political Finnish was really beyond my comprehension. However, I knew what she was going to say even before she started. The occasional Finglish or English word I recognized in her presentation indicated to me at what point she was at in her argument.

Finland gave women the right to vote in 1906, perhaps the first nation in the world to do so. The organizational meeting of the Finnish-American Socialist Federation, held in Hibbing (Minnesota) in 1906, unanimously passed a resolution in favor of woman sufferage. Subsequent national and regional conventions affirm that stand. I am surprised, considering this early support of women's rights, that I can only recall two independent-minded women in the Gardner Finnish community.

The first generation women always seemed to me to be so self-reliant, so capable of independent action. They certainly never took a back seat in the family life but they did not, in general, express themselves in the political, social, and cooperative organizations that existed in the Finnish community. And the number of women in prominent positions—board of directors, convention delegates, managers, and editors—in the Finnish-American community could have been counted on one hand.

REMEMBRANCE OF THINGS PAST

Before *Isä* and *Äiti* acquired the boardinghouse the evening before Thanksgiving was one of great anticipation for us kids because the next day we were going to have Jello. When the Kilpi Grocery Company delivered the Jello packages I was like a little puppy who, because his joy is so great, shakes his whole body to wag his tail.

Jello! I was in seventh heaven when, in the evening, *Äiti* let me open the Jello packages and pour the fragrant powder into a big bowl. My mouth was full of saliva as I watched her pour hot water into the bowl and stir the mixture to dissolve the powder.

I knew that tomorrow everyone would be allowed to eat all we wanted to of the shimmering dessert covered with real whipped cream. Jello was a far more important food treat for me and my brothers and sisters than the Thanksgiving Day turkey. I think I ate the turkey only so that no one could question the amount of Jello I consumed. We were lucky, I thought, to be able to afford this "expensive" dessert.

I was fourteen before I discovered *Äiti's* Jello deception. *Isä*, because of my deep interest in the consumers cooperative movement, allowed me to do some of the grocery shopping for the boardinghouse at the United Cooperative Store. I was a comparison shopper and bought everything at the Co-op that was cheaper or the same price as the A&P. When I first saw the price of Jello in the co-op, I thought the price on the moulding was wrong—two packages for 9¢!

I asked *Äiti* on my last visit about her "Jello Deception". Why didn't you serve Jello, a cheap dessert, more often when I was a kid?" She looked at me blankly for awhile. I prodded her memory and then she smiled broadly. "Oh, I remember. I wanted Thanksgiving and Christmas dinners to be memorable occasions. One day, when I used to do the washing and cleaning for Mrs. Cohen, she gave me some Jello for lunch. I was surprised that it was so inexpensive but I decided to make it an extra special dessert to be served only at Thanksgiving and Christmas."

Äiti did bake the juiciest blueberry pie (fresh in season and from home-canned ingredients otherwise). No corn starch or pectin to thicken the ingredients. And her apple pie has no competitor today. But my favorite pie was chocolate; a flavor *Äiti* didn't make. I don't mean the chocolate pie that is served in restaurants today. Today's chocolate pie is made for appearance, not for eating. Today's chocolate pie is thickened to keep the chocolate firm so that none of it runs when a piece of pie is removed from the tin.

I discovered, when I was twelve or thirteen, that the Blue Moon Cafe, a short order restaurant about three blocks from our boardinghouse, served chocolate pie for ten cents a slice. The chocolate in that pie "ran". It oozed when a piece of it was cut and served. The counter man would, on request, serve the last piece of pie right in the pie tin. That was a great bargain because the tin contained all the extra chocolate that had oozed out of the other pieces. I became a steady chocolate pie customer at the Blue Moon Cafe but only for the last piece of pie in the pie tin.

Whenever the chocolate pie urge overwhelmed my sense of guilt about deserting Äiti's cooking *and* I had a dime to spend, I always checked the Blue Moon Cafe to see how many pieces of chocolate pie were left in the tin. Usually I didn't even have to climb on the stools to peer into the iced pie cupboard because a counter man, spotting me, would say, "Two more to go. Come back in about an hour. I'll save the tin for you."

I would then go outside, and if other temptations didn't arise, I would walk impatiently up and down in front of the Blue Moon Cafe—a solitary chocolate pie picket. I would check, anxiously, every few minutes to see if anyone had ordered the next to last piece of pie. I soon learned that the best time for my surveillance was around 3 P.M., when many men took an afternoon coffee break.

Usually I didn't have enough money for coffee or milk but even if I did, I wouldn't have bought either anyway since there was so much free coffee and milk only three blocks away. Besides, the counter man on duty almost always set a glass of milk next to my pie tin and accepted my ten cents in full payment for the food.

Äiti laughed when I told her about my disloyalty to her cooking. "Why didn't you tell me about your fondness for chocolate pie? I could have learned how to make it. Cooking comes very easy for me. Do you remember how I learned to make those *pasties* (meat pies) Toivo always talked about when he came back from Hancock (Michigan)?"

ÄITI'S FAREWELL PARTY

I was a forty year old math major in my senior year (1960) at UCLA when my sister-in-law Rita phoned me, "If you want to see Äiti," she said, "You better come home to Gardner right away. She's going downhill very fast."

I interrupted my studies and went to visit Äiti for the last time. Äiti, a mere shadow of the dynamic and energetic woman of my youth was propped up in her bed which had been placed in the library. Äiti was in excellent spirits during my two-week visit. She knew she was terminally ill but that knowledge did not affect her morale. She spoke of her impending death but once to me, "Reino, don't go around here with such a long face. Let's enjoy your visit. I have no fear. I have been always ready to go whenever the Good Lord decides to call me. I shall always obey His Will."

What does one say? I tried to pooh-pooh the situation by giving Äiti that old blarney, "Oh, you'll be up and around before you know it. There's no question in my mind that you will live to be a hundred. In fact, I think if you conserve your strength you might be able to cook a delicious old-fashioned New England baked bean and frankfurter supper this weekend," even though anyone could tell with a single glance that the little old lady, propped up in that bed, was never going to be able to cook another meal.

Äiti paid no attention to my rubbish. Other things were on her mind. She said, "I would like a family reunion next Saturday night. Of course, I won't be able to help with the food but I think that Lilja, Vieno, Rita, and Helen can manage very well without me."

That evening when Rita gave Äiti her evening bath, Äiti said she wanted to see Bobby, one of Rita's sons. Robert dutifully visited his grandmother the next day. She told Robert in her best English, "You bring band Saturday night, Bobby. Band play."

Robert who, with his brother Richard, played in a five-piece band, was taken aback. He immediately consulted his mother. "Hey, Mom, Äiti wants me to bring the band for the reunion. What should I do?"

"If Äiti wants your band to play Saturday night, then let your band play. She'll love it."

Äiti's boardinghouse was full of people that Saturday night for the last time. The whole downstairs—the living room, the library, the dining room, and the kitchen—was packed with members of her immediate family and a few close friends. The boardinghouse served its last complete meal that night, perhaps the only one Äiti had not cooked.

Robert's five-piece band played the most popular tunes of the 1960's. The band members had positioned themselves by the living room bay window with the drummer, Richard, seated with his drums on the elevated window seat. Äiti's bed had been placed so that she had a full view of the chaotic and noisy activities going on in the living and dining rooms. Äiti beamed as she watched her more than 20 grandchildren, all ages and sizes, milling around in the three rooms. She even complimented a few of the older girls who showed her how well they could dance to the tunes played by the band.

Äiti fell asleep a little after ten-thirty even though the party was still quite lively. A few weeks later she was gone. Her Lord had commanded, "Come Home."

Chapter Eight

THE TOY TOWN STRIKE

President Franklin D. Roosevelt signed the National Recovery Act, popularly and fondly known as the NRA, into law on June 16, 1933. NRA was one of the many pieces of social legislation—called the New Deal—which caused American society to change its "mental attitudes" and direction. The New Deal destroyed most of the remaining remnants of nineteenth century Social-Darwinism as federal, state, and local governments became more responsive to the needs of their poorer citizens.

Under NRA, the various industries—coal, steel, textiles, furniture, grocery, etc.—formulated *fairness codes* for their respective fields. These fairness codes specified, among other things, the maximum number of hours an employee might work and the minimum wages an employer might pay. The greatest achievement—the one that FDR (Roosevelt) was most proud of—was the abolition of child labor. A special section, called Section 7a, gave the workers of every industry the right to join any labor organization of their own choice.

One of the immediate benefits of the passage of NRA was very beneficial to a great many workers in the Greater Gardner area. They received a raise in pay! Many workers had their pay raised to the minimum wage—$13.60 for the forty-hour work week established for the furniture industry. Another effect, slow in surfacing, was a growing restlessness of American workingmen (including those in Gardner) because NRA, greeted with tremendous enthusiasm by the working people, failed to live up to their expectations.

MEMBER

U.S.

WE DO OUR PART

NRA was ushered into law with one of the largest parades ever held in New York City. But almost as soon as the marchers put down their banners, the employers began to chisel on the codes, especially in those localities and industries where there were no strong labor organizations to guarantee enforcement of the law. Some of President Roosevelt's administrators felt that over 90% of the American big businesses were not obeying the codes for their industry even though the leaders of those industries had themselves formulated the codes. Small businesses found it difficult to obey the law and compete.

The only enforcement of NRA, except for the unions, was public opinion. Businesses which obeyed the code were allowed to display the NRA symbol, a *Blue Eagle* poster, in their places of business. Conforming manufacturers were also allowed to stamp the Blue Eagle insignia on their products.

A business that violated the NRA code lost all rights with respect to the Blue Eagle. The posters were removed from the business establishment. A manufacturer who violated the code was not allowed to stamp the NRA insignia on his products. The government apparently felt that the public would boycott those establishments which lost the right to display and use the Blue Eagle insignia. The loss of public patronage, it was felt, would force the code violators to conform.

It didn't work out that way. Henry Ford, who refused to sign the code because of Section 7a which gave the workers the right to organize, obeyed all the other NRA standards for the auto industry. His cars sold even though none of them carried the Blue Eagle endorsement. The other car manufacturers who signed the code but disregarded Section 7a and chiseled on the established standards never lost their rights to the Blue Eagle insignia. Their cars sold also.

Did the factory owners and managers in the Gardner area honor their agreement to abide by the NRA code for the furniture industry? I don't know. Perhaps the Gardner workers expected too much from the Blue Eagle. But whatever the reason, the restlessness of the Gardner area workers soon crystallized into many strikes and even, once, into sabotage. The sabotage, however, was very minor.

The first NRA strike—the first strike in many years in Northern Worcester County—started, not in Gardner, but in a small toy factory in Winchendon (Massachusetts). The strike was *spontaneous;* I mean that the workers in the factory had no organization of any sort. They just walked off their jobs in protest against the low pay they were receiving.

There was no Finnish-American socialist organization in Winchendon at the time although there had been one in 1907-1910. The organization had been disbanded when most of the Finnish-Americans had moved out of the community. They had left behind, however, one first generation Finn—Leon Winehill—born Lenni Jacoby Viinimäki in Kurikka (Finland). Leon gave the strikers his total devotion.

Leon Winehill was a truck driver for the Mason and Parker factory (the struck company). He was better paid than most of the employees and he lived in a company-owned house when the workers walked off their jobs. But, without hesitation, he joined the strikers and tried to organize them into an effective labor union.

Leon wasn't alone. There was a small community of Italian-Americans in Winchendon, many of whom worked in the Mason and Parker mill. These Italian-Americans had considerable organizational experience but they, too, had very little practical knowledge about union and labor activity. These Italian-Americans had organized a lodge called the Matteotti Lodge in honor of the leader of the Italian Social Democratic Party, Giacomo Matteotti, who had been murdered on orders given by Benito Mussolini. The Winchendon Matteotti Lodge also served to give notice to the community that the Winchendon Italian-Americans did not support Mussolini's fascism.

These fun-loving and high-spirited Italians also had a consumers cooperative named the United Cooperative Society of Winchendon. The cooperative had, at that time, two grocery stores, one on Front Street in downtown Winchendon and the other, a country style store, on Glen Allan Street in Winchendon Springs. Salvatore Nimmo, the president of the cooperative, said that the conservative-minded Italians threw away their business sense during the strike. The members of the cooperative, very sympathetic to the strikers' cause, insisted that the strikers be given credit during their six-week walkout. This altruistic, but unwise policy, almost forced the co-op to close its doors.

After the strike had been in progress for about a week, the workers sent a delegation to the Gardner socialist local (English-speaking branch) to ask for assistance. The local, since its members were busy working in the Gardner factories for their own livelihood, forwarded the request for help to the state chairman, Alfred Baker Lewis, of the Massachusetts Socialist Party.

Leon Winehill, now past seventy years of age, wrote me his reminiscences of the strike:

> We had a tough fight. All the meeting halls were closed to us. The police, who in those days considered strikers as criminals, would break up any open-air meeting we held in the fields or other public places.
> Once a Methodist minister—I think his name was Reverend Deale—told us to come to his church. "My church is open to you," he said.
> All of us strikers followed the minister into his church with the Chief of Police bringing up the rear. The minister, however, closed the door in the Police Chief's face, saying, "We don't need your protection

in here."

The Socialist Party, through Alfred Baker Lewis, sent three organizers to help us out. They were Reverend John Hall (a Unitarian minister), Leslie Richards, and—of all things—a poet named John Brooks Wheelwright. We held group meetings at night and, quite often, those meetings were held in some bar because there was no other safe place for us to meet.

My association with these three idealistic socialists was exciting and glamorous to me. I breathed in every word they said. I sang songs of rebellion with them—a new world was about to be born.

The enthusiasm to educate and help the downtrodden was very great within me, like a fire burning inside me. I wrote stirring slogans in letters of fire; solidarity, democracy, arise, unite, let justice rule the world! See! The strike awakened the poet in me.

Although I was not a leader of the strike, most things fell on my shoulders. I lived in a company house. They served me an eviction notice every week but I stayed put. We had a loudspeaker in my front yard across the street from the mill which we used to urged the few scabs to join us.

We made very small gains from the strike. The company, though, began to weed out the strike leaders soon after we went back to work. I was let go. I had to leave town to find employment. I stayed away for ten years, then I came back and went into my own business.

I should mention that the Italian cooperative store gave the strikers credit during the strike. I think the bill was originally presented to me. Alfred Baker Lewis paid that bill because he didn't want the co-op to go down the drain. That must have been something.

It's too bad the people never understood socialism. The system we finally got has 1/3 of the people on welfare, 1/3 on social security. The politicians are mostly crooks and those who work are taxed up to the limit to pay for it all. Socialism would have been a much better alternative. Maybe the next time around people will see the light.

I don't care if you use my name. I fear no embarrassment. I was always on the side of the downtrodden. Here is the poem you asked me to write for your book.

O Fates that mark the days of men,
When my time comes to depart this vale,
Cast me into the fiery furnace of a steel mill,
Blend my spirits and temper into the molten metal,
Send me out on the song of the Rolling Mill
To be shaped into a steel girder
For the top tower of a sky scraper
Where I may challenge the winds,
Where I may touch the face of God.

THE UNITED FURNITURE
AND ALLIED TRADE WORKERS

The furniture workers in Gardner were just as restless as the toy workers in Winchendon. The furniture workers didn't strike, however, because—strange as it may seem—the socialists did their best to convince the workers to stay on their jobs. "Don't walk off your jobs until we have built an effective union," was the gist of the socialist argument. The workers, unhappy and disgruntled, did wait.

I heard one of the workers, annoyed with the socialist admonitions: Wait! Organize! Build a strong union! Formulate your demands, negotiate from strength, strike only if necessary; assert, "Oh, the hell you say! We got the goddamn Blue Eagle. The government's on our side. Those fucking factory owners are breaking the law. They'll cave in the minute we walk out!"

But they waited because no organization, except the Socialist Party, was willing to help the Gardner workers organize their union. The members of the small English-speaking branch of the SP (as the Socialist Party was fondly called by its adherents) had no previous experience in labor activity. They made plenty of mistakes but they learned by doing.

There were several members in the large Finnish socialist local in Gardner who had considerable experience in union work which they had gained in the numerous strikes that had occurred in the Finnish-American communities in the West and Middle West. These first generation Finns, now middle-aged and with a somewhat comfortable lifestyle and handicapped by a tremendous language barrier, were reluctant to participate directly in the organizational work or the strike activity that followed. They did, however, always offer their hall—Ash Street Hall—to the union, free of charge, whenever it was needed.

The English-speaking Socialist Party members bore the brunt of organizing the Gardner furniture workers although it really didn't take any great effort to sign the workers into the union. The workers seemed to flock into the union. Each had his own personal list of grievances. They joined because they were convinced the union could remedy the injustices they faced on their jobs. After all, wasn't the Blue Eagle supporting the union!

Although the principal industry in Gardner was furniture, it seemed as if everybody in town—regardless where they worked—wanted to join the union. Applications for membership came even from several maids and at least one housekeeper. I do think that many of the workers were under the impression that President Roosevelt and the Blue Eagle endorsed the union. They felt joining the union was a patriotic thing to do since the Blue Eagle's slogan was WE DO OUR PART. We certainly didn't try to correct these impressions.

Employees of factories that did not make furniture—Florence Oil Stove, Simplex Recorder—and even mechanics and drivers from Flanagan Bus Lines joined the union which, in order to accommodate all these workers, named itself the *United Furniture and Allied Trade Workers*. The socialists of Gardner began to dream the old Finnish-American fantasy of "One Big Union". A hopeless dream, of course, since the other international unions would come into town to claim their own workers as soon as it was practical to do so. We were only doing their spade work for them.

How diligently we socialists worked to organize that union! I realize now that we were organizing a union for workers in a marginal industry, an industry with very little political or financial "clout". A furniture workers union is certainly needed if the employees of that industry are going to have any reasonable hope of fair wages and fair treatment on the job. But I doubt that even a strong union can gain the furniture workers an "honest day's pay for an honest day's work". The industry is just too weak.

The socialists were deeply concerned about red baiting during this organizational period. The issue was hotly debated in the socialist local when the time for the election of the first union officers approached. Should a socialist be nominated for the union presidency? There was no question in anyone's mind in the local that we socialists could elect any man we nominated. Finally, after considerable soul-searching, the local decided to support Axel Bachman, a non-socialist second generation Finn-Swede. There is no question that Axel Bachman was the right man for the job. Axel was and remained devoted to the interests of the Gardner furniture workers for the entire tenure of his office.

THE GARDNER GENERAL STRIKE

Finally the union felt strong enough to present a list of demands to the O.W. Siebert Company. The union wanted a small pay increase—not much more than 5¢ an hour—and the recognition of the union as the sole bargaining agent for the Siebert employees.

The company, just as the union expected, didn't even bother to reply to the union's request for a formal negotiating meeting. The company refused to admit that the union even existed although I recall they issued a highly idealistic statement which went somewhat as follows: "The management has always welcomed discussions about hours of work and pay scales with its employees. The management has always listened very attentively to all suggestions given it by its employees and has endeavored to put into practice all those suggestions it deemed beneficial to both the company's and it's employees' welfare. The management, however, is not willing, under any circumstances, to force its employees to pay tribute to an outside organization as a condition of employment."

All but two of the two hundred or so workers in the Siebert factory responded to the strike call when the deadline for the beginning of the negotiations expired. These men and women, mostly first and second generation hyphenated Americans, were on strike for over six weeks for union recognition—supposedly guaranteed by the NRA—and for a five-cent-an-hour raise in pay!

No middle class liberals—no teacher, no minister nor priest, no lawyer, and no doctor—ever uttered a single word in support of the Siebert strikers. No organization, except the two socialist locals—Finnish- and English-speaking—gave any financial help to the Siebert strikers. The Finnish socialists, even though their branch was extremely hard pressed to meet its own financial obligations such as the mortgage payments and maintenance costs of their large hall, generously offered the union its facilities free of any charge for weekly benefit dances. All the proceeds from the dance went to support the strike. But aside from that aid, the strikers and the embryo union were completely on their own.

Have times changed? The students of Gardner High School, even though most of them were children whose immigrant parents worked in some Gardner factory, never identified themselves with the strike. Not a single high school student, with the exception of the three members of the Gardner *Yipsels* (Young Peoples Socialist League), ever appeared on the picket line. Nor, as I remember, did they ever even talk about that strike. These students wanted to enter American society and a labor struggle was not the door to that society. They may have been right.

Even though the students were not there, about 400 people showed up each morning and afternoon to march double file the entire length of the O.W. Siebert factory. The pickets were loud and lusty in the cold snappy mornings. We *Yipsels* passed out mimeograph song sheets to the pickets and soon many of them were singing the labor songs of the Great Depression with great gusto. My favorite song, because I really believed the working people could run all industry themselves, was *Solidarity Forever* (sung to the tune of *The Battle Hymn of the Republic*):

When the Union's inspiration
through the workers blood shall run,
There can be no power greater
anywhere beneath the sun,
Yet what force on earth is
weaker than the feeble strength of one?
But the Union makes us strong!
Chorus:
Solidarity forever!
Solidarity forever!
Solidarity forever!
For the Union makes us strong!

Two other songs, *On the Picket Line* sung to the tune of *Polly Wolly Doodle* and *Please, Mr. Boss*, were popular with the strikers. I give only the chorus of *On the Picket Line* since it was the only part of the song we sang.

On the line, On the line!
Come and picket on the picket line.
We'll win our fight,
Our fight for the right
On the picket, picket line.

Waddya gonna do when you want more pay,
Please, Mister Boss?
Waddya gonna do for a chance to play,
Please, Mister Boss?
Waddya gonna do for a shorter day,
Please, Mister Boss?
No! It's strike, strike, strike, strike, strike
Strike, strike! NOT—
Please, Mister Boss.

The strike lasted a little over six weeks but to me the time seemed interminable. Never, however, did I notice any drop in the strikers' morale. The workers were militant but nonviolent. They were convinced their cause was just. And they were convinced the government was 100% behind them, too.

The impasse was finally broken when the Siebert Company obtained a temporary court injunction forbidding the union from picketing in front of the plant or otherwise interfering, in any manner, with the conduct of the struck business. The injunction named the union, all its officers, and several active members as respondents.

I believed then, and I still believe that there was something fishy about that injunction. It may not have been an illegal injunction but it certainly wasn't "judicial". I mean it wasn't fair. The judge was partial to the company's side. I think even the judge knew he would have to dismiss the injunction when the court hearing was held about it some weeks later—but by that time it wouldn't matter. The strike would have been broken.

If the judge had wanted to give everyone equal rights under the law, it would have been very simple for him to recess his court, visit the picket line, and observe for himself the action there. I was on that line every morning before school and I never saw any violence. There was no need for violence. Only two workers entered that plant each morning and the police had a very easy task when the two non-strikers arrived. They just stopped the picket line, formed a little path to shield the two brave but misguided non-strikers as they entered the plant.

The judge didn't do that. On what then did he base his judgment that an injunction was needed in the Siebert strike? I think I know. Does the following anecdote suggest how and why the injunction was obtained?

I became extremely interested in wrestling when I was about thirteen because there was a Finnish wrestler named Otto Huhtanen who was billed as *The Fabulous Finn*. He became my hero. I marvelled at his ability not only to stand on his head but also to do a complete split. Quite often an opponent, trying to give him a "spread-eagle", would strain mightily to push Otto Huhtanen's legs farther apart. The Fabulous Finn would resist while feigning great pain. Slowly the legs would give way then suddenly Otto Huhtanen would spread his legs into a straight line. The movement was so fast, the legs so far apart that his opponent lost his grasp with a loud snap. The audience, anticipating the action, would roar with delight at his opponent's consternation.

There was a wrestler nicknamed *The Terrible Turk*—a man I found to be extremely obnoxious—who was often matched against Otto Huhtanen. The Terrible Turk gave me the impression that he was very envious of Otto Huhtanen, a good-natured

Nordic type. Usually, but not always, Otto Huhtanen won the bout—two falls out of three—from the Terrible Turk.

Never did I see Otto Huhtanen take unfair advantage of any opponent, not even The Terrible Turk. In fact, many times—if my memory serves me correctly—when his opponent was momentarily dazed or off balance, the Fabulous Finn would wait even though under the rules he had a perfect right to charge in and pin his opponent. No, Otto Huhtanen always waited until his opponent "had gained his ready". When a Fabulous Finn's opponent was pinned, it was done in a sportsman like way.

The Terrible Turk always entered the arena with a prayer rug which he set down with extreme care, kneeled on it, and prostrated himself several times in the direction of Mecca. He took every advantage of his opponent using—especially when the referee's back was turned—irregular tactics, tactics that had no place in a wrestling match. He was, of course, loudly booed for these actions. The booing was exceptionally vociferous whenever he won a fall from the Fabulous Finn. The booing, however, didn't faze The Terrible Turk one bit.

Whenever Otto Huhtanen wrestled in the Old City Hall auditorium I was there with a bunch of other kids on the fire escape peeking through the second story windows. One night after the bout was over I spotted the Fabulous Finn as he left the auditorium. I dashed up to him and asked him in Finnish to shake my hand. He laughed, took my hand, grasped it tightly, and replied in Finnish, "It's a great pleasure to shake your hand. Don't take the wrestling too seriously. Enjoy it. Have fun. But don't forget to study hard and do all your homework."

I was on cloud nine! For a few weeks I went around pestering my friends—young and old, Finns and non-Finns—"Shake the hand that shook the hand of Otto Huhtanen!"

It all ended one night in the men's common room of the Oriole Street steambath (sauna). I had been shooting baskets at the Ash Street Hall when I suddenly remembered *Äiti* had given me a quarter and said to be sure I had a sauna before I came home. I guess I went to the Oriole Street steambath—not my usual sauna place—because it was the closest commercial sauna to Ash Street Hall.

I was dressing quite slowly, trying to keep cool after finishing my bath, so that I wouldn't start sweating again. Two professional wrestlers walked into the dressing room, one was the Terrible Turk and the other a French-Canadian whose wrestling name and real name I have forgotten. They were in such high spirits—talking and joshing one another—that they didn't see me sitting on the bench. Or if they did, they didn't think I mattered. Then I caught some words.

"Yeh, I know Otto doesn't make a very good bad guy. That's because he doesn't like to be booed. But shit, he's got to learn. He can't always be the hero. I don't think there's a single Finn up in Keene and that town has a helluva lot of Canucks. He...

"What the hell is taking him so long?"

"Oh, balls! Hold your horses! He may have to go more than one place to get it. You better take out your little prayer rug and pray before you come into the steambath with me. I like a fucking red hot steambath.

"Bullshit on you. Otto's trained me. Christ! Does he like it hot! How in the hell do those fucking Finns take so much heat?"

"They pick it up in Finland. It's suppose to be cold enough up there to freeze the balls off a brass monkey. The steambath is the only place those poor bastards can keep warm."

Do judges and lawyers discuss their cases like wrestlers, outside their arena, the court room? Sure they do. They're not supposed to but they do. Naturally, they are more discreet. The judges and lawyers usually have a better education than wrestlers so that they know a young boy may have a tremendous curiosity and very big ears even though he is very quiet.

I don't know where the doctors, lawyers, judges, and other members of the middle and upper class in Gardner socialized back in 1935. I know they didn't patronize the Finnish commercial saunas. (What an adventure they would have had if they did!) I conjecture, though, that Gardner's elite socialized in the Colonial Hotel and the Unitarian, Methodist, and Congregationalist Churches.

Or perhaps they met in some country club to play some golf because in my mind's ear I still overhear the following conversation. Did such a conversation actually take place?

"Hi, Ed! You certainly look peaked. Have you lost your best friend? Maybe I better give you a bigger handicap today."

"Hi, Judge."

"Look, Ed, take it from one who knows. Don't let that strike get you down. Fifty years from now it won't matter one way or the other."

"Maybe, Judge, maybe. But the going is pretty rocky right now. We got some cancellations on a few Christmas orders this morning. The first, but there'll be more. Still the association wants me to stand firm a little longer. I agree with reason—we just can't let that damn union get a foothold in this town. But I hope it doesn't break me trying to stop them. It gives one a strange feeling to have the federal government help those damn reds fight against legitimate American businessmen. I'm going to work like hell to get rid of that Roosevelt come 1936!"

"You really think a little more time will help you?"

"The association thinks so. I think we need some kind of action to shake that union to pieces. Something to scare them, something to knock them off guard. I wanted to get an injunction against picketing. That would of really hampered their style."

"Well, why don't you?"

"Counsel doesn't think we have a good case. And besides the Norris-Laguardia..."

"It certainly wouldn't hurt to try. Every man should have his day in court."

I recall March 7, 1935 as a very dark, gloomy, dismal, and forbidding day. It didn't rain but dark clouds blotted out the sun so effectively that the evening darkness seemed to come much earlier than usual. Actually, March 7, 1935 may have been a beautiful pre-spring day in Gardner. I recall that day as dark and dismal because that became my mood when I heard the Supreme Court had declared the NRA (National Industrial Recovery Act) unconstitutional.

I was frightened when I heard the news. I remember walking along Main Street in front of Bent's factory, disconsolate and depressed, looking for someone to grieve with about the evil days that were about to engulf the country. Although I had little long-term faith in President Roosevelt's reforms, I felt much of his legislation was a sincere effort to help the working people. Now I doubted that Roosevelt would be able to salvage much of his reform legislation from a court so devoted to the protection of the moneyed interests. Beware, I thought, of the Ides of March!

I had exactly the same feeling about the day the judge provided Sieberts with their anti-picketing injunction. That day too—about a year earlier—was dark, gloomy, dismal, and depressing. I had been absolutely convinced that we were going to win the strike. The strikers' morale was excellent. Victory was on the horizon! I hadn't had the slightest suspicion that the courts would intervene on the side of the employers. I remember thinking when I heard the news, "Equal rights under the law. Bullshit!"

I hurried to the union hall where workers from all over Gardner were gathering. The union members, coldly angry, were ready to mount the barricades. The mildest epithet I heard that afternoon was, "The goddamn judge is a traitor to the country. He wants to destroy the Blue Eagle!"

Another muttered angrily, "I sure hope Roosevelt makes the Blue Eagle shit on that fucking judge." Who was to know that in a year's time higher judges would destroy the Blue Eagle itself when they declared the NRA unconstitutional.

The English-speaking Socialist Party local, in an hastily convened caucas, decided to defy the injunction after an inspiring speech, "...we face the same diabolical dilemma faced by Eugene Victor Debs when Grover Cleveland was President. We are damned if we do and damned if we don't. They have given us no choice, so let Debs be our inspiration. Let's go down with our banners proudly unfurled, waving defiantly.

"Some of us will go to jail. The union will be destroyed. But our conscience will be clear. We tried. We tried to help the Gardner workers gain a measure of dignity and fair play. ...Let every socialist be on the picket line tomorrow!"

Axel Bachman, the union president, stated that he was also wiling to defy the court issued injunction against picketing if the union members would sanction such action in an open meeting.

The Union hall, the entire second floor of the Ryan Building, was packed that night with hundreds of workers. It was impossible to check anyone's credentials that evening as the impatient workers poured into the hall.

The thirty or so folding chairs had been stacked away. Everyone except the secretary, who sat at a table, had to stand. The staircase leading to the second floor meeting hall was jammed with members unable to gain admittance. At least a hundred others, I was told, were on the street in front of Rose's Furniture Store.

Although I don't think 90% of the members heard him, Axel Bachman carefully explained the "pickle" the union was in. The injunction, he insisted, was not fair but, even so, those who defied it were liable to go to jail. Every union official, he added, was willing to defy the injunction because there was no reasonable alternative. The officials were willing to go to jail. Did the union members stand behind their leaders?

A roar of approval from the people who could hear Bachman swept the hall. The roar was picked up by the members in the rear of the hall and passed on to those on the stairs and in the street. They all shouted back their approval. No one had to hear Bachman. The union members were willing to support their officers. That's why they came to the meeting.

My brother Toivo, treasurer of the union, jumped up on the secretary's table and yelled as loud as he could, "I move that the United Furniture and Allied Trade Workers declare a general strike in support of the O.W. Siebert strikers! All union members will be on the picket line tomorrow!"

The motion was never seconded. A tremendous roar sounded again throughout the hall as the workers yelled their acclamation. Several union members jumped on the table and shouted, "General strike tomorrow! General strike tomorrow!"

The words "General strike!" echoed through the building and into the street. The workers of Gardner were venting their anger against the injunction and the judge.

The next day the factory workers in Gardner responded to the union's general strike call in numbers far beyond anyone's expectation. They left their jobs and marched, usually in a group, to the O.W. Siebert factory. The union officers were amazed as group after group of marching workers joined the picket line. The picket line grew so big that it extended around a complete city block—up Main Street to Sherman, from Sherman to Logan, from Logan to Washington, and from Washington back to Main.

The continuous circle of defiant pickets were in extremely high spirits. They sang, shouted, and joked as they walked around and around the city block. They were not class-conscious rebels. They were patriots, defenders of the Blue Eagle. They were marching to protect the Blue Eagle which had promised them a greater equity in society. No judge was going to destroy the Blue Eagle. It belonged to the people.

A few days later the O.W. Siebert Company agreed to a 5¢ per hour wage increase and to recognize the United Furniture and Allied Trade Workers as the sole bargaining agent for its employees. The union has passed its first big test. It was in Gardner to stay. There were other strikes but my interests turned to other directions when I graduated from high school.

Chapter Nine

THE TEMPERANCE SOCIETIES

The first Finnish immigrants to arrive in Gardner were strike-breakers who came to take the jobs of some striking Yankee furniture workers. These strikebreakers were housed in an old decayed brick building that was located on the corner of Pleasant and West Broadway, near the outskirts of the city. One moonless night, shortly after their arrival, the angry Yankee strikers bombarded the strikebreakers' residence with rocks, stones, bricks, and other missiles. After the barrage was over, the strikers rushed the building, forcing the strikebreakers to flee.

The above account which I have translated from Elis Sulkanen's excellent history of the Finnish-American labor movement agrees with the stories I heard as a boy from the older Finns with a few exceptions. Elis Sulkanen says the Finnish strikebreakers were not culpable because they didn't know about the labor dispute. "Not so," I was told. The Finnish strikebreakers were ignorant about the labor movement not about the strike in progress. They soon learned though. Some of those strikebreakers became devoted members of the Gardner local (osasto) of the Finnish Socialist Federation. A few became charter members.

After the labor climate returned to normal and after the ire against the Finnish strikebreakers subsided, additional Finnish immigrants came to Gardner so that by 1905 there were over 1000 Finns in the Gardner area. The Finnish community continued to grow in Gardner so that by 1920 more than 10% of the population in Gardner was of Finnish extraction. It is interesting to note that each Finnish community tended to attract immigrants from the same locality in Finland. Gardner, for example, attracted Finns from Pieksämäki, Fitchburg tended to attract Finns from Toholampi, Fairport (Ohio) from Kryölä, etc.

The fight against Demon Rum and John Barleycorn was the most important concern of the early Finnish-American leaders. The young male immigrant, free from the watchful eye of the Lutheran Church and with no place to socialize, began to be a weekend saloon habituè. The reputations of all Finns began to be destroyed as the hard drinking became disturbing to the American public. The heavy drinking amongst the Finnish workers in Gloucester (Massachusetts), for example, caused a local newspaper to ask in print, "Are Finns human? Does a Finn have a soul?"

Temperance organizations that urged total abstinence were started in almost every Finnish-American community to provide social, cultural, and educational activities which, it was hoped, would entice the young immigrants out of the bars. These temperance societies, as the Finnish name *raittiusseura* was translated by the second generation, usually adopted sentimental names. The name of the largest temperance society in Gardner was *Rauhan Aarre* which means A Treasure of Peace.

Below is a sample of some of the names adopted by the temperance societies in various parts of the country. There must have been more than 500 Finnish temperance societies in the United States and Canada. Many communities had more than one group.

FINNISH NAME	ENGLISH NAME	TOWN
Aamunkoitto	Day Break	Fitchburg
Armonlähde	Fountain of Grace	Tarrytown, New York
Auringon Säde	The Sun's Ray	Rock Springs, Wyoming
Erämaan Tähti	Desert Star	Clear Creek, Utah
Erämaan Helmi	Desert Pearl	Cumberland, Wyoming
Hyvä Toivo	Good Hope	Calumet, Michigan
Iltahetki	Eventide	Lead City, South Dakota
Kaiku	The Echo	Bessemer, Michigan
Kansan Onni	Peoples Luck	Pierre, South Dakota
Kukoistus	The Blossoming	Fall River, Mass.
Kupari Ruusu	The Copper Rose	Centennial Heights, Mi.
Kultala	The Treasure	West Gardner, Mass.
Lännen Rusko	Western Glow	Carbon, Wyoming
Lännen Taimi	Western Seedling	Diamondsville, Wyoming
Lännen Tähti	Western Star	Eureka, Calif.
Laaksonkukka	Flower of the Valley	Red Lodge, Montana

Niemen Ruusu	The Peninsula Rose	Millstone, Conn.
Niemen Kukka	The Peninsula Flower	South Carver, Mass.
Onnen Aika	Time of Happiness	Republic, Michigan
Rauhan Aarre	A Treasure of Peace	Gardner, Mass.
Rauhan Vesa	Peaceful Growth	Allenport, Penn.
Saaren Kukka	The Island Flower	Kearsage, Mich.
Sovinto	Harmony	Eureka, Calif.
Toivon Tähti	Star of Hope	Fitzwilliams, N.H.
Tyven Satama	A Peaceful Harbor	Hoquiam, Wash.
Tähti	The Star	New York City
Voiton Lippu	The Victorious Banner	Monessen, Penn.
Valon Säde	A Ray of Light	Milford, N.H.
Valo	The Enlightment	Ironwood, Mich.
Vuoriston Ilo	A Mountain of Joy	Sand Coulee, Montana
Vuoriston Ruusu	Mountain Rose	Hanna, Wyoming
Valon Lähde	The Fountain of Light	Rock Springs, Wyoming
Valon Leimu	The Glowing Light	Rockport, Mass.
Vuoriston Toivo	A Mountain of Hope	Marlboro, N.H.
Valon Säde	A Ray of Light	Twilight, Penn.
Valonkipinä	A Glowing Spark	Iron Belt, Wisconsin
Uljas Koitto	The Valiant Endeavor	Quincy, Mass.
Yksimielisyys	Harmony or Unity	Marquette, Mich.

The first temperance society organized in Gardner was named *Pyrintö* (Endeavor) but since the leadership of *Pyrintö* forbade dancing or other merry social activities the youngest and most recently arrived immigrants organized a new temperance society named *Väinölä* in honor of the land where *Väinämöinen* was born and lived. Both temperance societies were on fairly good terms with each other and met in the same hall at 175 Nichols Street—two doors away from the building where *Isä* had his soft drink business.

Rauhan Aarre, the largest temperance group to exist in Gardner, was formed because the leadership of *Pyrintö* refused to join the Eastern League of Finnish Temperance Societies. The liberal *Väinölä* and *Rauhan Aarre* purchased the Miller's Opera House on Pine Street. The Miller's Opera House, the first real Finn hall in Gardner, became known as the *Suomi Hall*. The *Pyrintö* temperance society disappeared from the scene when both *Väinölä* and *Rauhan Aarre* moved their activities to Suomi Hall.

Schisms of this type were common in almost all Finnish-American communities.* They are a product of intellectual and

---

*The history of the Gardner Finnish-American community, except for the initial strikebreaking phase, is typical of the history of the Finnish-American communities elsewhere.

social ferment. And the intellectual and social ferment in the early Finnish-American communities were so high that schisms—major and minor—became a way of life for the Finns from 1900 to 1920. This narrative covers two of the major schisms that shook the Finnish-American communities. I leave the last one to future historians.

Around 1903, a spectre began to haunt the Finnish temperance movement. Many of the members in all parts of the country began to evince an interest in the rapidly growing labor movement in the United States. A labor lodge called the *Amerikan Suomalainen Työväenliitto Imatra* (Finnish-American Labor Lodge Imatra), founded in Brooklyn (New York) in 1890, was the catalyst that transformed many of the temperance societies into labor lodges.

I have translated *työväenliitto* to *labor lodge* because Imatra was a lodge. Other writers have translated *työväenliitto* to *labor league* or *labor association* but I don't think that makes sense. *Imatra*, according to one of its founders, was organized to provide: 1) mutual aid in case of unexpected difficulties; 2) an opportunity to develop intellectual aspirations; and 3) occasions for social enjoyment. *Imatra* was not a socialist organization but the use of the word *työväen* (working class) suggests that *Imatra* was liberal or reformist in its attitude and ideology.

Imatra became the first national Finnish-American labor organization in 1903 when delegates to a founding convention that was held in conjunction with the Eastern States Finnish Temperance League's summer festival (in Gardner), adopted bylaws and selected Brooklyn as the national headquarters. Each local lodge had the same name as the parent organization in Brooklyn. A number suffixed to the end of the name distinguished the lodges. The Brooklyn lodge was, of course, number 1. The name of the Gardner lodge was Finnish-American Labor Lodge Imatra 3 *(Amerikan Suomalainen Työväenliitto Imatra 3)*.

The temperance movement left its mark in the new labor associations. All of them kept the principle of total abstinence from liquor as a basic part of their creed. None of the organizations, to the best of my knowledge, ever served alcoholic beverages at their affairs or allowed any type of alcoholic beverage to be sold on any property they owned except the Brooklyn Imatra Lodge itself. And even that lodge did not acquiesce to the sale of alcoholic beverages in the Imatra Hall until 1930 when, faced with the loss of the hall itself because of the lack of revenues, the so-called "Booze Party" faction gained the right to open a bar on the second floor. In other Finnish localities, the principle of total abstinence remained part and parcel of *Finn Hall* philosophy. In Gardner liquor was never sold (not even beer) in the Labor Temple (Ash Street Hall) even though that Finn hall was finally lost on the auction block.

Imatra had 36 local lodges in the East and Middle-West at the height of its influence. Another Finnish labor organization—with ambitions to become a national Finnish organization too—was formed in Duluth in 1904. The Duluth organization was, however, much more political in nature than Imatra. The central question at the very first convention of the Duluth group was: "Shall we join the Socialist Party of the United States?" The "Nays" won the day but the convention, as a compromise, did authorize a call for a national conference of all Finnish labor organizations to discuss and resolve the issue of Finnish-American affiliation with the broader American labor movement.

THE FINNISH-AMERICAN WORK ETHIC

Many of these early independent Imatra-affiliated workingmen's associations (as well as a good number of temperance societies) conducted their membership meetings in a ceremonial fashion, a manner common to American lodges. The Saima Labor Society *(Työväenyhdistys Saima)* of Fitchburg (Massachusetts), in the years before Saima affiliated with the Socialist Party, conducted its meetings in the ceremonial manner specified in its handbook. The chairman opened the meeting by reciting:

> Worthy fellow-workers! Since the days of Adam and Eve we have been directed, "Work!"...
>
> The Gospel of Work is as ancient as the Gospel of Peace. Work was honorable. Adam sowed and Eve gathered. The old patriarchs were shepherds. History tells us that the ancient Romans chose their chief while standing by their plows...
>
> Sometime ago, a damaging vanity, which takes many forms, descended on humankind. It is evident in the desire for power, and it has resulted in the bondage of much of mankind...
>
> Capital and labor once cooperated together because work is the motivating force for all humanity. But this cooperation no longer exists. No longer is a laborer worthy of his hire! The owners of capital band together to keep workers in bondage...

Since the owners of capital have organized to control the government; we workers must respond by forming associations that, too, will try to influence the government.

We meet again, with harmony and love, to study and to discuss the problems faced by all workingmen. For that reason, I now invite all of you to take part in our important discussion.

The membership would then arise and sing before the association's business was considered.

New members were initiated into *Saima* in much the same manner as I was initiated into the Elks—only the words and the attitudes were different. The candidates for membership were queried ritually by the sergeant-at-arms, "Do you, of your own free will, solemnly swear to obey and to uphold the principles and ideals of our association, principles that are based on mutual aid and ideals that motivate us to improve the society we live in?"

The sergeant-at-arms, after hearing an affirmative answer, would escort the candidates to the initation circle where he would recite to the chairman, "Mr. President, I have the great honor of sponsoring these candidates for membership. These are all worthy candidates."

The president would then intone:

Welcome to our ranks! We are indeed extremely joyful that you have accepted our values and attitudes as your own. Let this association be as your home...

Our noble purpose is to improve both the spiritual and the material life of all working men and women. We give moral and material assistance to one another as good brothers and sisters should. We want to improve, by all legal and peaceful means, the lot of the worker in this country, help each other when strikes or other labor difficulties occur, and to provide support to one another when illness presents itself...

You have now joined our ranks and you have the same rights and privileges as any other member.

But the candidates were not yet installed. The sergeant-at-arms would then escort them to the "oldest member's" chair where they were admonished by the ancient wisdom:

Work and pray! Remember these words, the Lutheran motto, taught us by our fathers. We believe the workingman's best shelter is work and the fear of God...

The unity of our brothers and sisters in this association gives us additional assurance. We are, remember, a group of your fellow workers who will be true to you, who want to stand by your side whatever the vicissitudes you may face in life's struggle. Now that you have joined our ranks, Be at home!

Then the vice-president had to have his say;

> We are all workers in life's large arena. We are all equal, children of the same God. We note that our greatest responsibility is to live in harmony and love with our fellowmen. We must behave in a civilized and temperate manner to our fellow citizens as we work for the improvement of ourselves and our nation. We obey the one truthful commandment: Do unto others what you want done unto yourself.
>
> Friends! You have now been informed of the important principles of our association. You have assumed the duties of a member. Remember these duties are nothing more or less than that which we all owe to society and to each other.
>
> Members of Saima, please arise and welcome these candidates into our midst by singing.

A STORM HITS ROCKPORT

The national Finnish-American Labor Lodge Imatra *(Amerikan Suomalainen Työväenliitto Imatra)* had a very short life. All of the local lodges, except the headquarter's lodge in Brooklyn (New York)—Imatra #1—joined the rapidly growing socialist movement led by Eugene Victor Debs.

The harbinger of Imatra's demise was the organization *Mrysky* (Storm), the first Finnish socialist association in the United States or Canada. And, ironically, *Mrysky* was started because of a small comedy of errors which involved the Lutheran clergy and one Dr. Antero Ferdinand Tanner. A doctor of natural science and a Finnish pioneer in sex education, Tanner was forced to flee Finland because he had given some lectures about the "theories of idealistic free love."

Dr. Tanner went to Rockport (Massachusetts) where one of his former classmates, Rev. P. Airaksinen, was the pastor of a Lutheran congregation. Rev. Airaksinen, much to his future sorrow, invited Tanner to lecture on natural science at the popular educational courses sponsored by the church.

The pastor was well aware of Tanner's brilliance but he did not realize that Tanner actually believed in all the "new science" of that era even when that science conflicted with the teachings of the Bible. The explanation provided by Rev. Airaksinen to excuse his association with Tanner was understandable but didn't the pastor know Tanner had to flee Finland? Wasn't he the slightest bit curious why Tanner had to leave?

Can you imagine the turmoil and consternation in the conservative Finnish religious atmosphere of 1900 when Tanner gave forth on evolution and the age of the earth? After all who wants to sacrifice the precious gift of eternal life for some unproven scientific speculations? The Lutheran Church officials labelled Tanner "the evil apostle of the Devil!" And then dumped the catalyst into the situation by calling Tanner "an abominable socialist!"

Tanner, who had not espoused any socialist ideas in his lectures was taken aback but he admitted, "Yes, I am a socialist by conviction." This admission forced Tanner to give one more lecture in order to explain what socialism was about and why he accepted its tenets. The lecture was given in the Rockport Finnish Temperance Hall even though the clergy demanded that the temperance society's facilities be denied Tanner.

The clergy's demand went unheeded because Tanner intrigued the young Finnish immigrants in Rockport. He had, in his natural science lectures, made "water burn and changed the nature of oil so that it would not ignite." Surely such deeds can only be the work of the Evil One. So Tanner's lecture on socialism was packed with Rockport Finns. After all, if the Devil gave a lecture, wouldn't you, dear reader, make it a point to hear what he had to say? Oh, I suppose most of the young immigrants came to the lecture hoping to hear and see a good scrap between Tanner and the Lutheran clergy. Anyway, the hall was packed that night.

The principles and ideals of socialism—which we might call a new religion to the immigrants—appealed to many in the audience so Tanner made several converts that night. What did he do with his converts? Well, a few weeks later the tongue-twisting Rockport *Suomalainen Sosialidemokraattinen Yhdistys Myrsky* (Finnish Social Democratic Association-Storm) was in existence with about a dozen members. The group immediately applied for affiliation with the Socialist Labor Party of the United States.

Myrsky (Storm), Tanner claimed, was the first Finnish organization in the world to use the socialist name (social democratic is a synonym for socialist). No sane group would have dared, at that time in Czarist-ruled Finland, to use such a dangerous name in public.

Tanner himself, in a humorous mood, reminisced:

> ...of all things! The ruling class in Finland sent this writer to America to bring the first socialist message to the American Finns.
> It all happened in that very remarkable year 1899. I had scarcely

become acquainted with the new labor movement which was developing in Finland at that time. Nor had I read very much about socialism, when they sent me to evangelize for socialism across the sea.

Actually, even then, I doubt if I would have recognized my "great calling"—since I had made up my mind to retire into a studious life upon my arrival in America—except that the Lutheran clergy in America urgently requested me step forward and be heard. So I did.

I was completely amazed and enchanted when I discovered the great appeal socialist evangelism had for the poor. People [Finns] loved the doctrine. They were converted in droves.

The Fitchburg people [Finns] were especially interested and very curious. There were always over a hundred people in the audience when I lectured there. Even though I had to pay five cents a person (from the collection) to the temperance society as hall rent, I still found two dollars or so left for my travel expenses.

UNCLE MATTI (MATTI-SETÄ) HENDRICKSON THE APOSTLE OF SOCIALISM

The conversion of one Martin Hendrickson, a twenty-eight year old shoemaker from Kivijärvi (Finland), was Tanner's most important proselytizing achievement. Hendrickson, who became the foremost Finnish-American apostle of socialism, characterized Tanner as a "crazy educated fool" after listening to Tanner's first lecture on natural science. The socialist bug, however, bit Hendrickson at one of Tanner's lectures. But, then, Hendrickson was an easy mark because he needed something to believe in, something to work for with his whole heart and soul. After several personal meetings with Tanner, Hendrickson announced his conversion to socialism.

We might say that Hendrickson accepted Tanner as his socialist "guru". The two men, almost inseparable for several years, carried the socialist message to every Finnish-American community with high spirits and much humor. Hendrickson continued his efforts alone and went on to an unusual fate after Tanner, somewhat disillusioned by his inability to start a Finnish socialist newapaper, returned to a private life in Chisholm (Minnesota) where he died in 1919.

Matti-Setä (Uncle Matti), as Hendrickson became fondly known among Finnish-Americans, kept traveling throughout the United States and Canada. He visited most Finnish communities several times. Sometimes, when he visited a community that appealed to him—such as Fort Bragg (California)—he found employment and became a resident until the urge to carry the socialist message

Martin Hendrickson

became too great to ignore.

He preached the socialist gospel with a good deal of humor, poked fun at the Finnish-American conservative leaders, and laughed at the harassment he sometimes faced from the Finnish Lutheran clergy—even when the harassement inconvenienced him. He organized dozens of workingmen's associations, each with a definite socialist orientation.

His preaching was interrupted twice. Once because he was given a ten week jail sentence for helping out some South Carver (Massachusetts) striking cranberry workers. The second interruption occured in 1902 when he joined the idealistic Finnish commune *Sointula* (Harmony) on Malcolm Island in British Columbia. Matti Kurikka, the leader and the life force behind Sointula, made a tremendous impression on Hendrickson. But there was no role for Hendrickson to play in Sointula. He was much too restless and energetic to settle down in such a quiet place; so a few months after his arrival on the island, he resigned from the commune and returned to his socialist proselytizing. He claimed he was utterly disappointed and disillusioned by the political attitude and philosophy of the commune.

Finally the seeds planted by Hendrickson, Tanner, and the other early Finnish-American evangelists flowered into a vigorous socialist organization, the largest and most influential Finnish organization in the Finnish-American communities. This organization, named *Suomalainen Sosialistijärjestö* (Finnish Socialist Federation), had its golden age in the years from 1906 to 1920 when it dominated Finnish-American community life. We shall see (next section) that Hendrickson and the other socialist evangelists didn't do it alone. They had tremendous assistance, involuntary though it was, from the apostle of *Kalevala*, Matti Kurikka.

I have used the word *evangelist* to describe these early Finnish socialist agitators because these young organizers were imbued with a deep religious conviction about socialism. This deep religious feeling was even noticed by the early Finnish journalists since they used the Finnish word *herättäjät* which means *evangelists* to describe these young men and women also.

This deep religious spirit of the young Finnish socialists was clearly noticeable at the founding convention of the Finnish Socialist Federation in 1906. Since many of the delegates arrived in Hibbing (Minnesota) a few days before the formal opening of the convention, they held several street corner meetings in various parts of the city so that the "socialist presence would be felt in Hibbing."

The most surprising aspect of these outdoor meetings where speeches were given in both Finnish and English was, according to the participants, that the police did not interfere in any way with the activities "even though some of the outdoor rallies were held right next to the Hibbing City Hall." These committed young people were quite ready to become martyrs for their cause. Perhaps they thought they were in ancient Rome. Anyway they began to learn how to function in the American democracy.

The founding of the Finnish Socialist Federation—the official Finnish name was usually abbreviated to *SSJ* since *Suomalainen Sosialistijärjestö* was more than a mouthful for even a Finn—was celebrated by a huge festival in the Finnish Workers Association

Park. The delegates, accompanied by two Finnish labor group brass bands—one from Chisholm (Minnesota) and the other from Hibbing—and hundreds of enthusiastic supporters, marched along the city streets to the festival grounds.

Excitement was in the air! A mutiny of Russian army officers (called the *Viaporin Kapina* in Finnish) had taken place in Finland shortly before the convention opened so both the Russian secret police and the American authorities carefully monitored the festivities and the convention. The police agents, ignorant of Finnish, had to have interpreters to explain what was going on in the park and on the convention floor. The minutes of the meeting noted this fact by "... secret police, with their interpreters were everywhere trying to understand what was going on but they were quite civil, not the least bit hostile..."

The Finnish Socialist Federation grew rapidly from the 58 charter locals to 264 within a few years. At one time or another, over 300 communities had a Finnish socialist *osasto* (local). And the Finnish *osasto* usually acquired a hall which became the center of Finnish-American cultural and social life in the community.

What happened to our socialist apostle, Martin Hendrickson, in this prosperous and growing organization he helped develop? Well, Hendrickson did not find a proper niche for himself in the socialist federation. He was much too anti-establishment and too restless to find comfort as a day to day functionary in a stable organization. When the first schism *(Ensimmäinen Hajaannus)* shook the federation in 1914, Hendrickson chose to leave with a sizeable minority of Finnish socialists to embrace the tenets of the International Workers of the World.

A few years later, during the First World War, Hendrickson was forced into the side lines as the IWW's effectiveness as a labor organization was destroyed by persistent Federal, State, and local persecution of its members. Hendrickson, more fortunate than hundreds of his fellow "wobblies", escaped a prison sentence.

Can you imagine Hendrickson, the socialist evangelist, as a Florida real estate agent? He was. Uncle Matti was the first Finnish real estate agent in Florida. He was one of the forerunners of all those first and second generation Finns who, determined to escape the cold weather, have settled around Lakewood and Lantana.

Oh, Martin Hendrickson continued to evangelize but now he

preached about the virtues and beneficial effects of the Florida sun. Armed with a projector, picture slides of Florida, and his own special brand of humor he returned North (in good weather) to propagandize his old socialist friends. "There are no dangerous snakes in Florida! The pigs take care of them. But beware! There are dangers that lurk in that wonderful land—a land so warm you walk outside in your shirt sleeves at Christmas time. Yes, there are dangers to entice the unwary! Watch out! Watch out for the beautiful women!" And he would flash a picture of a scantily dressed woman on the screen.

But our story does not have a happy middle class ending. Martin Hendrickson did not die in the comfortable surroundings of a fairly successful real estate agent. No. An ironic fate awaited him. The Russian Revolution did him in although it took fourteen years or so for that revolution to devour him.

The Russian Revolution excited Hendrickson as it did millions of other East Europeans who had lived under the rule of the Czar. Hendrickson joined the Communist Party. He believed the Soviet Union was now the worker's paradise. Exploitation no longer existed. After all, didn't the workers themselves own the means of production? How can you exploit yourself?

In the 1930's, in the midst of the Great Depression, Father Stalin issued a call to all communist Finns, "I need your help! Come to Finnish Karelia with your skills and your tools. Help me build a strong socialist Karelia!"

Hendrickson, now in his early sixties, replied, "I am an old man. I want to see socialism in action before I die. I am going to Karelia."

So Hendrickson, with thousands of other American, Canadian, and Finnish Finns—nobody knows how many thousands of Finns—answered Father Stalin's call. They emigrated to Karelia. They voluntarily entered Stalin's domain? Had they, following Rev. Nikander's injunction, "imprisoned their minds?"

Very little is known about the fate of the Karelian immigrants. Shortly after their arrival, great purges swept the Soviet Union sending millions to their death and prison. Nothing was known about Hendrickson's fate until Aino Kuusinen defected from the Soviet Union and published her memoirs—*The Rings of Destiny*.

Yes, Martin Hendrickson met an ironic fate. Do you recall that Hendrickson's socialist teacher—Dr. Anton Ferdinand Tanner—was expelled from Finland in 1898 because he, Tanner, espoused "free love"? Well, Martin Hendrickson was expelled from the Communist Party of the Soviet Union because he criticized the sexual mores of the Russians. He thought the Russians were too permissive in their sexual behavior. They had no restraint. "The Russians," he said, "are a bunch of goats."

Hendrickson's explusion from the Communist Party was equivalent to a death sentence, Aino Kuusinen wrote, because "expelled from the Communist Party, he couldn't find employment and those who didn't work in Karelia in the 1930's didn't eat." But Hendrickson didn't lose his sense of humor. He continued to preach to the end. Aino Kuusinen relates, "...Hendrickson dwindled away to a skeleton and could scarcely walk. He kept his sense of humor, however. One day he was going along the road to Petrozavodsk with some American Finns, when they met a billy goat. He wagged his finger at it and said: 'Pay attention, my friends, and don't tell anyone that you are a goat or you'll surely be in trouble.'"

THE APOSTLE OF KALEVALA -
MATTI KURIKKA

It was the "gospel of Kalevala", not socialism—although socialism reaped the harvest—that germinated the intellectual development of the young Finnish immigrant at the turn of the twentieth century. Matti Kurikka, the apostle of Kalevala, attracted thousands of young Finns to his rostrum where they heard him denounce both "materialistic socialism" and the "twisted dogma of the Lutheran Church". He called for the return to the "spiritual nobility of our heroic Finnish ancestors" as depicted in the epic *Kalevala*.

> We should develop our spiritual idealism because spiritual idealism enables an individual and a people to preserve moral purity even in the midst of deception and fraud...
>
> Even though the capitalist system imposes a harsh burden on each of us—a burden that forces us to struggle fiercely for our livelihood—it is imperative that each of us live by the teachings of Jesus so that our life will be pleasing to God...
>
> Personal responsibility and personal morality, the highest ideals of Kalevala, are the heritage we have received from our ancestors. The Lutheran Church, of course, tries to destroy these virtues, our people's most previous heritage, by trying to distract our attention from Kalevala's idealistic words and forcing us to pay homage to the Old

Matti Kurikka

Testament's savage barbarians. But the ideals of Kalevala are much deeper in our people than the clergy realizes...

We can bring new force and vitality to the teachings of Jesus and bring help to those who lack peace and love in their nature by preserving our national character; the character we inherited from our ancestors. We can preserve that character even though the clergy tries to frighten us away from our true selves with their tales of horned devils, hellfire, and damnation...

The early Christian chose to live in moral purity and harmony but the clergy sold Christendom into godless imperial slavery, as we know from history. Strife then replaced harmony, hate and persecution replaced love...

Matti Kurikka looked like a prophet. True believers might say he had the appearance of a messiah. He was a tall handsome man with a dark complexion. "His skin was so clear, it seemed to glow," an old woman told me in her recollection of him. He wore his long luxurious crown of black hair shoulder length. His intense eyes, blazing forth, captivated his audience before he uttered a single word. Here was the Finn with a message. And he spread that message by speaking in all of the important Finnish-American communities in the United States and Canada.

No other immigrant Finnish leader—before or since, Canadian or American—spoke to such large crowds. He awakened the latent intellectual instincts of the former backwoods peasants of Northern Finland. He helped to destroy their prejudices and superstitions. He opened a new world for them.

Kurikka more than anyone else except perhaps the Lutheran clergy itself influenced the wholesale defection of the Finnish immigrant from the Lutheran Church. The socialists, even though they were alarmed at the time by the huge crowds Kurikka attracted, credited him with keeping the socialist torch burning brightly even though it was done unintentionally. When Kurikka left the scene, there was no other place for the young immigrant to go except into the Finnish-American socialist movement.

The Lutheran clergy harassed Kurikka wherever and whenever possible. The most memorable occasion occured in the Imatra Hall in Brooklyn (New York) where Kurikka was a guest of the Finnish-Amerian Labor Lodge. The incident occurred in 1902 shortly after President McKinley was assassinated by an anarchist. Two members of the Lutheran clergy who apparently abhorred Kurikka took action. I quote from a report which appeared in the *History of Finnish-American Organizations in Greater New York:*

> ...Another time the police walked into the Imatra Hall in Brooklyn, New York, where a meeting was in progress and ordered everyone out. On the stage at that time stood Matti Kurikka. ...Finnish pastors Blomberg and Blomgren found Kurikka's doctrine abhorrent; hence they combined forces and informed the police that a dangerous anarchist was lecturing at Imatra. Because an anarchist had quite recently assassinated President McKinley the police didn't waste any time taking action.

Kurikka was a man obsessed; obsessed with building an idealistic commune based on the ethics and morality that he believed were taught by the *Kalevala.* A commune, he insisted, was the only way the immigrant Finn might save some of his Finnish heritage in the New World. The commune would also be a refuge from the...

> ...capitalistic and materialistic class struggle. It will be a refuge from the Church with its false doctrine...
>
> In this commune we will build a rich cultural life with freedom—away from the priests who have defiled the morality of Christianity, away from the Church that has destroyed peace, away from the evils of the outside world...
>
> We will build a lucky colony, Sointula, where we will be at peace! We will laugh at the outside world! Why? Because we have turned our backs to the world's evils; we have gained the right to laugh at its foibles.

Matti Kurikka left the scene, after kindling the intellectual fires of the Finnish immigrant, to build his idealistic commune Sointula. The immigrant Finns kept their eyes on Sointula and when

The Co-op store in Sointula

Sointula was not successful, Kurikka lost prestige. He became a prophet without honor. And there remained no spiritual home for the Finnish immigrants except socialism; so they joined the socialist federation in unprecedented numbers. Martin Hendrickson's and the other socialist evangelists' spade work had paid off.

SOINTULA - THE KALEVALA COMMUNE

The Finnish coal miners of Nanaimo (British Columbia) were, at the turn of the century, exceedingly unhappy with their plight. They wanted no part of the coal mines which were completely alien to their background. They, just as over 80% of the Finnish immigrants who came to the United States and Canada (in 1890-1910), were peasants. They came from the land where they were used to working out in the open air.

They immigrated to escape a bleak future in the cruel, cold environment that existed in Northern Finland at that time. They had hoped to find better opportunities in the New World. And—irony of life—they were plunged into the starless black and dangerous night of the coal mine where many of them worked the entire shift without being able to stand up. It was an unnatural state for men of the soil.

Many of these British Columbian miners had heard about or had read articles by Matti Kurikka who, even in Finland, had promoted the building of idealistic communes. These miners also knew that Kurikka who was forced to flee Finland from his job on the Helsinki *Työmies* (The Workingman) newspaper was in

Australia where he was trying, without much success, to interest the Australian Finnish immigrants in forming a commune. The Nanaimo coal miners saw Kurikka as their salvation. They took action. They collected $150 from their meagre pay and sent the money to Kurikka with a message: "We want to get out of the mines. Come to Nanaimo. Get us out of these coal mines."

Matti Kurikka responded to the call. He came to Nanaimo in August, 1900. He immediately established a newspaper called *Aika* (The Times), lectured to raise money, and organized the People of Kalevala Colonization Company, Limited. The company was actually chartered under its name in Finnish—*Kalevalan Kansan Colonization Company, Limited*—but I shall use the English translation of the name in this narrative.

Matti Kurikka also began to negotiate with the British Columbian and Canadian officials for a grant of land for the commune. *Väinämöinen* must have been hovering around using his magic because these officals gave Kurikka a very favorable ear even though they delayed an actual grant for several months. Kurikka used the time, given him by the delay, to travel to all the important Finnish communities in the United States and Canada to exhort the Finnish immigrants to join him in his great adventure.

Finally on November 21, 1901, *The People of Kalevala* was granted Malcolm Island in the name of His Majesty, King Edward VII of England. The long delay had a cause. A paper mill company had been given extensive timber rights in all the areas of Northern British Columbia including Malcom Island. The land grant to the commune was made only after *The People of Kalevala* agreed to sign a contract with this paper company. Both sides, the paper company and the commune, felt they had made a good deal. The People of Kalevala thought the logging operations would help them clear the land for agriculture while the paper mill company had high hopes of getting very cheap labor for their logging enterprises.

But I suspect Matti Kurikka had been astute. Did he insist, with deep insight, that the grant be made in the name of His Majesty, the King of England? If he did, it was a stroke of genius that almost paid off.

So, in November 1901 *The People of Kalevala* had the right to colonize Malcolm Island which is about 185 miles north of the City of Vancouver—about midway between the mainland and

Directors of The People of Kalevala

Vancouver Island. Malcolm Island, itself, is fifteen miles long and has an average width of two and one-half miles. Its 28,000 acres were covered with cedar, spruce, and hemlock. Visions of great cultural achievements and complete freedom from "wage slavery" were deep in the minds of these first Finnish pioneers as they viewed their beautiful, isolated fertile island.

Although life was not easy for the pioneers on the Island during the first few months of the commune's existence, *Väinämöinen's* magic had its effect. About six months after the first settlers arrived a change took place in the political administration of British Columbia. The paper mill company lost its rights to the timber on Malcolm Island as well as elsewhere on the mainland. The grant given to *The People of Kalevala* would also have been rescinded except the grant had been made in the name of His Majesty, the King of England. What the King has decreed, let no man tear asunder! The timber rights, too, on Malcolm Island now belonged to *The People of Kalevala*.

Alas! Dissension and backbiting, common elements in communal life, troubled Sointula, as the commune had been named. The dissension was actually a power stuggle between the "scientific socialists", led by one A.B. Makela who had been one of Kurikka's colleagues on the staff of the socialist daily *Helsinki Työmies* (The Workingman), and the "utopian socialist" followers of Kurikka.

In the commune's first two years, Matti Kurikka had the political strength to dominate the colony even though the pioneers suffered from short food rations, poor clothing allotments, and the lack of adequate housing. Then calamity struck.

Matti Kurikka, who was not nearly as good a businessman as he was a spellbinder, had made several disadvantageous business arrangements for the commune. A special meeting demanded by many members to discuss the commune's severe financial plight was held in *Cedar Hall*, a two story common building. It was January 29, 1903, an unusually cold day on Malcolm Island. Almost the entire adult population of Sointula was in the second floor meeting hall. The children were in the rooms below because Cedar Hall was the warmest place in the commune.

The discussion in the meeting, vocal and bitter, was interrupted by screams of "Fire!" The fire spread so fast that eleven people lost their lives, eight of the victims were children who had been playing in the rooms downstairs. The morale of the commune hit rock bottom.

Accusations of arson were made against both Matti Kurikka and A.B. Makela even though Makela was so badly burned that little hope was given for his survival. The accusers—soon to be labelled slanderers—claimed the fire was started deliberately in order to destroy the books that might have proved both Kurikka and Makela had embezzled the commune's money. The accusers were forced to leave the commune and the island.

The commune began to rebuild and the morale of its members began to rise but the expulsion of the slanderers had set a precedent. At the next annual meeting in February, barely a month later, Matti Kurikka threatened to resign and leave the commune unless two of his most vocal political opponents were expelled from the commune and "exiled" from Malcolm Island. The meeting decided to acquiesce to Kurikka's demands but the "scientific socialists" in the colony began to organize in earnest to oust the father of Sointula, Matti Kurikka, himself. The issue—free love.

Matti Kurikka had always preached a doctrine of free love, even in his Helsinki days. It was part and parcel of his anti-clergy bias. The church (nor its clergy) was needed to sanctify a marriage. Love was the natural criterion. A couple in love had the natural right to cohabitate. It was a sin to live in loveless wedlock. The doctrine is tame by the standards of the young generation in the 1970's but, in 1900, it was a bold and scandalous doctrine.

Let me quote at length from a pamphlet, *History of Sointula,* which is based on a Finnish history written by one of Sointula's pioneers.

> Kurikka had been writing articles in his newspaper Aika, on free love. People in the outside world got the understanding that it was practiced on the island. Even the government had been notified to this effect. The people of Sointula knew, of course, that such wasn't the case but they also knew that Kurikka and his followers had been advocating it.
>
> Sober-minded men and women arose against such tendencies. At the end of September when the bridge gang had returned home the issue was taken up at a special meeting. By now definite sides had been formed, those for Kurikka's ideas regarding the matter and those against it. Makela's and Kurikka's wills clashed at this meeting, with the result that Kurikka resigned from the colony and left Sointula, never to return.
>
> But he didn't leave alone. Almost half the members left with him. Kurikka went to Finland some time afterwards, got married and returned to America. He died about ten years later in the State of New York, leaving his wife and one daughter.

The commune, head over heels in debt—now with its labor force, its only source of money, drastically diminished—was doomed. Bankruptcy seemed to be the only solution so on May 17, 1905, *The People of Kalevala* held its last meeting. The commune was dissolved. Each of the remaining pioneers was given an allotment of land. The rest of the island was returned to the commune's benefactor, His Majesty, the King of England, whose receivers sold it at $5.00 an acre to pay off the commune's debts. Only about 36 families elected to remain in Sointula.

I made my pilgrimage to Sointula in 1977 when Malcolm Island was still somewhat isolated. At that time there still wasn't a paved road all the way to Port McNeil where there is a ferry to Malcolm Island. The town of Sointula reminded me of the Finn halls of my youth, somewhat old and worn down but still extremely functional. The first generation Finnish-Canadians who founded Sointula, almost all gone now, seem to haunt the place.

The largest building in town, a three story wooden edifice built on a hill that overlooks the sea, is the old Finnish socialist hall. The socialist name is, of course, no longer attached to it. It is now known as the Finnish Organization Hall. In its socialist heyday the hall was the center of community life. Something—play rehearsal, choir preparation, brass band or orchestra practice—was going on in the building every night. The week's ac-

Sointula

tivity—all so typical of Finnish hall activity—was climaxed by the Saturday night social and dance.

Another large building houses the consumers cooperative which the pioneers of Sointula organized in 1906, shortly after the People of Kalevala commune was dissolved. The cooperative is one of the oldest continuing consumer's cooperatives in the United States and Canada. Its two retail stores do a thriving business since it is, except for a small restaurant and a tiny variety store, the only business in town.

The Lutheran Church has no membership in Sointula. In fact Sointula was without a church until about 1960 when the Sointula community church was organized for the "benefit of those who wish to participate in church or Sunday school work."

The cemetery, where most of the old pioneers lie buried, is at *Koti Niemi* (Home Point) about a mile from the center of town. It is an unusual cemetary since the cross is so conspicuous by its absence. I seemed to feel the presence of the old Finnish pagan gods there as I walked around looking at the gravestones. These gods seem to be keeping watch over the final resting place of their own people.

I had to coax the Sointula residents to speak Finnish but when they did I discovered their mastery of Finnish was much better than my own. But no wonder. The language of Sointula was Finnish until sometime in the 1930's. Even children whose parents were not Finnish had to learn the language in order to belong to their peer group.

One lady told me, "...Finally the school board passed a rule

The large white building in the center is the Sointula Socialist Hall.

which forbade the children to speak Finnish in school or anywhere on school property. For a while, once off school property, we used to burst into Finnish but after a few years we found ourselves talking English except when we spoke to the old timers."

Matti Kurikka is an unhonored prophet in the community. The Sointula museum (which has hundreds of books used by the intellectually hungry pioneers) did not even have a picture of the founder of the community. No picture of Kurikka appeared in the semi-official History of Sointula published by the Sointula centennial committee. None of the second, third, and fourth geneation Finnish-Canadians would be in Sointula if Matti Kurikka had not passed this way. Yet, he is ignored. Maybe in the future, when time has mellowed us all, they'll put his picture, framed, on the museum wall.

THE ALBUM

A Glimpse Into the Past

A Parade Was a Celebration

Summer Festival parade in Maynard — 1912

Freedom Parade in Aurora, Minnesota — 1911

Summer Festival parade - 1912, Fitchburg, Massachussets

Gardner Summer Festival parade — 1923

Summer Festival parade in Fitchburg, Massachussets — 1915

Nashwauk, Minnesota Finnish-Socialist little theatre presents "Volga Boatmen" 1926

Gardner Finnish-Socialist little theatre presents "The Gypsy Princess"

The Ash Street Hall little theatre presents "The Resurrection"

Fifth Avenue Finn Hall. Eugene Debs was nominated for President here in 1920

Berkeley Finn Hall — largest building constructed by volunteer labor in the United States

The Finn Halls Were Packed

The Maynard Osasto members celebrate the opening of their Finn Hall

The Quincy Osasto celebrates the anniversary of their Finn Hall — 1918

Private Collection

*Isä and Äiti with one of their
24 grandchildren*

*Oskari Tokoi, first prime minister of an
independent Finland*

The Finnish Brotherhood Hall in Berkeley, California

The Idealistic League

The Gardner Ash Street Hall Idealistic League (Ihanneliitto)

Ishpeming Finnish Idealistic League (Ihanneliitto)

Äiti's House

The Raivaaja Building (1913-1969)
Fitchburg, Massachusetts

Frans Syrjälä (1880-1931)

Doctor Tanner after opening his hospital in Chishlom, Minnesota where he practiced medicine until his death in 1918

New England Finnish Summer Festival parade in Gardner — 1923

Imatra, the Maynard Finn Hall Band

The Negaunee Finnish Labor Temple

Finn Hall in Deadwood, Alaska — 1910

Chapter Ten

INTERLUDE

The main purpose of the next two chapters is to develop further one of the underlying theses of this narrative. This thesis, simply stated, is that the Finnish immigrants of 1890 to 1914, intelligent but unskilled, found themselves in a new world—Canada and the United States—where the dominant philosophy, the philosophy of the ruling establishment, was *Social-Darwinism*. These immigrants inevitably came into a headlong clash with this philosphy in their efforts to improve their economic status. These Finnish immigrants did not pick an easy foe and at some point in the struggle that followed the Lutheran Church deserted them. In fact a case can be made that the Lutheran Church worked against the aspirations of the immigrants who, therefore, began to look elsewhere for spiritual sustenance. They found it in a new "religion"—socialism.

The Finnish immigrant found the socialist doctrine appealing for several reasons. Socialism claimed to be scientific, a useful attribute in the rational period around 1900. The socialist doctrine also explained why exploitation and oppression existed. And since ruthless exploitation and oppression did exist in the United States and Canada during the 1900's, the socialist painted picture hit home. Most important, socialism promised them a better life here and now which encouraged them in their struggle to improve their immediate environment. These Finnish immigrants, therefore, converted to socialism in unprecedented numbers. And they built one of the largest labor movements—in proportion to population—anywhere in the world.

I do not think one can understand this early American Finn

unless one understands the Social-Darwinian philosophy that dominated industry and government at that time. That philosophy extends the Darwin's theory of *natural selection* to human society. That is, the Social-Darwinists claim that the process of natural selection (which they call *survival of the fittest)* functions in human society to weed out the weak and to ensure that the very best percolate to the top. Only the fit survive. The others die and disappear. Only the best reach the top. The other survivors, I suppose, find their proper niches in society. Dr. William Graham Sumner, the foremost Social-Darwinist in the United States (1840-1910) put it this way, "The millionaires are a product of natural selection."

Social-Darwinism developed in England. Its father (or inventor) and foremost advocate was Herbert Spencer (1820-1903) who coined the phrase *survival of the fittest.* Spencer taught that it was a mistake to help the weak and the lame because such aid interfered with the natural processes that weed out misfits, a process that improves the race. Spencer, when accused of championing a cruel philosophy replied, "I am simply carrying out the views of Mr. Darwin in their applications to the human race."

Spencer was very influential in England since Social-Darwinism justified all the evils existing in nineteenth century English society. But in the United States...Let me quote John Kenneth Galbraith:

> His numerous books were influential in England but in the United States they were very little less than divine revelation...Spencer was the American gospel because his ideas fitted the needs of American capitalism like the celebrated glove, perhaps better.

I have provided a few references about Social-Darwinism for those who might want to do additional research. The best place to begin is *The Age of Uncertainty* by John Galbraith. Bear in mind as you read this narrative that the socialism of 1900-1920 was a product of the Social-Darwinism of that time. If the first generation Finns were arriving on American shores today, they would probably be liberal democrats.

THE SOCIAL-DARWINIAN ENVIRONMENT

The young Finnish immigrants whose average age was less than 20 years found themselves in a New World where life was dominated by a philosophy that justified greed, cruelty, and exploitation in the name of *nature*. Life was a struggle for the survival of the fittest so why bother to make the coal mine a safe place to work.

John D. Rockefeller, Sr. once explained the Social-Darwinian struggle to a Sunday school class:

> The growth of a large business is merely a survival of the fittest...The American Beauty Rose can be produced in the splendor and fragrance, which brings cheer to its beholders, only by sacrificing the early buds which grew up around it...This is not an evil tendency in business. It is merely the working-out of a law of nature and a law of God.

Avaricious exploiters were not, of course, a strange class to the new American Finn. There had been plenty of them in his former homeland. The ruling group there, at that time, still retained a vestige of feudal attitudes—perhaps influenced by the autocracy of the Russian imperial court, even though feudalism as a social institution had never existed in Finland.

Poverty and hunger, especially hunger, were the reasons that drove most of the Finnish immigrants to the United States. Lahtinen, the left wing symphathizer in Vaino Linna's *Unknown Soldier,* brought to my mind remembrances of the attitudes of many first generation Finnish-Americans when he said,

> Hunger is a goddamn tradition in Finland...The rich have convinced the poor that hunger is sacred. We Finns have gone to battle for over six or seven hundred years with hunger continually gnawing at our guts and with our bare asses visible through our rags. First we created history for the Swedish ruling class...

The young new American Finn had not been able to fight back in Czarist-ruled Finland. As the same Lahtinen put it, "They would have put us in jail and given us a copy of the New Testament to read." In America, though, these Finns found a new ingredient in the social milieu. The law of the land recognized the right of dissent. The law of the land recognized the right of an individual and of a group to protest and to fight any oppression, injustice, and cruelty that existed. And the new dynamic American Finn did just that. He fought back. His actions and his attitudes are best epitomized by that Yankee slogan: *Don't tread on me!*

The new American Finn, who undoubtedly would have joined Daniel Shay's Rebellion had he emigrated during the Revolutionary War years, came into headlong clash with the Social-Darwinian philosophy which had been embraced by the captains of industry. The captains of industry believed in the Social-

Darwinian philosphy with great gusto because that philosphy justified their actions which, more often than not, violated the law of the nation as well as individual human rights.

Reforms? Why reforms? Reforms would only interfere with the forces of Nature that slowly, but inexorably, elevated the best of the human race to the top of the heap and washed away, into the archaeological fossil pits the inferior, the defects, and other mistakes of *Nature*.

The state? The state was a necessary evil whose only function was to ensure that the "orderly" processes of *Nature* continued without "outside" interference. Of course, these captains of industry made sure, whenever they could, that they, themselves, controlled the state. In many instances, in the early part of this century, the dominant business in a community did own the local government lock, stock, and barrel. The big trusts—especially the ones that owned the railroads, the mines, and the forests—often controlled the state governments in the West and Midwest. And it is very easy today, in this new era, to underestimate their influence in the federal government.

Listen to Alexander Agassiz, the largest shareholder in Calumet and Hecla, the bonanza copper mining company involved in the 1913 Great Copper Strike in the Upper Michigan Peninsula. Thousands of Finns participated in that strike which many claim was a landmark in the Americanization of the Finnish immigrant.)

Yes, listen to Alexander Agassiz, "If it were a question of bribing a State legislature, I should regard it in the same light as the removal of a bank of sand."

Did these Social-Darwinists make profits? They certainly did and it was income tax free too. Andrew Carnegie made 25 million dollars in 1900. That must be close to half a billion dollars today. John D. Rockefeller, starting from scratch, had accumulated 900 million of those turn-of-the century dollars by 1913.

But, in 1912, when 20,000 employees (including women and children) walked out of the textile mills in Lawrence (Massachusetts) to protest a new wage cut, half of these workers were earning less than $7.00 for a 54 hour work week. Yet the Pacific Mills, one of the struck companies, paid 12% dividends regularly on its stock and had declared 36% in extra dividends in the six years between 1905 and 1912. And, in addition, Pacific Mills had accumulated an undistributed surplus which was three times greater than its original capitalization. More? Yes. The company had depreciated the cost of its factories to nothing, that is the value of the factories was zero on its books.

There is no question that the Pacific Mills management had accomplished great goals for capital. The death rate, however, for children under five years of age in that same city—Lawrence (Massachusetts)—was 176 per 1000, almost 20%. Most of the deaths were caused by tuberculosis. One out of every five children who went to work at around 11 or 12 years of age in a textile mill could expect to die of some illness within the next five years.

The Social-Darwinists of that era—which included most factory owners, most managers of industry, and most government officals—had no intention of interfering with the workings of *Nature*. The establishment was completely heedless of the conditions existing in Lawrence. They felt that any interference was not only futile but also dangerous. Tuberculosis was, after all, a method by which the weak and the defective were swept away by the *Natural Process*. (Attitudes have changed, haven't they?)

The working people made many attempts to better their conditions by joint effort but the men who controlled industry were not about to share their power nor their profits with anyone, especially not labor. It is extremely difficult for us, today, to understand the paranoia that seized hold of an industrial baron whenever his employees made a joint effort to request better working conditions. The leaders of the organized workers were fired and blacklisted. In many instances these leaders were forcibly removed from the locality after being "tarred and feathered." If the workers went on strike, they found the entire establishment—church, press, courts, police, and other government officials (local, state, and federal) solidly arrayed against them. It took great courage for a working man to dissent in those days. The first generation American-Finn had that courage.

The conflict betwen capital and labor broke out into actual warfare at the turn of the century. When, for example, Henry C. Frick, President of Carnegie Steel, decided to cut wages in 1892, he had a high wooden fence erected around his Homestead (Pennsylvania) Steel Works. The top of the fence was strung with barbed wire. Apertures were cut in the fence at strategic points for riflemen. Search lights were mounted on several towers inside the grounds. Then, two days before the wage cut took effect, Frick locked out his workers. Three hundred Pinkerton armed detectives were imported to Homestead to guard the steel mill.

A conflict between the irritated workers and the Pinkerton detectives resulted in several deaths. Henry Frick felt he needed additional help so he merely telegraphed Harrisburg, the State Capital, for reinforcements and the Government of Pennsylvania sent 8000 state troopers to Homestead. These state troopers became virtually employees of Carnegie Steel. The union no longer existed in Homestead at the end of the month. The wage cut went into effect.

When the silver and lead miners in Coeur d'Alene (Idaho) were about to win their strike in 1899, President Harrison rushed several thousand federal troops to the rescue. All known union men in the area were arrested. Several hundred of them were imprisoned for months in camps surrounded by barbed wire. Twelve of these arrested men were said to have been lucky. They were sentenced to a regular jail for contempt of court. The others were starved and mistreated in their bull pens. The United States Army prohibited the mining companies from hiring any miners suspected of being union men. The strikers, when finally released from behind the barbed wire, found themselves blacklisted throughout the industry.

The tragedy at the Ludlow (Colorado) mines in 1914, mines important to the Rockefeller estate, was the most brutal display of terror against any interference (read: union activity) with the "normal process of *Nature*" ever seen in this country. Ludlow was a company town, so the evicted strikers set up a tent colony in a meadow near the town. They then moved their wives and children into their new "homes."

On April 20, 1914, the Colorado State Militia attacked the tent colony without warning. The entire meadow was raked by machinegun fire. After the fusillade, the Militia charged forward to burn the tents in the colony. The soldiers shot, bayonetted, or clubbed anyone—man, woman, or child—whom they encountered in the assault.

A great many Finns lived in Colorado in those days. Several took part in the strike which must be why Ellis Sulkanen wrote quite extensively about the Ludlow Massacre in his Finnish-

American Labor History. I translate from that history:

> ...Later an investigating judge spoke about the tragedy, "The true story of what happened may be too terrible to print...One miner found his young son's body in a military encampment. The boy's head had been shot off and his body was partially burned. Some soldiers threw him the body, shouting, 'There, take it home.'
> "...Mothers who rushed to aid their children were shot or bayonetted...Man's barbarianism of ancient times could not have been worse than what transpired at Ludlow...' "

THE DISSENT AGAINST SOCIAL-DARWINISM

Intellectual dissent against the prevailing Social-Darwinian philosphy in industry and government flourished in parallel to the labor protests to which, as I have indicated, were so ruthlessly put down by the authorities. A great deal of this intellectual dissent, incidentally, was religious in nature although that fact apparently went unnoticed by the Finnish Lutheran Church in America.

Some of the Protestant Christian clergy, especially ministers in big cities, began to preach a social gospel because with their direct knowledge of the brutalizing and oppressive environment in the metropolitan slums; these ministers recognized that it made little sense to talk about Christian morality and ethics to the working men who, to make "ends meet" (even in their sordid habitat), were forced to put their wives and their young children to work in the sweat shops of that era.

The dissent in America seemed unbounded at the end of the nineteenth century. Thousands of middle class citizens were attracted to the highly idealistic and romantic reform movements nurtured by Edward Bellamy's best seller, *Looking Backward*. The single tax movement had its greatest influence at the turn of the century after Henry George, an intensely religious man, published his critique of the American society, *Progress and Poverty*. This book, which outlined Henry George's single tax as a cure for society's ills was full of moral indignation against the treatment given those who worked for a living.

The Populist movement was at its greatest strength. The American farmers, angry at the control Wall Street had over their economic well-being, banded together to try to diminish the influence big business, especially the railroad trusts, had with the Federal government. And they wanted, in some states, to "wrest" control of their own state capitals from these same railroad tycoons. California was not freed from the tutelage of the Southern Pacific railroad until about 1920 when Hiriam Johnson succeeded in getting elected U.S. Senator from that state.

The muckrakers had their heyday around 1912. The scandals they dug up never seemed to end. Upton Sinclair's *The Jungle* shocked the American public into an awareness that the Social-Darwinian philosophy did not protect them from adulterated food. What was good for the meat industry was not necessarily appetizing to the American public. Profits came first in the meat packing industry. The public (and labor) was considered if profits were not affected too much. Reform legislation to regulate the food industry, especially meat packers, won overwhelming public support.

Big city politicians, absolutely corrupted by their absolute power, began to face angry coalitions of political reform groups. Tom Johnson, a single taxer, was elected mayor of Cleveland and immediately began to clean house. His mentor, Henry George, barely lost the mayoralty of New York City in the 1888 election. His campaign was supported by a broad coalition of reformers, liberals, single taxers, radicals, and socialists. Henry George may actually have received the majority of the votes cast but Tammany Hall, the Democratic party organization that controlled the ballot boxes and counted the votes, may have stolen the election as they had many others.

Christian socialism was at the peak of its influence in the United States. The movement, an outgrowth of the idealism generated by Edward Bellamy's *Looking Backward*, began to advocate a social gospel program for the Christian churches. The largest such organization, the interdenominational Christian Socialist Fellowship—founded in Louisville (Kentucky) in 1906—published a nationwide magazine, *Christian Fellowship*, which had considerable influence with the Protestant clergy. The purpose of the Fellowship and its magazine was "to permeate the churches and other religious organizations with the social message of Jesus."

The Christian Fellowship editorialized (in commenting about the labor strife at Ludlow, Colorado where the militia so indiscriminately fired into the tents of the striking miners), "contemptible as Rockefeller is, he acts strictly in accordance with capitalist morality. The dead were but human sacrifices laid at the altar of his worship. He chants a hymn to capitalism as they die among the flames."

John D. Rockefeller, Jr., in testifying before a Senate committee about the Ludlow Massacre stated, "If I had failed in my duty, I would resign but my conscience utterly acquits me." The Christian Fellowship commented, "His (Rockefeller's) conscience is determined by his pocketbook and since his pocketbook prospers, his conscience acquits him." That magazine concluded that to Rockefeller (in accordance with the then prevailing Social-Darwinian philosophy) the "deaths of women and children in Ludlow are their own fault. They got in the way of his god and his god crushed them."

THE DISSIDENTS UNITE

The dissidents and protesters against the evils of Social-Darwinism seemed to permeate into every nook and cranny of American society in 1900. Reform movements sprang up everywhere. But it was the Socialist Party of the United States, led by Eugene Victor Debs, which united middle-class dissent with labor and farmer protest into a strong vital crusade that challenged, frightened, and finally helped erase Social-Darwinism as an effective philosophy in American life.

The Socialist Party was gaining adherents in the United States at such a rate in the early 1900's that most socialists, and a good number of conservatives as well, were convinced that Eugene Victor Debs would be elected President and the Socialist Party would become the dominant political force in the United States by 1920 or sooner.

The growth of socialism was a worldwide phenomenon and the largest idealistic mass movement to arise in the West since Christianity. The working people of Europe flocked to the socialist banner in such large numbers that it seemed as if all Europeans, as well as Americans, would be living in a socialist democracy in a short time. The First World War, however, destroyed the tremendous impetus of the movement.

It is interesting to note that the international socialist movement had been able to stop at least two wars before 1914. In 1906 the socialist parties of Norway and Sweden forced their respective governments to settle a dispute peacefully and in 1912 an attempt to ignite a Balkan brush war was squelched by the international socialist movement. Alas! Nationalism proved to be a stronger force in 1914 when each socialist party (except the party in the United States) endorsed and supported its own country's participation in World War I. Incidentally, the European countries that remained neutral in the war and whose governments were dominated by socialists have the highest standard of living in the world today. These countries are, of course, Sweden, Norway, and Denmark.

The Socialist Party of the United States had so much influence (or generated so much fear) in the 1912 election that every major presidential candidate—Wilson, Roosevelt, and Taft—was forced to run on a liberal or progressive platform. The Americans were so fed up with the Social-Darwinian philosophy that no presidential candidate promised to return the country to the "good old days" of 1900!

Nor did any candidate promise to maintain the status quo. All candidates campaigned for drastic reforms, new freedoms, and for laws that would protect the weak from the rampages of the strong. Each candidate promised to break more trusts and to regulate the activities of the "captains of industry" by stricter laws than his rivals. The specter of a socialist America put great pressure on the major political party candidates.

Eugene Victor Debs, the socialist candidate, drew larger audiences than Taft, the President of the United States, even though the Socialist Party charged admission to all of Deb's indoor campaign rallies. Debs even attracted a larger audience in Taft's home town, Cincinnati (Ohio). The young socialists on Debs' campaign staff could not avoid playing the game of one-upmanship. They offered to share Eugene Deb's platform with President Taft. That way, they said, Debs would have a wider audience to speak to. President Taft, surprisingly, was alert enough not to accept the offer.

The 1912 campaign was the beginning of the end of Social-Darwinism in American although the various governments—federal, state, and local—continued to be influenced by vestiges of that philosophy for a few decades. Most of the remaining traces of Social-Darwinism were finally swept away in the intellectual and social revolution that occurred in the Great Depression. A new era was ushered in during the first two terms of

Roosevelt's presidency. Many of the benefits of socialism were given to the people but without assigning them the associated responsibilities. That fact may some day lead to disaster.

THE SOCIALIST PARTY OF 1912

Let us now take a closer look at the Socialist Party of the United States in the beginning of the century. We will see that the first generation American Finns did not join a tiny sectarian protest movement against the establishment. They were attracted to a vital organization that had widespread support in all areas of American life.

The American Finns had to negotiate long and hard with the Socialist Party officials because they were dubious about allowing the Finnish or any other language group to join the party as a federation. The bulk of the party's membership was native born; still the party was quite sensitive to the accusations that socialism was a foreign ideology. Finally, after months of negotiations, the party officials agreed to have the Finnish Socialist Federation join as a foreign language affiliate—but each Finnish local (called, remember, an *osasto*) had to join their respective state organizations. Although a Finnish-speaking liason person was employed by the Chicago national headquarters of the Socialist Party, the Finnish Federation had no vote in the national affairs except through their membership in the local state socialist parties.

The Finnish Socialist Federation set the pattern for the admission of other language groups. By 1913, there were fourteen foreign language federations in the Socialist Party. The Finnish federation was by far the largest. Only the Jewish federation rivaled the Finnish federation in size but then there were a great many more Jewish immigrants than Finnish. The Finnish Federation membership was larger than the combined memberships of all Socialist Party foreign language affiliates except the Jewish and German federations.

It may surprise you to learn how strong the Socialist Party was in 1913. Over 300 periodicals, mostly weekly newspapers, supported the socialist cause. Three English language daily newspapers were socialist oriented. The weekly socialist *Appeal To Reason* had a circulation of 761,747 in 1913. The *National Rip Saw*, another socialist weekly, had 150,000 subscribers.

The highly literate Finnish immigrants supported four daily

socialist newspapers in 1913! These were the *Toveri* (The Comrade) published in Astoria (Oregon), *Työmies* (The Workingman) published at first in Hancock and then in Superior (Wisconsin), *Raivaaja* (The Pioneer) published in Fitchburg, and *Sosialisti* (The Socialist) of Duluth (Minnesota). In addition there was the daily, *Työkansa* (The Working Class) published in Canada.

The Socialist Party itself had over 118,000 dues-paying members who carried the red Socialist Party card in 1912. Most of the socialist strength was in the Midwestern states—especially concentrated in Oklahoma and Texas—where the adherents of the Populist dissent againt Social-Darwinism embraced the socialist doctrine in great numbers. Oklahoma had thousands of dues-paying socialists, almost all native born Americans, organized into 961 locals. They had already managed to elected (by 1910) five of their members to the Oklahoma legislature.

Was it just a "radical response"—as some Finnish historians have called it—when the first generation Finnish-Americans of Berkeley (California) organized a socialist local in 1906? Berkeley had a socialist mayor, a Christian minister. And Berkeley was not an isolated instance. At least 200 cities had elected socialist mayors at one time or another in the period from 1900 to 1912.

In 1912 socialist mayors were on the job in such large cities as Minneapolis, Milwaukee, Reading (Pennsylvania), and Schenectady (New York)—where the socialist and famous electrical genius, Charles P. Steinmetz, was the president of the city council. Even small Midwestern towns such as Conneaut (Ohio), Lorraine (Ohio), Girard (Kansas), Des Lacs (North Dakota), and Butte (Montana) had socialist mayors during this period.

Socialism was the American "fad" in the period from 1900 to 1920. Name a prominent intellectual or writer of that period and you are most likely naming a member or supporter of the Socialist Party. The prolific historical writer and philosopher, Will Durant, was a member of the Socialist Party at that time. And in his *Dual Autobiography* (written with his wife, Ariel Durant) he states, "I am still a socialist..."

Upton Sinclair, Lincoln Steffens, Norman Hapgood, Jack London, Finley Peter Dunne, John Dewey, and Charles A. Beard at one time or another supported the socialist movement. Charles A Beard wrote in 1913 that this was an age when socialism "was admittingly shaking the old foundations of politics the world over and is penetrating our science, art and literature."

Many Finnish-American historians suggest that the young new American Finns of 1900 were naive. Their education, they suggest, did not provide them with enough ability to evalute critically the socialist doctrine. That may very well be the case. But then those young American Finns were in excellent company. Other naive people were H. G. Wells, George Bernard Shaw, Sidney and Beatrice Webb, and Bertrand Russell. All of them shouted in unison, "Hey, there's something wrong with this system. There must be a better way to do things." And, remember, we today are enjoying the benefits for which those early socialists and dissidents worked and sacrificed.

Chapter Eleven

THE FINNISH IMMIGRANT

The new world enticed more than 300,000 Finns to leave their homeland in the years from 1890 to 1914. They represented more than 10% of Finland's population. They came from the northern part of the northernmost country in the world. Some of them recalled the horrible famine of 1866-1868 when an irresponsible government allowed about 100,000 people to starve to death. These immigrants had a stubborn streak of independence and self-reliance, attributes needed for survival in the harsh, cold environment in the Finnish rural areas at the turn of the century.

They left because in Finland they were nothing. They belonged to the lowest class. The only avenue open to them was emigration. But these immigrants had a rude shock in the New World. The conditions of life in many communities where their unskilled labor could be used were often worse than the conditions they had left behind. Only the pay was better.

They found the English language with its multitude of prepositions just about impossible to pick up. The vast majority never did become proficient in the new tongue—not even after living here for fifty years. I think the reason was because Finnish is an unusual language, one of the most unusual languages in the world. Most of the immigrants were prisoners of their native tongue.

Finnish has no articles—no, *a*, *an*, or *the* to place in front of a noun. It has no gender, no pronouns like *he* or *she*. One pronoun *han* must suffice for both sexes. There is no future tense and only one or two prepositions. Prepositions are inferred by changing the endings of the nouns, pronouns, and adjectives. There are, therefore, at least fifteen cases, each of which requires a different ending on the nouns, pronouns, and adjectives. The endings also change to signify singular or plural, positive or negative, polite or familiar form, and question or emphasis. The Finnish language is so difficult that only a child growing up in a Finnish environment seems to be able to master it. And once mastered, the Finnish language can be a prison—at least it was for the Finns who came to the United States in 1890-1914.

The Finnish peasant brought with him a deep respect for work. By *work*, I mean hard physical labor. He and she were proud of their stamina to perform difficult and monotonous manual labor. I think they glorified work. This deferential regard for manual labor (and their low social and economic status) made them somewhat distrustful of the "gentlemen class" whose members earned their livelihood without soiling their hands.

Oskari Tokoi, who emigrated to the United States when he was a little over 17 and who was destined to become the first prime minister of an independent Finland told the following story in his autobiography—*Sisu, Even Through a Stonewall*—which gives an impression of the Finnish peasants' attitudes about work—hard physical labor—and about education in the 1880's.

Young Oskari was such a brilliant grammar school student that the village leaders (the pastor, the druggist, the schoolmaster, and the town merchant) of Lestijoki in central Ostrobothnia offered to send him to the city of Vaasa for an advanced education. But they needed his father's permission. The village committee, therefore, sent a message to young Oskari's father who was shovelling iron ore on the docks in Ashtabula (Ohio) requesting permission to send his son to a Vaasa lyceè.

The reply came back promptly. It was negative even though the village committee had offered to foot the entire bill. Let Oskari Tokoi tell his own tale, "The reply from America came back promptly. It was brief and it was negative. Father wrote that as soon as I had learned reading, writing, and arithmetic; I was to learn how to work. In America, he said, he had seen too many *gentlemen* who did not know how to work with their hands or how to support themselves in an honest fashion. 'My son will not be brought up to be a *gentleman*.'"

No wonder Eugene Victor Debs was the idol of the first generation Finnish-American socialists. Debs held the very same sentiments as those early American Finns. He often said, "As long as
there is a working class, I shall be part of it." and "I don't want to
rise out of the working class, I want to rise with the working class."
This attitude made the Finnish-American communities a fertile
field for the socialist evangelists.

THE WHITE ROSE TEMPERANCE SOCIETY STRIKE

Strikes were a common occurrence in the mining areas and
lumber camps around 1900. Finns participated but the effects of
the strikes on the Finnish-American attitudes about politics and
religion was minimal. Then the White Rose Temperance Society
strike *(Valkoruusu Raittiusseuran Lakko)* erupted in Rockland
(Michigan). This strike became a cause *celebrè* in the Finnish press
throughout the country, both because most of the strikers were
Finnish and because of an attempt to accuse several of the Finnish
strikers of murder.

It all started on July 4, 1905, when the White Rose Temperance
Society held a summer festival to celebrate the American In-
dependence Day. The day was spent in a typical Finnish-
American summer festival manner. Songs were sung, poetry was
recited, and the Finnish brass band of Rockland, *Mehiläinen* (The
Honeybee), played stirring patriotic tunes.

It was typical of Finnish-American organizations in those days
to grant speaking privileges to almost anyone. A Finnish-speaking
Western Federation of Miners organizer asked for and was given
an opportunity to address the festivities. The organizer gave a pro-
vocative talk. At the end of the month, 280 of the 300 miners
were on strike. It was the Finns—the *Mehiläinen* band, the
Valkoruusu Raittiusseura, and the Lutheran Church—against the
mining company.

The sheriff hurriedly deputized a group of local citizens to protect the mines. Many of these new deputy sheriffs, according to
the strikers, were habituès of barrooms. Nevertheless the sheriff
provided them with firearms. On the last day of July the miners
went to picket during a change of shift and the armed deputy
sheriffs became a gang of vigilantes. They stopped the picketing
miners and forced them to run a gauntlet while they fired their

revolvers. Two people were killed in the meleè, a striker and a deputy sheriff. It was later proved that the deputy sheriff was killed by a stray bullet from a gun fired by another deputy sheriff.

That evening the sheriff illegally rounded up 110 Finnish miners from their homes, placed them under arrest, and incarcerated them on the second floor of the Rockland fire house. Thirteen of these men were charged with the murder of the deputy sheriff. The Finnish press throughout the country came to the defense of the accused. Most Finnish-American communities rallied to support the White Rose Temperance Society strikers. The English language socialist and labor press also took up the cause. Even the Russian consul (the Finns were then Russian nationals) in Chicago intervened with a battery of eight lawyers. Finally, on May 30, 1907—almost a year later—the men were acquitted but the White Rose Temperance Society strike was lost.

The entire Rockland Finnish community was forced to move elsewhere because the company flatly refused to hire any more Finns. The Finnish Lutheran Church, the White Rose Temperance Society, and *Mehiläinen* (The Honeybee) Brass Band were dissolved. The strike, however, had changed the attitudes and feelings about unions, strikes, and society in every Finnish-American community.

THE SCHISM BETWEEN CHURCH AND LABOR

The warfare between labor and the Social-Darwinists was fought almost continually in the mining areas at this time. Strikes were commonplace and most of the strikes were lost. The first generation Finn, conspicuous in the strike activity, began to find his name on blacklists. "Blacklists, circulated to steel and mining companies as far west as Montana and east to Pennsylvania and West Virginia, singled out for special attention Finns who had been unionists and strikers." Finns in the Mesabi Range (Minnesota) changed their surnames to hide their national origin in order to get jobs. The Finnish-American labor press began to encourage a back-to-the-land movement which, because of the blacklists, had considerable success in getting the Finns out of the mines and back on the land.

This prejudice against the Finns because of their activity in the labor movement resulted in an attempt to keep Finns from gaining United States citizenship. In 1908, District Attorney John Sweet of St. Paul (Minnesota) asked the United States District Court to deny citizenship to a John Svan and sixteen other Finns because, it was claimed, Finns were Mongolians and, hence, not eligible for United States citizenship. The District Attorney based his case on a law—since declared unconstitutional—that was enforced then to keep orientals from obtaining United States citizenship. John Svan got his citizenship. The judge ruled . . .

> . . . If the Finns were originally Mongolians, modifying influences have continued until they are now among the whitest people in Europe, . . . The applicant is without doubt a white person within the true intent and meaning of such law. The objections . . . should be overruled, and it is so ordered.

This ruling—which displays the racist attitudes of that era—did stop the extension of the blacklisting of Finns into other areas.

At some point during this period Lutheran Church officials began to evince a distaste for the union and labor activities of the first generation Finnish-American. I think if the strikes had been successful in the vicinity of the central headquarters of the Lutheran Church, the total alienation of the liberal and socialist Finns and the Lutheran Church would not have occurred. But the mining companies were not compliant so strike after strike was lost by the workers which caused the Finnish Lutheran officials to take a closer look at the industrial fiefdoms in the mining areas. They looked at the unusual amount of power wielded by the absentee owners and their managers—and exclaimed, *"Herrankin Herra!"* (The Lord of the Lords!)

What could be a better way to serve God, the Church, and these lowly-born depressed Finnish immigrants than to accomodate ourselves to the power exercised by these lords of the New World. Didn't Martin Luther himself say:

> What is more ill-mannered than a foolish peasant or a common man when he has enough and is full and gets power in his hands . . . The severity and rigor of the sword are as necessary for the people as eating and drinking, yes, as life itself . . . The ass needs to be beaten, and the populace needs to be controlled with a strong hand. God knew this well, and therefore he gave the rulers not a fox's tail, but a sword.

I used the word "fiefdom" in the last paragraph. I did not use the word lightly nor did I use it to make a point. And lest you, dear reader, think this is only my point of view, I call your attention to the June 1978 issue of *National Geographic* in which that

The Finnish-American socialist periodicals

magazine called Pennsylvania of 1900 a "series of industrial fiefdoms". These fiefdoms, or "feudal estates"—moderated somewhat by the very liberal Constitution of the United States—were created for the aggrandizement of the copper, coal, steel, silver, and lumber industries. And in many respects these fiefdoms resembled the capitalist society portrayed by Karl Marx.

The Mesabi Range (Minnesota) strike of 1907-08 widened the chasm between the Finnish immigrant workers and the Lutheran officials but I believe that cleavage could still have been bridged. The strike started when the Oliver Mining Company—a subsidiary of U.S. Steel—fired 300 of the most active union members when the Western Federation of Miners (*Lännen Kaivosmiesten Liitto*) requested a negotiation session. The list of proposals and grievances presented to the management included an eight hour day, a minimum wage of $2.50 per day, a small premium pay for those miners who worked underground, and an end to the petty bribes the miners were forced to pay to stay in the good graces of the straw bosses.

Although there was nothing very revolutionary in these demands, the company reacted as if the miners were going to seize the mines. The Oliver Mining Company imported its own armed labor detectives who worked in close cooperation with the local police. Several strikers were killed but no one was ever brought to account for these deaths. After all, the dead were only immigrant strikers.

The strike had the usual unhappy ending for the miners. They lost. The Finnish miners, conspicuous in the strike because of their militancy, lost the most. The Finns, among the most desired of workers before the strike, were blacklisted. A local newspaper helped to taint the image of the Finnish miners with "...fully ninety percent of those in line (a strike parade) were Finlanders...fiery followers of the Red Flag."

The Finnish business community and the Lutheran officials were disturbed by this discrimination against the Finns but instead of protesting the discrimination, the clergy and businessmen organized a movement to diminish the influence of the socialists and labor people with the Finnish miners. They took the name *True Finns* because they claimed "they were the true spokesmen of the Finnish-American community."

The True Finn League (*Tosisuomalaisliike*) sponsored Peoples'

Meetings (*Kansalliskokouksia*) in the various Finnish-American communities in the Middlewest where resolutions were passed criticizing the socialists and labor activists as unAmerican and not representative of the American Finns. The contention for the allegiance of the Finnish immigrant between the socialists who now had their socialist federation and three daily newspapers and the Lutheran Church began in full earnest. The socialists labelled the resolutions passed at the True Finn Peoples' Meeting with the infamous name *Judas Resolutions*.

The dispute was bitter but reconciliation was still possible. The Lutherans labelled the socialists as atheists, anarchists, and advocates of free love. The socialists very carefully stipulated in their 1909 convention that religion was a personal matter. They also pointed out that anarchism was incompatible with socialism. Then the convention went out of its way to deny the Lutheran charge that the Finnish Socialist Federation advocated free love. Were the socialists handing the Lutheran leaders an olive branch? The Suomi Synod Lutheran officials didn't see it that way and the rancor continued unabated.

Then, in 1913, came the greatest tragedy to hit a Finnish-American community, a tragedy that touched the heart of every Finnish-American. About 15,000 miners, a good majority of Finnish descent, went out on strike in the Upper Peninsula (Michigan) in July, 1913. In many ways that strike seemed to be a struggle between the Finnish Lutheran Church and the Finnish Socialist Federation. The Lutheran Church had organized an antisocialist league which cooperated during the strike with a newly formed vigilante group called the Citizens Alliance. The armed labor detectives hired by Calumet & Hecla, the struck company, cooperated with the Citizens Alliance. The labor detectives marched in the parades of the Citizens Alliance whenever that organization staged demonstrations in support of "law and order."

Christmas came. What a bleak Christmas it was going to be! To brighten things up a little, the union decided to hold a Christmas Eve party in the Calumet Italian Hall for the women and children. During the height of the festivities, someone yelled "FIRE!" and almost simultaneously, the town fire signal sounded throughout Calumet.

A panic broke out as everyone in the Italian Hall rushed to the only door which, unfortunately, opened inward. Seventy-four persons died in the stampede. Most of them were trampled to death near the exit door. Forty-seven were women and children of Finnish descent.

The Finnish socialist newspapers—*Töveri* (The Comrade) in Astoria, *Työmies* (The Workingman) in Hancock, *Työkansa* (The Workingclass) in Canada, and *Raivaaja* (The Pioneer) reported the tragedy with screaming headlines. The headline in *Raivaaja* read: "96 CHILDREN MURDERED". Those headlines meant that many American Finns were gone from the Lutheran fold forever. Reconciliation was no longer possible.

Who yelled "FIRE!"? Was it an organized harassment of a union affair? After the tragedy, the Citizens Alliance abducted the union president Charles Moyer and ran him out of town after shooting him in the arm. And the local police force, backed by the deputized Waddell-Mahon Agency's armed detectives, illegally raided the offices of the Finnish daily newspaper in Hancock—a few miles from Calumet—and forced it to cease publication.

The Michigan legislature conducted a hearing about the Christmas Eve tragedy but was unable to reach a definite conclusion about the facts. Such a verdict was not surprising. Could this legislative body, regarded as a "bank of sand" by Calumet & Hecla's largest stockholder, have reached any other decision?

After all, a much stronger force—the Michigan state militia—sent to Calumet early in the strike to maintain law and order, with over two thousand men organized into two battalions of artillery, two troops of cavalry, three regiments of infantry, and three brass bands was not able to guarantee the safety nor the civil rights of Charles Moyer, the union president. Neither did this strong, and undoubtedly proud, body of men have the courage to protect the First Amendment to the United States Constitution which guarantees freedom of the press without which there is little meaning to "law and order".

So, even if the legislative body of the Commonwealth of Michigan had thought the Citizens Alliance culpable in the Calumet Christmas Eve tragedy, do you think it would have had the courage to oppose the wrath of Calumet and Hecla, in that company's own industrial fiefdom, when its own militia—the Michigan State Militia, over two thousand strong—was so timid in "keeping the peace"?

THE MOUNTAIN ROSE TEMPERANCE SOCIETY WINS A VICTORY

Not all attempts to organize the miners ended in defeat. The Mountain Rose Temperance Society *(Vuoriston Ruusu Raitiusseura)* of Hanna (Wyoming) was successful in organizing the coal mines in that area. The temperance society and the Finnish *Kalevala Brotherhood* had both been secretly organizing the miners who worked in the Union Pacific captive coal mines. Organizational meetings had been held covertly in an old run down saloon about two miles outside Hanna.

It was decided on June 8, 1907 to hold an open meeting in the Mountain Rose Temperance Hall in Hanna (Wyoming) the very next day. The audience in the hall the next day included Finnish and non-Finnish miners. The meeting became extremely tense as a report reached the Finn Hall that the company officials, accompanied by armed body guards, were approaching the hall.

The railroad officials, however, had come to the hall to recognize the union. They were willing to sign a contract. Bedlam broke loose in the meeting. A report, written by one of the Finnish organizers named John Malo, stated:

> ...the chairman shouted, *"Hurratkaa, pojat, yhtio on tunnustanut union!* (Cheer, brothers! The company has recognized the union!)"
> It was like the first ray of light in the long dark night. Cheers rose from hundreds of miners. Old calloused gnarled miners leaped to their feet as if they were young boys. Many stood on their chairs, waved their arms, and cheered. The dark depressed atmosphere had disappeared. A victory had been won. The miners had gained the right to hold meetings and to organize. The miners had gained some dignity.

SOCIALISM - HISTORY IS GOD

What did these Finnish-American converts to socialism believe in? Let's take a look at the philosophy which displaced Lutheranism from their lives.

There were socialist long before Karl Marx appeared on the scene. Karl Marx labelled these early socialists *Utopian Socialists* and their doctrines as *Utopian Socialism*. To differentiate his ideas from the Utopian Socialists, Marx called his doctrine *Scientific Socialism*. He and his converts became known as *Scientific Socialists*, or *Marxists*. (The Marxian doctrines are, of course, no more scientific than the ideas of the Utopian Socialists but Marx

177

was no charlatan; he really believed he had discovered the basic truths that underlie history and economic systems just as Sigmund Freud felt he had uncovered the purpose of dreams.)

History is god for the *Scientific Socialists*. *History* can be understood, or we might say the *Truth* in *History* is only revealed to those who use an economic interpretation. Or as Oscar Ameringer used to write in the old socialist *American Guardian*, "If you want to understand what's going on; just find out whose got the nickel under his foot."

History has a purpose. *History* is dynamic. That is, societies are always in a process of change. *History* is dynamic because there exists a *Force*, a mysterious force, called *Dialectical Materialism*. *Dialectical Materialism* transforms one society based on a particular class structure into another society based on another type of class structure. There is nothing you or I or anyone else can do to prevent that transformation. It is inevitable.

Dialectical Materialism consists of three parts—*thesis, antithesis,* and *synthesis*. From the existing social, economic, and political conditions in society (the *thesis*), there arise human needs and desires (the *antithesis*) which react on the existing conditions to set up a course of action which results in a change (the *synthesis*). *History* is the story of change caused by the class struggle inherent in each type of society that has a class structure. *History* causes a change from slavery to feudalism to capitalism to socialism.

Socialism is the ultimate end. When the human race attains the socialist commonwealth, the class struggle will cease because there will be no classes. The brotherhood of man will have arrived. The political state will slowly disappear since government, an instrument of the ruling class, will no longer be needed. When *Socialism* is achieved, then the *Real History* of the human race will begin.

Bear in mind that this step by step evolution from slavery to feudalism to capitalism to socialism is inevitable. That is, socialism is inevitable. It will come. *Socialism* will be triumphant no matter how strong the forces arrayed against it seemed to be. Socialism may be delayed. That is, *History* may be deflected but *History* cannot be denied. Since *Socialism* will be triumphant one day, why not get in tune with *History?* Why not jump on the bandwagon of *History?*

There is no reward, though, for believing in socialism, no punishment for disbelieving. When socialism is attained the true believer and the non-believer will be equal. Oh, you'll be, I suppose, allowed to mildly admonish those non-believers with a playful "I told you so!" but you cannot condemn a non-believer to eternal damnation because under socialism all men and women—believers and non-believers—will be equal and free.

Is *Scientific Socialism* scientific? Science, it seems to me, has a predictive capability. I mean someone should be able to predict (or deduce) something about future behavior from the scientific knowledge known today. When Einstein, for example, proposed his relativity theory there were plenty of skeptics. But one could test that hypothesis or test the deductions made from his hypothesis. One of the results that could be deduced from Einstein's theory was that light rays from the stars would bend toward the sun as those light rays passed the sun on their way to the earth. The bending is caused by the sun's enormous gravitational pull.

Some scientists tried an experiment in 1919 during an eclipse of the sun to test the bending light rays hypothesis. And you know the story. Those light rays did bend towards the sun! Einstein's theory was much more plausible now. It had weathered a major deduction made from it. Had the light rays not behaved as predicted, then Einstein would have had to go "back to the salt mines" to do more research and more thinking.

Is *Scientific Socialism* scientific in the sense described above? Is Marxism really a science? Marx thought so—so did and do a countless number of his disciples. Let's take a look at some of Marx's predictions.

Marx predicted that as the capitalist system matured, the wealth would become concentrated in fewer and fewer hands. This concentration of wealth would displace members of the middle class. These displaced people would be forced to join the ranks of the growing (in number) working class. As capitalism matured, the workers would become poorer and poorer.

The development of labor saving devices and other improvements in the productive facilities would merely widen the wealth gap between the owners of capital and the workers. That is, as society built better machines the rich would get richer and the poor poorer faster. The innate conflict between the two important classes in society—the owners of capital and the workers—would become a *conscious* class struggle when the workers find themselves no longer able to sustain themselves at the levels *to which they had become accustomed.* The resulting confrontation between these two classes in a *fully mature* capitalist society would result in a new era for man—*socialism.*

Much of Marxist theory hit the spot in the United States in the decades 1880-1930. The workers were ruthlessly exploited. Their wages were kept as low as possible. The wealth was accumulated by a few families such as the Rockefellers and the Carnegies in astronomical amounts.

Capitalism was maturing! The revolution did come! But, surprise! The revolution did not occur in any mature capitalist nation such as the United States, England, France, or Germany. The revolution did not occur in any one of the four most industrialized and mature capitalist nations in the world. It occurred in a nation that Marx considered one of the most backward nations on earth—Russia.

The last vestiges of feudalism had not even died out in Russia. The old feudal lords, not capitalists, held the dominant power there. Then, 30 years later, the revolution came to China which, if anything, was more backward industrially and socially than Russia. These two nations didn't even have much of a working class. The dispossessed in China and in Russia were not an industrial proletariat but a landless peasantry.

Something went haywire with Dialectical Materialism. The "socialist" revolution took place in the wrong society at the wrong time. We might say, The light rays did *not* bend towards the sun. If Karl Marx were alive today, we would have to say to him, "Sorry about that! Back to the salt mines! Back to the British Museum for more research." And do you know what? I believe he would have gone back to that library to try to unravel the error in his hypothesis.

Marx's prediction of the woeful condition of the working class in a mature capitalist society is way off base, too. The working class in the United States should be growing larger in number and poorer in wealth. But, the working class today is far better off than it was in 1900, 1920, 1930, or even 1950—in spite of inflation. In 1938, for example, it would have taken almost my whole year's wages as a grocery clerk (working sixty hours per week) to buy a new car. Today a retail grocery clerk can easily buy a much better car for twenty (forty hours per week) weeks' work. And there are plenty of other examples that illustrate this point.

The working class in the United States should be growing larger in proportion to the population as the middle class is diminished by the concentration of wealth into fewer and fewer hands. The working class, however, is getting smaller! Less than 40% of the people who are gainfully employed grow and make the things we eat and the things we use. And that percentage keeps getting smaller. (I don't know what the other 60% who draw pay checks do. Let's hope it's something worthwhile!) One might well ask the question: Will the working class disappear altogether?

It is true, though, the wealth of the country is being accumulated by large industrial corporations but strange to say, most of those corporations have more shareholders than workers! Standard Oil of California has 268,000 stockholders and only 38,283 employees, not all of whom can be classified as workers. The United States Steel Company, that former lord of the fiefdom of Pennsylvania, has 248,986 shareholders and only 165,845 employees. One of the wealthiest and biggest corporations of all, IBM, has 581,500 shareholders and only 310,150 employees.

What is the significance of these figures? Well, Karl Marx said that the working class created all wealth. The capitalist class tacked on a value—called the *surplus value*—to a commodity before the commodity was sold. The wealth of the capitalists came from their accumulation of this surplus value. Marx never visualized a world where there would be more people getting surplus value than were creating it.

TWELVE ATTRIBUTES

What did these first generation Finnish-Americans believe in? I mean: What is socialism anyway? Well, the word is used in two ways. Sometimes the word is used to mean the organizations working to achieve the socialist commonwealth along with the literature, philosophy, and the methodology developed by these organizations. In this sense socialism means the *socialist movement*.

One speaks, for example, of British socialism of 1900. What is meant is the character of the British socialist movement of 1900. I am, to give another example, writing a good deal about Finnish-American socialism, the Finnish-American socialist movement of 1900-1920. Many writers, incidentally, label the Finnish movement in the United States and Canada as *hall socialism* because most of the activity revolved around the Finn Hall. (This is an apt term although many of the writers used it disparagingly in an attempt to belittle that movement.) One also hears the Finnish socialists called *bread-and-butter socialists* which tends to imply that they were more concerned with immediate goals instead of the far-away dream. As you see, the word when used in this sense is easy to define.

The word socialism is also used to signify the goal, the end result—the new society sought by the socialists. Socialism, when used in this way is almost impossible to define. At least I have not been able to find or create a satisfactory definition. I shall not attempt to do so now. I list, however, 12 attributes that must exist in a society if that society can claim to be socialist.

Five of these attributes were developed by me and the janitor of the Ash Street Hall (along with my buddies in my Yipsel study circle) many years ago. Some I have compiled from answers to a questionnaire I sent to some friends who are still socialists. I have no way of knowing, of course, but I feel confident that most of the first generation Finnish socialists would accept my list of attributes as a litmus paper test to determine if a society is truly socialist.

SOME ATTRIBUTES OF SOCIALISM

1. *Public ownership, either cooperative or state, of all basic industry and natural resources.*

2. *Local control of local industrial units.*
   Comment: The control of each local industrial unit will be vested in the people who work in the local unit. These local workers shall determine the number of and choose the supervisors in their unit. The pay of each worker will be based on the efficiency of the industrial plant in which he or she works.

3. *Equitable distribution of all wealth distributed in the society. The ultimate goal will be: From each according to his or her ability, to each according to his or her need.*
   Comment: No individual, no matter how important his position, shall be paid more than a reasonable multiple of the lowest compensation received by any full-time worker in the society. The top manager in a local industrial unit, for example, might not be paid more than, say, 5 times the amount paid to the workers on the lowest notch of the unit's salary scale.

4. *Complete freedom of speech, religion, and press.*

5. *Limited return on capital.*
   Comment: All capital (savings) will be paid at a fixed rate of

return. This rate may fluctuate year to year depending on society's need for capital but capital will never share in the distribution of society's earnings. The use of capital will be an expense of doing business.

6. **Complete freedom of emigration.**

7. **Limited Inheritances.**
Comment: No one will be allowed to inherit vast accumulations of wealth directly nor in trust. Inheritance of property will be limited to personal property such as homes, books, papers, furniture, and other personal belongings. Society shall inherit all capital above a maximum amount—this includes all monies left in trust.

This socialist attribute will discourage the creation of dynasties based on wealth such as the Rockefellers, the Kennedys, etc.

8. **State ownership of all land.**
Comment: The title to all land will be vested in society. Taxes (or rent) on land will be instituted to discourage speculation in real estate since the people, society itself, creates all real estate values by the activity of the people.

9. **Equal opportunities for all.**
Comment: All people, without consideration of sex, race, or creed, will have equal opportunity for employment and equal access to the educational, recreational, and health facilities.

10. **Limited private enterprise.**
Comment: Individuals will be allowed to engage in such businesses which seem naturally suited for private ownership. Some of these businesses may even compete with state-owned or cooperatively-owned businesses in the same field. The entrepreneurs of these private firms may even hire others to work for them but no entrepreneur may profit from the labor of others.

The entrepreneur's income from any privately owned business will be limited to the going interest rate for the capital used in the business plus compensation for the services (work) performed by the entrepreneur himself.

11. **Special incentives to encourage extraordinary contributions.**
Comments: Special incentives will be developed to encourage individuals to contribute, beyond a citizen's normal duty, to the enrichment of the society's cultural, spiritual, and economic life.

12. **Dignity of all work.**
Comment: No labor, no matter how menial, shall be paid less than the minimum amount provided by law. The minimum pay paid will determine the maximum compensation that may be received by society's leaders.

Chapter Twelve

THE FINN HALL

The first generation Finnish-American had an obsession about halls. They built or acquired them by the scores. The halls had to be very functional since they were in constant use. They had to be large enough to allow several activities to go on at the same time. The auditorium had to be spacious enough to accomodate dances, athletic events, and the celebration of weddings and anniversaries. A stage, on which the Finn hall little theatre might present its productions, had the highest priority.

The hall had to have a rostrum for the many itinerant speakers who visited the community for no Finn in the early days was denied the right to present his point of view. There had to be ample room for the informal social evenings devoted to poetry reading, recitals, musical entertainment, and—of course—some discourse from an orator or two. These social evenings were called *illanviettoja* and it was at such an *illanvietto* that many a Jussi found his Karoliina.

The Finn hall had to have a coffee lounge too since every event held there was interrupted by a coffee intermission when the refreshment committee served *kahvia ja pullaa* (coffee* and cake). The refreshments were usually free of any additional charge. There is no question in my mind, as I recall the amount of coffee

---

*Finnish is the only language that has a word for coffee that is made from secondhand grounds. *Sumppi* is coffee made from used coffee grounds. It is also the name for the grounds left after a pot of coffee has been brewed. We, the second generation boys, used to to tease our girl friends with "This isn't coffee, it's *sumppi*."

consumed, that the Finnish-Americans were the first coffee addicts in this country. I believed they introduced the coffee break and the coffee intermission into American life.

No other ethnic group in the United States owned and built as many halls as did the American Finns even though the number of Finnish immigrants was small in comparison with other nationalities. A Finn hall was often purchased on the open market if the building satisfied the organization's needs. When necessary the Finn hall was built by volunteer labor in a *talkoo* (work bee).

The largest building constructed completely by volunteer labor in the United States is the old Finn hall on Tenth Street in Berkeley (California). It was built by members of the Berkeley Finnish socialist local in 1906. That Finn hall—known in the 1930's as the Red Finn Hall—is still standing and has recently been noted in the California Historical Registry as an historical monument.

A Finnish owned hall was usually called the *Finn Hall*, although at times in some communities, one had to qualify the name to Socialist Finn Hall, IWW Finn Hall, Communist Finn Hall, or Temperance Society Finn Hall to be sure that the correct Finn hall was identified. Two aspects of the Finn halls impressed me—no matter where they were located or who owned them—they all seemed to look and feel alike.

The local socialist Finn hall became the new church for the greater part of the Finnish-American community during the golden age *(loistoaika)*—1906 to 1920—of the Finnish Socialist Federation. In the West and Middlewest, the Finnish adherents of the IWW (International Workers of the World) gained control of a great many socialist Finn halls in the so-called First Schism *(Ensimmäinen Hajaannus)* that hit the Finnish Socialist Federation in 1914. The Finnish-American communists captured a majority of the remaining Finn halls (as well as the new ones built to replace those lost to the IWW) in the *New Schism* (Uusi Hajaannus) of 1920 that ripped asunder the entire American socialist movement including the Finnish Federation. But on the eastern seaboard where I grew up, the Finnish democratic socialists retained control of most of the Finn halls. These Finnish halls owned by the local branches of the surviving Finnish Socialist Federation dominated Finnish community life until the demise of most of the first generation.

I do not mean to imply that the Finn hall was a socialist invention. It wasn't. The American Finns were busy building halls long before they converted to socialism. In the Greater Gardner rural area which probably is typical of other Finnish-American rural areas, the young farmers and their wives built at least two small Finn halls to serve their needs. The first one was a tiny hall near the Templeton town line west of Gates Hill. The second, a much larger hall, was built in Pitcherville as more Finnish people moved into the area.

After the first hall was built the farmers held a raffle; the prize: the privilege of naming the new Finn hall. My godfather, Aati Poikonen, won the cherished honor. He christened that building with the prettiest name ever given to a Finn hall—*Tupsunpera* (The End of the Tassel). This hall was so small that the musician, usually an accordian player, had to play his musical instrument on a tiny platform elevated above the dancers' heads.

THE FINNISH SOCIALIST CONGREGATION

Frans J. Syrjala, one of the early Finnish-American socialist leaders, published an informative article in 1924 about the nature and function of the Finnish Socialist Federation and its local branches. Mr. Syrjala held the opinion that the Finnish socialist movement in the United States and Canada educated and uplifted the Finnish immigrant peasant. He believed, as I do, that the socialist movement changed the hard-working, independent, sometimes obstinate, and often hard drinking Finn into a knowledgeable, concerned, and able American.

I have translated the following excerpts from this essay, *Minkä-moinen Laitos on Suomalainen Sosialisti Osasto?* (What Is The Nature Of The Finnish Socialist Branch Organization?)

> Each branch of the Finnish Socialist Federation is actually a small community as can be easily verified by examining its bylaws, the real estate it owns, and the activity that goes on in its domain. Each socialist branch supports an extremely wide range of activities. It has to, because each socialist branch is the center of Finnish-American secular life in its community.
>
> The largest branches, as expected, support the widest range of interest groups. It is not unusual for a large branch—and there are many large branches—to have a little theatre group, a brass band, an orchestra, one or more choirs, a performing gymnastic group, an athletic organization, a sewing circle, an idealistic school (*Ihanneliitto*—the socialist version of the Sunday school), and a youth league. Even the smallest branch has at least a little theatre group and a sewing circle.

Every branch maintains a Finnish library.

...Most of the interest groups have so many members that they are divided into smaller groups. The *Ihanneliitto* (idealistic school), for example, has four grades which meet at least once a week (usually Sunday) in a study session. The youth group has two age levels—teenagers and children. The gymnastic teams and sports organizations have members whose ages ranges from five to sixty so activities and sports are sponsored for many age levels—children, teenagers, young adults, and the old timers *(ikämiesten)*. The women have, in many branches, formed their own athletic and gymnastic classes.

The brass bands and the orchestras in many branches have a beginners and an advanced section. Quite often a branch will have a paid director in charge of the musical program. Since so many people are attracted to musical endeavors, some branches have a full time salaried musical director. The choirs, the brass bands, and the orchestras present public concerts in the local socialist Finn hall and often travel to neighboring Finnish-American communities to give recitals.

The drama group, or little theatre attracts the largest number of participants and is the most active section of almost every socialist branch in the Federation. In many communities the socialist little theatre *(näytelmäseura)* stages a play every Saturday night to a capacity audience in the Finn hall.

...A large Finnish socialist branch organization *(osasto)* may well have up to forty different committee meetings, rehearsals, or practices of some kind each week. At least a couple hundred people are involved in planning or taking part in these activities. The socialist Finn hall, a little community, is a very busy place.

...I note that there has been a branch of the Finnish Socialist Federation at some time in the period from 1906 to 1920 in the following places:

Alaska - Juneau

Arizona - Globe, Miami, Lowell

California - Albion, Eureka, Fort Bragg, Los Angeles, Pudding Creek, Redwood Valley, Rocklin, San Francisco, San Pedro, West Berkeley, Reedley

Colorado - Denver, Leadville, Telluride

Connecticut - Canterbury, Collinsville, Hartford, New Haven

Florida - Jacksonville

Idaho - Enaville, Elo, Larson, McCall, Mullan

Illinois - Chicago, De Kalb, Juliet, Waukegan, El Dorado

Indiana - Clinton, Muncie

Maine - Cushing, East Waldoboro, Long Cove, Monson, Rockland, Thomaston, Vinal Haven, Union, West Paris, West Rockport

Maryland - Baltimore, North East, Wilmington

Massachusetts - Abington, Allston, Amesbury, Ashburnham, Ashby, Chester, Clinton, East Boston, East Cambridge, East Douglas, Fall River, Fitchburg, Gardner, Gloucester, Hingham, Lanesville, Lawrence, Lowell, Maynard, North Adams, Norwood, Peabody, Pittsfield, Quincy, Rockport, Sagamore, Sandwich, South Carver, South Royalston, Springfield, Waltham, West Wareham, West Fitchburg, Winchendon, Worcester

Michigan - Ahmeek, Amasa, Arnold, Bessemer, Calumet, Chassel, Crystal Falls, Daggett, Detroit, East Branch, Grand Rapids, Green, Hancock, Herman, Imperian, Iron River, Ironwood, Ishpeming, Kaleva, Kenton, Kreeton, Marquette, Mass City, Michigamme, Neguanee, Newberg, Paynesville, Princeton, Rock, Rudyard, Sault Ste. Marie, South Range, Squaw Creek, Suomi, Tri Mountain, Verona, Wakefield

Minnesota - Angora, Angoratown, Aurora, Bates, Besset Town, Biwabik, Bovey, Blackberry, Brainerd, Brookston, Buhl, Calumet, Cheen, Cherry, Chisholm, Clinton Town, Cloquet, Corbin, Crosby, Crystal Bay, Cuyuna, Deer River, Duluth, Ely, Embarras, Eveleth, Fairbanks, Floodwood, Florenton, Gilbert, Gowan, Hibbing, International Falls, Isabella, Keewatin, Kettle River, Kinney, Lawler, Leipold, Little Marais, Little Swan, Little Sturgeon, Markham, Max Menahaa, Mesaba, Minneapolis, Mountain Iron, Naswauk, New York Mills, Northland, Orr, Palo, Pike River, Poupore, Perch Lake, Release, Sandy Lake, Sandstone, Sawyer, Sebaka, Soudan, Sturgeon Town, Squal Lake, Sucker River, Thomson, Toimi, Toivola, Two Harbor, Vermilion Lake, Virginia, Wagoner, Wawina, West Duluth, Winton, Wright, Zim

Montana - Belt, Bonner, Bear Creek, Butte, Geyser, Hamilton, Helena, Red Lodge, Roberts, Round Up, Sand Coulee, Stocket, Vendalia, Wickes

Nevada - Goldfield, Round Mountain, Tonopah

New Hampshire - Fitzwilliam, Harrisville, Lebanon, Manchester, Marlboro, Milford, New Ipswich, Newport, Troy, West Concord, Wilton

New Jersey - Bergensfield, Bogota, Englewood, Jersey City, Morristown, Newark

New York - Albany, Bronx, Brooklyn, Bridgeport, Buffalo, Jamaica, New Rochelle, New York City, Port Chester, Rochester, Schenectady, Scotia, Spencer, Staten Island, Van Etten, White Plains

North Dakota - Belden, Bracket

Ohio - Ashtabula, Ashtabula Harbor, Akron, Aurora, Chardon, Cleveland, Conneaut, Fairport Harbor, Girard, Jacksonville, Martins Ferry, Santoy, Warren, Youngstown

Oregon - Astoria, Marsfield, Park City

Pennsylvania - Bessemer, Bristol, Coal Center, Daisytown, Donora,

Aberdeen (Washington) Finnish Socialist Festival — 1911

Erie, Fayette City, Glassport, Monessen, New Castle, Nanty Glo, Philadelphia, Pittsburg, Woodlawn

Rhode Island - Pawtucket, Providence, Westerly

South Dakota - Fredericks, Lead

Utah - Bingham, Eureka, Park City

Vermont - Bethel, Graniteville, Hardwick, Proctor, Ludlow, Winousky

Washington - Aberdeen, Ballard, Black Diamond, Brush Prairie, Carbonado, Deep River, Everett, Hoquiam, Independence, Ilwa Co., Issaquah, Jaunita, Kirkland, Pearson, Poulsbo, Raymond, Roslyn, Seattle, Spokane, Wilkinson, Woodland

West Virginia - Clarksburg, Weirton, Wheeling

Wisconsin - Allouez, Brantwood, Brule, Carey Town, Clifford, Eagle River, Eagle River, Hartford, High Bridge, Iron Belt, Kenosha, Madison, Maple, Marengo, Milwaukee, Oulu, Phelps, Park Point, Racine, Red Granite, Silver Creek, Superior, Waino, Washburn, Wentworth

Wyoming - Carneyville, Cumberland, Diamondville, Dietz, Elkol, Frontier, Gunn, Hanna, Lion, Reliance, Rock Springs Sublette, Superior

...Even after the New Schism, the communist Finnish-Americans who left the New York Branch of the Socialist Federation had the strength and the motivation to build the $225,000 (1920 dollars) Finn hall on 126th Street and Fifth Avenue. These left-wing secessionists also built a $125,000 and a $60,000 Finn hall in Detroit and Worcester

(Massachusetts), respectively. They also built numerous smaller Finn halls in several other communities.

"Some Finnish-American communities now have three sects of the labor movement, each with its own Finn hall, competing for the attention of the Finnish population. The activities at each hall—IWW Finn Hall, Communist Finn Hall, and Socialist Finn Hall—are about the same. The competition between these sects obliges each organization to plan the best possible entertainment and activities they can in their respective Finn hall. The division of the small Finnish-American comunity into three groups, however, tends to weaken all Finnish activities in the community.

"The New York branch of the Finnish Socialist Federation was once the largest local with 617 members. Now [1924] the Finnish Labor Society Saima of Fitchburg is the largest local with 550 adult members, 200 Sunday school (Ihanneliitto) participants, and about 80 Yipsels. Saima is the largest Finnish-American organization in the United States.

"...The socialist Finn hall has often been the only meeting place available to the workers during a labor dispute. Other halls are usually closed to strikers or the charge for renting them is beyond their capacity to pay. The Saima Labor Society loaned both Saima Finn Hall and Saima Park to the textile workers during their long strike in 1922. And we also raised several thousand dollars in support of this strike.

"The leaders of industry have often looked at our generosity with jaundiced eyes. They have often harassed us about minor matters in order to frustrate our efforts to help the workers in a labor dispute. Sometimes they take drastic [illegal] action as they did in Weirton (West Virginia). During the great steel strike of 1919, the Finnish socialist branch loaned its small Weirton socialist Finn hall to the striking steel workers. In retaliation, the Finn hall was seized and searched by the state police.

"The state troopers 'discovered a large cache of arms and ammunition' in the hall. At least this is how the metropolitan newspapers reported the event with large headlines. The large cache of arms and ammunition, however, consisted of only some wooden shotguns, an old rusty revolver, and some blank theatrical bullets. The officials of Weirton, however, compelled the entire Weirton Finnish population to move out of town for their sin which was to let the steel strikers use the Finn hall."

"...The major importance of the Finnish socialist branches was that they provided a forum where the young immigrant Finnish workers could discuss their common problems and other topics of mutual interest. The Finn hall also provided a place where the young immigrant could express his esthetic sense. Here was a place where he or she could act, sing, or play musical instruments.

"The forums and discussions in the Finn hall gave the young immigrant an opportunity to engage in intellectual activity, a chance to acquire leadership skills, and an opportunity to develop ability in public speaking. No subject, no topic was so trivial that it didn't give rise to a heated discussion in the forums. And everyone—the pros and the cons—had a chance to express their points of view in front of the whole group.

"The comradely criticism faced by each speaker was not always gentle but it helped to thicken sensitive skins. The 'books always balanced' since if one received harsh criticism after one's talk on some evening, the 'tables were turned' a few evenings later when one's critic stood at the podium. Those who were able to stand the heat grew in stature intellectually and spiritually.

"The socialist branches soon recognized, in those early days, that a strict discipline was a necessity when dealing with the raw and unsophisticated immigrant. The roots of the old life which consisted of noisy hostility and drunken indulgence had to be eradicated by its roots. Organized workers striving to build a better world, we taught, had to be responsible for their own actions and their own order.

"The young unruly gangs and wild ruffians who came to the Finn hall hankering for a fight found themselves in the tight grip of sober strong arms. If they persisted in their behavior they were hurled, unceremoniously, out the back door.

"The Finnish Socialist Federation and its branches educated its members and followers. The socialist organization gave the young Finnish immigrant a sense of importance. It taught him and her self-discipline. Our Finnish socialist branches converted 'beasts of burden' into alert thinking men and women who believed in high ideals about life and society. That is the greatest achievement of the Finnish Socialist Federation."

THE FINNISH-AMERICAN LITTLE THEATRE

Show business was the first item on the agenda in the Finn hall. The class struggle, basketball, and other matters had to wait in the wings of all Finn halls—the IWW hall, the socialist hall, and the communist hall—until the drama society was done. First things first. The drama society, the little theatre of the Finn hall, had first priority. They dominated and saturated the Finn halls with their show business.

The Finnish-American little theatre presented one act plays, three act plays, light opera, musical comedy, satire, and heavy drama to capacity audiences. The presentation rarely carried a social message. The audiences, usually mesmerized during a performance, were insatiable. They wanted more and more. The little theatre worked overtime to try to satisfy that demand.

No other group in the United States or Canada, native or foreign-born, before or since, has devoted so much time and so much effort to the little theatre as did the first generation Finnish-American. The drama society was at it night and day. "No, you can't practice basketball because the drama society is putting on a dress rehearsal. The upstairs hall is yours after 10 P.M."

In 1920 the Gardner socialist branch reported its little theatre had held 35 business meetings during the year to discuss their activities. They called 197 rehearsals which resulted in 27 actual productions. Thus, the Gardner Finnish little theatre met 259 times in a single season.

"What evening did you have off?" asked the president of the branch.

"Only Thursday evening and then we all went to the coffee hop where we danced until 11 P.M." was the instant reply. (The coffee hop was the weekly Thursday night dance in Ash Street Hall. The admission price was 15¢ which included coffee and *pulla* at intermission).

I have adapted the rest of this section from another historical essay written by Frans Syrjala which he published in his book *Historical Essays About the Finnish-American Labor Movement*. The excerpts are from the essay *Suomalainen Sosialisti Osastojen Näyttämöt* (The Finnish Socialist Little Theatre). Mr. Syrjala was keenly interested in the Finnish Little Theatre. He translated Gilbert and Sullivan's *Pirates of Penzance* into Finnish. That musical comedy, *Merirosvot*, was presented to several packed audiences at the 1921 New England Socialist Summer Festival held in Fitchburg.

Bear in mind when you read these excerpts that many of the actors—the leading ladies, the leading men, and the supporting casts—were working men and women. These actors went into the chair factories, the textile mills, the woolen mills, the coal mines, etc. at about 7 A.M. They weren't coddled on their jobs either—a coffee break was almost unheard of in those days. Many of them didn't have an eight hour day either, at least not until Franklin D. Roosevelt gave them the NRA. And even if those workers did get home by 5 P.M., they had to eat supper before transforming themselves into actors and actresses. Now here is Mr. Syrjala:

"There are exceedingly few plays published in the Finnish language, be they short skits or long dramas, that have not been presented on a Finn hall stage by at least one of the many little theatre groups associated with the Finnish Socialist Federation. The Finn hall stage has tried to interpret all types of dramatic composition. Sometimes they failed. Sometimes they succeeded. When they failed, they failed because of the lack of personnel and theatrical apparatus; never did they fail because of lack of interest. Thousands who have followed the efforts of this little theatre have many cherished memories of the great moments on this stage.

. . ."The American Finn has gained great joy and even shed a tear or two watching the countless number of plays presentd by the socialist little theatre. This is good evidence that our actors and actresses have, at least once in a while, achieved an artistic effect which has taken the audience out of their everyday existence, enriched their intellectual life, and helped sow the seeds of a spiritual renewal.

"The actors, actresses, directors, and other participants of the little theatre have accumulated and increased the spiritual capital and distributed it to tens of thousand of immigrants who, because of their dire circumstances in Finland, had to leave their homeland to find their daily bread, and in many cases they had to emigrate before they had gained spiritual and intellectual maturity.

"A spiritual awakening drove them to create their own unique culture, a Finnish-American culture. They were not able to participate directly in the American culture because of their inadequacy in the English language. The most remarkable thing about this new culture was that it was created by laborers! It was created by men and women who left Finland without any working skills.

"Yes. The little theatre and the Finnish-American culture were created by unskilled laborers, by men and women who worked with their hands to earn their daily bread. That culture was not created by the "educated" Finnish middle class—the clergy and the merchants. The men and women of this middle class evinced little or no interest in the promotion of any art nor did they support any educational or cultural program that was not sanctioned by the Lutheran Church.

"The clergy considered the theatre sinful. The merchants were too busy trying to make money to spend time with the cultural aspirations of the Finnish-American people. The "educated" middle class was, therefore, left way behind both spiritually and intellectually. One of the consequences of this was that it became very easy for a brand new leadership—an unschooled leadership—to develop in our communities.

"The officials of the church tried to harass the little theatre because they considered the stage evil and sinful. There is a great deal of evidence to suggest that the Lutheran clergy and their followers kept the police alerted about the Finnish socialist little theatre in the hopes that this theatre might be suppressed.

"The Saima Labor Society in Fitchburg almost lost its theatre permit when the local police did not consider a satire about Bolshevism and Bolshevik terror suitable for viewing by the Finnish audience. Imagine, even an anti-Bolshevik satire was considered degenerative and sinful!

"Earlier, in a few other communities, the local Finnish little theatre had to cancel its programs and had to explain the substance of the drama to the police. In all cases the Lutheran clergy or other members of the middle class had informed the police about these plays. At most times the plays presented have had nothing to do with current events or politics. Some of the plays staged by the little theatre might even be considered religious in content but the police informers were too ill-informed and uneducated about our little theatre and about culture in general to appreciate this fact.

"A struggle existed between the little theatre directors (who were paid about the same as the clergy) and the Lutheran pastors to see who could capture the loyalty of the Finnish immigrant. The plays of the little theatre and the music in the Finn hall won the day easily. The Lutheran Church was too old-fashioned, too narrow-minded, too uneducated in cultural matters to keep hold of the inquisitive minds of the Finnish immigrants. The pastors preached against worldly evil to almost empty churches and the socialist little theatre staged its plays before packed houses in the Finn hall.

"...Capable professional theatrical directors had charge of the socialist little theatre in New York City, Maynard (Massachusetts), Gardner, Worcester, and Detroit. Several other branches of the federation have had paid part time professional help. Generally, however, most of our little theatre groups have been led by part time volunteers who, although not professionally trained, were devoted to their calling.

"The New York City and Fitchburg little theatres are the largest but the socialist little theatre in Gardner, Maynard, and Worcester are almost as big. The number of people interested in the local little theatre seems to depend on the size of the Finnish-American community.

"The activity of the Fitchburg Saima little theatre illustrates how widespread the interest in our drama society is. The Saima little theatre has, on the average, produced 36 large productions annually. These productions include plays, musicals, and satires. An example of their effort was the presentation of Gilbert and Sullivan's *The Pirates of Penzance (Merirosvot)*, which this writer had translated, at the 1921 Summer Festival.

"*The Doll, The Small Saint, Merry Widow, September Manoeuvers, Gypsy Queen*, and *The Suitors* are some of the light operas presented by the Saima little theatre. Many of these light operas have been shown three or even four nights in a row to a total audience of almost three thousand. There are barely three thousand Finnish speaking residents in Fitchburg which suggests that many saw the operas more than once.

"Historical plays, so difficult to stage, also drew large appreciative audiences. The most notable of these dramas staged by Saima are *William Tell* and *Daniel Horth*. The drama, usually restricted to Finnish drama, has included Eric Puke's *Ylösnousemus* (The Resurrection), *Isä* (Father), *Perintö* (The Legacy), and *Elinan Surma* (Living Sorrow). It should be obvious that this working class little theatre had the courage to stage some demanding drama. I should also mention that the Saima little theatre produced countless satires such as *Pirun Kirkko* (The Devil's Church). They even produced an occasional socialist propaganda play.

"How important was the socialist little theatre in the Finnish-American community? Well, in the 1923-24 season the Saima drama group presented 30 productions for which $6,000 was collected in admission charges. Since the average admission fee was only 40¢, about

194

15,000 tickets must have been sold. These figures suggest—since Fitchburg had barely 3,000 Finnish-speaking individuals (counting, men, women and children), that every Finn in Fitchburg, even those who believed the little theatre was sinful, must have seen at least one production.

"A rough nationwide estimate indicates that the Finnish-American little theatre associated with the socialist Finn halls and the IWW Finn halls put on an average of 3000 presentations in each of the peak years. An audience of over 500,000 watched these 3,000 productions! [Bear in mind that the Finnish-speaking population in the U.S. never exceeded 350,000—author.]

"To say the least, the little theatre was a profitable enterprise for the socialist branches. The directives which set up the little theatre did not, however, forsee the financial gain that would accrue to the branches. The directives merely asked the drama societies to pay their own way. 'Provide entertainment but don't become a financial burden to the local.'

"The number of men and women who participated in the socialist little theatre is so large and their accomplishments so great that a deeper study should be made of it. I find it almost embarrassing to reflect about the thousands of hours of free labor these actors, actresses, stage hands, and other participants gave to the little theatre week after week, year after year. The little theatre even captured the attention of hundreds of second generation Finns who, in order to participate, had to master the Finnish language thoroughly.

"Space does not permit me to tell about all the joys, woes, and triumphs of our little theatre. Let us, however, take a glimpse or two behind the curtain. I note that some leading ladies who received a bouquet of flowers from the audience were too proud, too haughty, to acknowledge the gift. But most leading ladies were so taken aback, so abashed by this tribute that all they were able to do was to cry like little children with their heads bowed in front of the flowers. How different are peoples' natures!

"Sometimes the leading man arrived a little tipsy. The director would take away his liquor flask so that he would be somewhat sober when the curtain rose. Some of these tipsy actors would threaten, 'Give me back my flask or I won't step a foot on the stage.'

"A Finnish word-rich quarrel followed. Usually a third person entered the argument who tried to cool the tempers of both the actor and director. And often he would turn to the tipsy actor in a comradely fashion and say, 'You have a choice, you know. Will you go on the stage and give the best performance of your life or do you want a beating—and I tell you, you'll get a good one if you disappoint us. This event tonight is an organized working class activity and not a drunken brawl.' Always the leading man was able, somehow, to conquer his fears, go on the stage, and perform as if he were in a frenzy. He knew the socialist local would not tolerate anything less.

"Finally, let me say that the great artists of Finland who wanted to present their talents to Finnish audiences in the United States had to come to us, the Finnish Socialist Federation, since we provided the only platform, the only stage that could and would support them.

Chapter Thirteen

THREE EPISODES

Two events occurred in the golden age (1910-1920) of the Finnish Socialist Federation which shook that federation to some degree and, in consequence, the Finnish-American community. These events have been given special names in Finnish: *Ensimmäinen Hajaannus* (The First Schism) and *Uusi Hajaannus* (The New Schism). A third event, which has not been given a name, occurred in 1930. This event changed the philosophy of the Finnish-American consumers cooperative movement.

The First Schism—a split between the adherents of the IWW (Industrial Workers of the World) and the parliamentarian socialists—was the result of a resolution passed in the 1912 national convention of the Socialist Party. The New Schism was the reverberation of the worldwide split of the socialist movement into two groups, the democratic socialists and the communists.

The First Schism had a much greater impact on the Finnish Federation than it did on its parent organization, the Socialist Party. A large percentage of the unskilled Finnish workers in the West and Middlewest were favorably impressed by the IWW. The split in the Socialist Party consisted of hundreds of individual resignations of IWW members but almost three score branches withdrew from the Finnish federation. And when those branches left, they usually took the Finn hall with them. The socialist Finn hall became the IWW Finn hall.

The second schism, the so-called New Schism, destroyed the Finnish Socialist Federation. A new one was organized but the new federation never had more than 60 branches, almost all of which were on the Eastern Seaboard. This schism, incidentally, was also the death blow to democratic socialism in the United States. Although the democratic socialist movement perked up a little during the Great Depression, the left shift of the Democratic Party in the 1930's nailed the coffin lid of the Socialist Party tight into place.

THE IWW AND THE FIRST SCHISM

The IWW was a native American product. That union with its philosophy was a uniquely American response to the imported Social-Darwinian doctrine used by the industrial tycoons to justify their greed and their oppressive actions. These industrial barons had all the power and as I have indicated, usually "owned" the local governments where their industries were situated. They did not hesitate to use the authority of these local governments to suppress efforts to organize the unskilled workers. If the local government was not strong enough to do the job, then the state and federal governments were called in. The IWW, the one big union movement, was a fervid attempt by the dispossessed to even the odds. The IWW activities were a series of Boston Tea Parties to protest "exploitation without representation". For many of the unskilled immigrant workers, the IWW was more than a union; it was a crusade for justice.

Bear in mind that no one spoke for the unskilled, the dispossessed in the mining towns, lumber camps, steel mills, textile factories, and other basic industries in the 1900's. The American Federation of Labor, almost a million strong in 1900, was afraid to organize them. The AFL labor leaders were afraid of a tussle with the industrial giants. The AFL, expedient, chose to organize skilled workers, especially those who worked for the smaller businesses. The owners of these small businesses lacked the power and the political clout to put down a labor organization. The AFL leadership sold out the unskilled workers and the American consumers as well in order to develop a privileged class of American workers.

Many members of the Socialist Party (among them Eugene Victor Debs), aware of the plight of America's unskilled workers, were ardent supporters of industrial unionism but their efforts to commit the Socialist Party to that task were unsuccessful. The opponents of industrial unionism, which included international presidents of AFL unions, local AFL business agents, and the leaders of important big-city socialist locals such as existed in Milwaukee (Wisconsin), New York City, and Reading (Pennsylvania), were able to defeat or table all resolutions in support of industrial unionism in the Socialist Party conventions.

One union, the Western Federation of Miners (*Lännen Kaivosmiesten Liitto*), was totally committed to industrial unionism. This miners federation called together over 200 delegates (representing about 60,000 workers) to the founding convention (June 1905) of the IWW. Included among the delegates were Eugene Victor Debs and the legendary Mother Jones, the United Mine Workers organizer who, only 75 years of age then, had 25 more years of organizing before her.

The dispossessed of America, the unskilled workers, finally had a spokesman. In fact, they had the most innovative spokesman any American labor group has ever had. The IWW organizers (and every member in good standing considered himself an organizer) were the rugged individualists of American society. They had a cause—the *one big union*. They were devoted to that cause. They wrote songs and poetry about their cause. They went into battle singing their own songs. They had complete faith their cause would triumph. That faith made them fearless. Their ingenuity brought them victories. Those victories sealed the IWW's doom.

The IWW organizational and tactical skill was demonstrated in the Lawrence (Massachusetts) 1913 textile strike, which began when the Massachusetts legislature passed a law that limited the work hours of women and children to fifty-four hours a week. When these women and children, who had been working fifty-six hours per week, received their first pay check under the new law, they found their pay reduced about 30¢.

"Short pay! Short pay!" resounded throughout the textile mills in Lawrence. The commotion led to a spontaneous walkout. The local AFL leaders sat on their hands, they made no move to help these textile workers. The immigrant strikers turned to the tiny IWW local in Lawrence. The IWW accepted the challenge, sent in some experienced labor people, ran the strike, and won it.

How did they win it? They won because they were innovative and unafraid. In spite of a clumsy bombing frame-up and a false arrest of the IWW leaders on a murder charge, the IWW found a strategy that brought the strike to a successful conclusion.

When the strike funds ran low, the IWW began to move the strikers' children out of town just as the children of London were moved to the countryside during the Nazi bombing of that city and as many children of Finland were moved to Sweden during the Winter War of 1939.

The resulting publicity shamed the Lawrence city fathers so much that they took action. They finally took notice of the children of the poor. Remember that Lawrence was the city where, at that time, the death rate among small children—those under five years of age—was 176 per 1000 (almost 20%) and where one out of every five children who went to work—at around 11 or 12 years of age—in a textile mill could be expected to die of some illness within 5 years! Yes, the city fathers finally noticed the children of Lawrence. What did they do? They passed an ordinance to protect the children from the IWW. No more children would be allowed to leave Lawrence. The exodus was declared illegal!

The IWW seldom obeyed unconstitutional laws. And they didn't obey this one. The very next day a new contingent of forty mothers and their children were at the Union Station waiting for a train that would take the children to Quaker homes in Philadelphia.

The Lawrence police confronted this "lawless" group of mothers and children. Then, according to the report of the Women's Committee of Philadelphia which was in charge of escorting the children, "...the police...closed in on us with their clubs, beating right and left, with no thought of the children, who were in the most desperate danger of being trampled to death. The mothers and children were thus hurled in a mass and bodily dragged to a military truck...where they were placed under arrest."

Public opinion swung around in favor of the immigrant unskilled strikers. The IWW, very uncharacteristically, appealed to Congress. Congress responded. The Socialist Congressman from Milwaukee, Victor Berger, led an investigation of the strike and the conditions that led to the strike. The textile mill owners, now under pressure, acceded to the union demands. The strikers, instead of receiving a short pay' discovered, on the average, 20% more in their pay envelopes.

Ah! But you protest! The IWW advocated violence, you say.

These are Negaunee (Michigan) Finnish Wobblies. They had the majority of one in the 1914 schism but a court injunction forbid them to enter or loiter around the Finn Hall.

They were always dynamiting something or somebody. *Terror* was the name of their game.

Well, the truth is that it was not so. The truth is that the press of that era—and many historical writers, too—did try and did succeed, at least to some extent, in creating a violent and even terroristic image of the IWW.

The wobblies, however, were usually the recipients of violence, the victims, not the sinners. The wobblies didn't preach nonviolence the way Martin Luther King did, but they did tell strikers "to keep your hands in your pocket as you picket." The wobblies were very much aware that violence would react against the union. The strikers in Lawrence were told, "Make this strike as peaceful as possible. In the last analysis, all the blood spilled will be your blood."

On the other hand, some of the AFL craft union leaders, men who piously denounced terror and violence publicly did not hesitate to use terror and bombing to gain their ends. One of the McNamara brothers, who bombed the Los Angeles Times building (1900), wiping out 20 innocent lives, was an officer in the AFL International Association of Bridge and Structural Iron Workers.

The Iron Workers union, by the way, had considerable experience in dynamiting. In fact, that is why the detectives were able to pick up the McNamara brothers' trail in the Los Angeles

Times tragedy. And, even though President Gompers and the other AFL leaders must have been fully cognizant of the Iron Workers terror tactics, that union was not even verbally reprimanded by the AFL. Louis Adamic had the following to say in his book *Dynamite:*

> Gompers could be hardly expected to behave with less duplicity than he did. It was inevitable in his position that he should, on the one hand, spout pious hokum and, on the other, indirectly and secretly participate in violence.

The wobblies were maligned. They didn't deserve the reputation they received. They weren't angels but the media of that day—beholden to the industrial barons and not anywhere near as free as it is today—associated the IWW name with terror and violence because these wobblies made a religion of their efforts to improve the lot of the most exploited classes in America. The wobblies were maligned because they were so direct, so innovative, so bold, and—much more sinful—because they were so successful.

It was guilt by innuendo. Consider this example. The Yale University Press published in 1921 and reprinted in 1971 *Armies of Labor* in which Chapter 9 is titled *The New Terrorism: The IWW.* But in that 30 page chapter the author does not give a single incident of terror perpetrated by the IWW in spite of the title. The author does, however, list about 20 incidents in which the wobblies were the victims of illegal action by bands of vigilantes and hired gunmen. The chapter is an excellent discussion of the IWW even if its contents fail to justify the title. Maybe the author intended no malice. He may have expected the Yale students to read more than the title.

The success of the wobblies frightened the industrial barons and the American Federation of Labor who, at times, supplied strikebreakers in IWW strike situations. The IWW also frightened the Socialist Party which, having gained great prestige with voters in the American middle class, became somewhat self-conscious about its image. At that time many wobblies held dual red cards— they belonged to both the Socialist Party and the IWW. The titular head of the IWW, William Dudley Haywood, even sat on the Socialist Party's executive committee.

The conservatives in the Socialist Party felt something had to be done, something that would not produce too much fanfare. Since the wobblies didn't have much faith in the political process anyway, why not get them out of the Socialist Party by making a belief in the political process a prerequisite for membership. So the delegates to the 1912 Socialist Party National Convention passed an amendment to the party constitution. Introduced by Rev. W.R. Gaylord, a state senator in Wisconsin, it read:

Article 2, Section 6

Any member of the party who opposes political action or advocates crime, sabotage, or other methods of violence as a weapon of the working class to aid in its emancipation shall be excluded from membership in the party.

This amendment was clearly directed at the IWW since the IWW pooh-poohed political action. The amendment, as the conservative socialists hoped, created no great hullabaloo in the Socialist Party except that William Dudley Haywood was forced off the executive committee and he and several hundred devoted IWW members resigned. But in the Western and Midwestern Finnish communities the convention's action caused a little disaster, a schism in the Finnish Socialist Federation.

The Finnish wobblies had no intention of remaining in an organization that didn't want them, an organization that had, they felt, compromised the struggle for socialism. Both sides might have gone their own way quite amicably except for the question: Who owned the socialist Finn halls? Who owned the socialist daily newspapers?

Many of the Finn halls had been built with volunteer labor, donated by both sides. The monthly hall mortgage payments had often been met by contributions from the members. Naturally, neither side was going to voluntarily walk away from their Finn hall. The ownership of the Finn hall, not socialist principles, became the bone of contention in many localities. In many towns the wobblies were the majority. They were able to convert the socialist Finn hall into an IWW Finn hall when they seceded from the federation.

In Negaunee (Michigan), the wobblies had a majority of exactly one vote in a showdown meeting. However, the socialists refused to accept their parliamentary defeat. The Michigan State Socialist Party administration intervened by revoking the charter of the Negaunee Finnish socialist branch and then obtained an injunction from the district court naming the majority, the Negaunee

Finnish wobblies, as respondents. The IWW faction was under court injunction. They were forbidden to frequent or loiter around the socialist Finn hall. The hall eventually came under control of the minority. The Negaunee IWW had to acquire its own hall.

I have not been able to determine how many branches seceded from the Finnish Socialist Federation before the *First Schism* had run its course. Because the IWW never allowed the existence of any language federation (after all, they claimed to be the Industrial Workers of the World) the Finnish wobblies were direct members of the one big union. The Finns, of course, did form an unofficial association of Finnish IWW organizations. The IWW was so loosely organized that this aberration was overlooked by the leaders of the union. The informal Finnish IWW association had about 55 branches in 1914. They were located in:

Minnesota - Aurora, Basset Town, Bessemer, Brainerd, Biwabik, Calumet, Clinton Town, Crobin, Crosby, Crystal Falls, Duluth, Ely, Embarras, Hibbing, Isabella, Keewatin, Kinney, Leopold, Menahga, Mesabi, Mount Iron, Negaunee, Pike, Thompson, Toimi, Two Harbors, Virginia, Winton.

Michigan - Daggett, Maple Ridge, Marquette, Squaw Creek, Wakefield.

Montana - Bonner, Butte, Hamilton, Red Lodge, Stockett.

New York - Bronx, Harlem.

Ohio - Ashtabula, Ashtabula Harbor.

Oregon - Portland, Marshfield.

Washington - Aberdeen, Ballard, Seattle, Spokane.

Wisconsin - Washburn.

Arizaon - Brisbane, Lowell.

California - Eureka, Fort Bragg.

Idaho - Enaville, Larson.

Illinois - Chicago.

The Finnish daily newspapers were another prize in the schism. The wobblies almost won control of the socialist daily *Työmies* (The Workingman). The wobblies claimed they did actually own the majority of the original shares. The socialists, they said, pulled off some capitalistic shenanigans. They "watered the stock" *(vesiosakekaupan)* in order to retain control of the *Työmies* corporation. I suspect there was some truth to the allegations. The whole story, however, has never been published in detail.

The Finnish wobblies started their own newspaper in Duluth

EDUCATION

ORGANIZATION—EMANCIPATION

The Work Peoples College at Smithville, Minn., near the city of Duluth, is the only institution in the United States that gives instruction in industrial unionism and also in all such theoretical and technical subjects that are necessary in the industrial labor movement.

This school is controlled entirely by members of the I. W. W. which is a full guarantee for the fact that this institution is serving the purposes of the organization of the I. W. W. and its membership by teaching various subjects pertaining to social sciences, economics, and technical matters which all are useful in the revolutionary labor movement.

The Thirteenth annual convention of the I. W. W. fully endorsed in principle this college and promised its moral support and publicity through the various publications of the organization.

All this shows that the Work Peoples College is the only place of learning for revolutionary workers, that it serves the revolutionary labor movement, and is, so to speak, one of the necessary organs for building up industrial democracy.

In order to emancipate ourselves from industrial slavery we must know our aim. Taking this into consideration the Board of Directors for the Work Peoples College sends an appeal to workers who wish to obtain education that they would make use of this in satisfying their desire for learning.

Following courses are offered:

COURSES OF INSTRUCTION

1. Scientific department.
2. Technical elementary sciences and practise.
3. English department.
4. Organization bookkeeping department.

SCIENTIFIC DEPARTMENT

Lectures in this department will be given on the following subjects: The construction and procedure of industrial unionism, commencing with the preamble of the I. W. W. and concluding in industrial society. Economics, Sociology, Geography and Biology.

KNOWLEDGE IS THE
MOTHER OF PROGRESS

PRACTISE DEPARTMENT

Among other work in this department, two hours per week will be devoted to correct pronunciation, reciting poetry, reading and platform department.

Two hours per week will be given to public speaking and presentation, debate, parliamentary drill, and organization work.

In addition to these hours the student body will arrange for two meetings per week in which subjects of the hour and other discussion will be carried on so as to give the students practise in speaking and conducting meetings according to parliamentary rules.

DEPARTMENT OF ENGLISH

The teaching of English language is divided into four classes. The first class learn the fundamentals of grammar, pronunciation and the diacritical marks.

The second class goes through the grammar thoroughly and in detail. Considerable attention is given to composition in connection with the points raised in the grammar. Attention is also given to sounds and the pronunciation.

The third class concentrates on composition with reviews now and then in grammar. Considerable time is given to reading.

The fourth class gives most of the time to the study of rhetoric; several long themes are written.

DEPARTMENT OF BOOKKEEPING

I. The duties of a delegate.

II. The duties of a secretary.

III. Fundamentals of double entry bookkeeping according to the Rowe system. The student can take up the work where he had formerly left off, or depending on his former preparation.

Additional information regarding the school year, fees, etc., may be obtained by addressing THE WORK PEOPLE'S COLLEGE, Box 39, Morgan Park Station, Duluth, Minnesota.

The Work People's College near Duluth
Courtesy: University of Turku, Emigration History Research Center

(Minnesota). They originally named it *Sosialisti* (The Socialist) but that name confused everybody. It was not long before the name changed to reflect the IWW attitude—*Teollisuustyöläinen* (The Industrial Worker). That name, a tongue twister for even a Finn, was soon shortened to *Industrialisti*, a good Finglish name.

The *Work Peoples College*, a Finnish-American socialist folk school, was captured by the wobblies in the First Schism. It was the biggest prize they gained in the split. The loss of this school was a severe blow to the federation. They never succeeded in establishing another folk school so the wobbly Work Peoples College was the only Finnish college in the United States whose entire financial support came from the Finnish-American immigrants.

The Work Peoples College was started as a *Suomalainen Kansanopisto* (Finnish Peoples Folk School) run by the (take a deep breath) *Kansalliskirkkokunta* (The National Church) in 1903 in Duluth and then moved to nearby Smithville. When the American Finns left the Lutheran Church in the wholesale exodus of the 1900's, the socialists took the school with them and renamed it *Työväen Opisto* which was translated by someone to Work Peoples College. A language consultant might have named it The Labor Folk School or some such other name. Well, it got a distinctive name which is easy to remember even though it does sound like broken English.

The Work Peoples College closed its doors in 1935. The *Industrialisti* was published until the early 1970's. For many years, though, the *Industrialisti* was the work of a single man, Jack Ujanen, who was close to 90 years of age when the last issue came off the press and the Finnish-American "one big union" ceased to exist.

THE NEW SCHISM

The slogan *Land, Peace, and Bread* destroyed, in a sense, the Finnish Socialist Federation. That slogan, invented and proclaimed by Lenin's Bolshevik Party, caught the imagination of the Russian workers, peasants, soldiers, and sailors in the chaotic period that followed the collapse of the government of Czar Nicolai II. These Russians responded to the slogan by electing enough Bolsheviks to the various soviets to give the Bolshevik Party working control of those councils. Once that control was assured, the Bolsheviks, calling for *All power to the soviets*, were able to instigate a successful and bloodless insurrection against the Provisional National Russian government.

The overthrow of Czar Nicolai II had even pleased President Wilson since the feudal autocratic Russian government was an extremely embarrasing ally in the war to make the world safe for democracy. Socialists all over the world cheered, of course, when the reactionary Russian government crumbled to pieces. But when Lenin grabbed power many socialists were sure the *Millennium* had arrived. It didn't matter one iota that Russia was one of the most backward industrial nations on earth. What did matter was that the working class had taken control of over 1/6th of the earth's surface.

The morale of world socialism, at an extremely low ebb because of the socialist failure to prevent World War I, rebounded to new heights. Even Lenin admitted to a sort of "dizziness in gaining power". The impact of the Bolshevik Revolution not only electrified socialists all over the world but the euphoria helped imprison a lot of minds everywhere. The socialist foreign language federations in the United States, especially the Slavic language federations, had a phenomenal spurt in membership. The first generation Slavic-Americans rushed to join the Socialist Party because they thought their membership would give them a passport to the new promised land.

When the Socialist Party in the United States dragged its feet in giving the Bolsheviks an unqualified blessing, most of the language federations withdrew their affiliation with the Party. Some of the federations were, however, expelled. The Finnish-American socialists, as excited about the Russian Revolution as any other East Europeans, debated almost two years before disaffiliating themselves from the Socialist Party.

A special five day convention, held in Chicago in November (1919), did pass a resolution to withdraw from the Socialist party. The vote was so close that, as provided by the bylaws, the issue was placed before the entire membership. This plebiscite surprised everyone; it vetoed the convention's action so the Finnish federation remained affiliated to the Socialist Party. But not for long.

The situation was extremely tense and delicate. Remember the socialist Finn halls were at stake. Pro-Bolshevik Finnish speakers visited each socialist branch decrying the Socialist Party's refusal to jump on the Bolshevik bandwagon. I don't think there was anything the parliamentarian-minded socialists could do to stem the tide. Nothing succeeds like success. And the Russian Bolsheviks were successful in hanging onto their power.

Another special convention held at Waukegan (Illinois) in December, 1920 voted overwhelmingly for an independent Finnish Socialist Federation. Only a few New England votes were recorded against the motion even though Frans Syrjala warned the delegates they were being led into the Bolshevik ranks. He was right, of course, but even Frans Syrjala did not recognize the fate in store for the proud independent Finnish Socialist Federation.

The New England Finnish socialists and their daily newspaper—*Raivaaja*—began to build a new democratic socialist association. It had to take a new name, *Yhdysvaltain Sosialistipuoleen Suomalainen Järjesto* (The Finnish Federation of the Socialist Party of the United States). The new organization had about 60 branches, almost all of them on the Eastern Seaboard.

It was a branch of this organization that owned and ran the Ash Street Hall of my youth. I know that I have given the impression that this group was a branch of the old Finnish Socialist federation. I was justified because all Finnish socialists on the East Coast felt that this new federation was merely a continuation of the federation organized in 1906. In a sense this was true since the seceding group no longer existed in the 1930's. It had been *Bolshevized.*

Yes, the old Finnish Socialist Federation, the seceding federation, was Bolshevized. It took several years of bitter struggle but that Finnish Socialist Federation built by those proud independent former peasants of Northern and Central Finland was Bolshevized.

I know you want to ask: "What does it mean to be Bolshevized?" The result to me was just as distressing and unpleasant as the word sounds. But let me give the insider's, the true believer's definition. He or she might define Bolshevization as the restructuring of an organization so that its members become highly disciplined effective communists working under a capable central leadership for the communist cause.

So this seceding Finnish Socialist Federation became the Finnish Federation of the Workers (Communist) Party. These new Finnish-American communists comprised 40% of the total membership of that party. But not for long.

The members of the new Finnish Federation of the Workers (Communist) Party, used to the free wrangling of the old democratic socialist days, were much too independent for the leaders of world communism. The Fifth Plenum of the Communist International announced the beginning of the *Bolshevization* process. The first step: All language federations in the Workers (Communist) Party were to be abolished. Each member of the Finnish Federation would have to join a *cell*, or communist *fraction* as it was sometimes called. The language used in these cells would be English. The Finnish Federation was to be dissolved.

These new Finnish-American "communists", these former peasants from Northern and Central Finland had the audacity to challenge the wisdom of the Comintern! *Eteenpäin* (Forward), a new Finnish communist daily published in Worcester (Massachusetts), urged the Comintern to reconsider the matter. "Good propaganda, not organizational changes, were needed," the paper editorialized. (That, dear reader, was like challenging the wisdom of God. "Say, God, Why don't you make good health catching, instead of disease?") Yes, the opposition, often bitter, of the Finnish-American communists to the arbitrary actions of the Communist International had begun.

Heads began to roll! The leaders with the best (most independent?) minds in the federation, those who opposed or doubted the Kremlin's wisdom, were expelled. The minds of the other leaders were shackled. Only about 2000 Finnish-Americans joined the communist cells. The rest, resistant, were allowed to keep their old federation under the name *Center of Finnish Workers Clubs*. Most of the 2000 cell members belonged to fractions (cells) organized within the Finnish Workers Club. The purpose of these cells was, in my opinion, to keep the Finnish Workers Clubs following the party line.

The pleasant Finnish cultural traditions continued to be followed in the now communist Finn halls. I do think, though, that the ownership of those halls was now vested in the central organization of the Finnish Workers Club so that no branch could rebel without losing its Finn hall.

THE FINNISH COOPERATORS DEFEAT BOLSHEVIZATION

The most dramatic fight to keep a Finnish-American organization out of the Comintern's control was the year long struggle between the Consumers Cooperative Exchange of Superior (Wisconsin) and the Comintern in 1929-30.

Ever since its founding convention in 1906 the Finnish Socialist Federation had urged its members to organize consumers cooperatives. There were more than 100 Finnish co-op stores in Minnesota, Michigan, and Wisconsin in 1929. These co-ops had banded together to build a wholesale business which provided the local cooperatives with grocery and other items in addition to some management services. The Central Cooperative Exchange*, as the wholesale was named, was a highly profitable business and it had experienced a rapid growth in business volume in the latter part of the 1920's.

When the Finnish Socialist Federation ceded from the Socialist Party, this cooperative movement began to reflect the new political attitudes of its members. A line of canned goods called the Red Star brand appeared on the shelves of the local cooperative grocery store. Red Star canned ground coffee roasted by the wholesale, was a big volume item.

The Central Cooperative Exchange even had a Red Star chorus. The chorus was composed of young women whose costumes included hats on which was embossed the twin pines symbol of the Cooperative League of the United States of America. The chorus delivered the cooperative message to the Finnish communities in northern Wisconsin, Michigan, and Minnesota. This cooperative movement, much to the chagrin of the national Cooperative League, was very sympathetic to the communist movement. Then the Bolshevik boom was lowered!

The Workers (Communist) Party directed the members of the communist cell in the Central Cooperative Exchange to secure a $5,000 loan for the Party from the Cooperative Exchange. The members of the cell refused! They refused to obey a party directive!

The majority of the board of directors of the Central Cooperative Exchange were members of the communist cell in the Exchange but this board, after a four day delay, instructed the manager, who was also a cell member, to send the following telegram to the party headquarters.

"Impossible to send money. Have no funds. Are borrowing ourselves."
George Halonen

Robert Minor, a top communist functionary, was sent to Superior (Wisconsin) to enforce party discipline. He told the Central Cooperative Exchange communist cell that the party meant

---

*Its name was later changed to Central Cooperative Wholesale.

business. He also informed them that the *Party* had now raised the ante. The Cooperative Wholesale was to contribute 1% of its annual sales to the *Party*. The communist cell, which included the top managers of the wholesale, told Minor that only an annual meeting of all the local consumers cooperatives that belonged to the Exchange could make such a crucial decision.

The local consumers cooperative in the Finnish-American communities were controlled by the members who belonged to the local Finnish Workers Club. The communist cells in those Finnish Workers Clubs had considerable influence on the rank and file members. However, they failed to generate support for the communist demand even though the newspaper *Työmies* (now a communist daily) urged the communist cells to work energetically for the Exchange's compliance with the Party directive.

Michael Karni, an authority on the affair, wrote:

> Events between the summer of 1929, when...the Workers (Communist) Party precipitated the crisis (by demanding a loan from the Exchange for party use), and April, 1930 when the Exchange's annual meeting decided the issue, were dramatic. Recalcitrant members of the Exchange's Board of Directors were called to Moscow to explain their position; the now polarized Finnish radical press rose to unprecedented heights of polemic and vilification; families split over the issue; delegate votes were courted assiduously; operatives were sent to Superior from Moscow and New York; cablegrams crossed the Atlantic frequently; sporadic violence broke out; and clandestine strategy caucuses were held almost nightly. A general air of anticipation and apprehension prevailed over the Finnish community from Sault Ste. Marie to International Falls.

The Board of Directors of the Central Cooperative Exchange was unanimously opposed to the communist directives even though, as I have indicated, a majority of the board members belonged to the wholesale communist cell. Then the solidarity of the ranks was broken when one of the directors, Matti Tenhunen, was called to Moscow to explain his recalcitrant attitude. Tenhunen changed his mind in Moscow and when the all-important annual meeting of the Central Cooperative Exchange took place, two other board members had also changed their minds.

Husky young American Finns, according to Michael Karni, were posted around the Workers Hall on Tower Avenue in Superior (Wisconsin) for all three days of the annual meeting. Only bonafide delegates were allowed into the building. Greetings to

210

the annual meeting came from the Comintern headquarters in Moscow and even from the Finnish Communist Party which, at that time, was in exile.

The crucial issue of control was decided on the third day when the three board members who had switched their support to the Workers (Communist) Party—and that included Matti Tenhunen—were removed from their positions by a vote of 167 to 89. The Finnish-American cooperators in the Midwest, even though they were sympathetic to the Russian Revolution, refused to be Bolshevized!

The Finnish communist cells in the local cooperatives and in the Finnish Workers hall had refused to accept *Party* discipline. They refused to allow the Comintern to interfere in their way of life. Their decision enabled the Finnish cooperative movement in Minnesota, Wisconsin, and Michigan to have a vigorous life, free of political entanglements, until its merger with the Midland Cooperative Wholesale in the 1960's.

Chapter Fourteen

THE COOPERATIVE MOVEMENT

Rochdale (England) was a gloomy dismal town in the 1840's. The only employment was in the Lancashire Cotton Mills. The hours were long and the pay was short. Men, women, and children worked from six in the morning until eight at night. Some workers received two shillings (worth about 50 cents in 1840) for their fourteen hour day but most cotton mill employees received slightly more than one shilling (12 pence). A parliamentary report stated that at least 1500 people in Rochdale were living on less than one shilling per day in the year 1841.

Business was booming in the England of 1840. The cotton mill owners shared in the boom. The mill owners, however, refused to share their prosperity with their employees so a group of weavers approached the mill owners to request a wage increase. The mill owners and managers gave those workers that age old "song and dance": A wage increase would ruin the Rochdale cotton industry; a wage increase would drive capital out of Rochdale and, worse, out of England; a wage increase would only raise prices and leave the weavers worse off than before.

The Rochdale weavers walked out of their meeting with their hats in their hands. Although they were very poor, these workers had trained themselves—in much the same manner as the Finnish-American workers had in the 1900's—to debate and handle intellectual ideas. And they did debate a course of action. They decided a strike was not in the realm of practical action.

Perhaps, some of the weavers conjectured, we could lower the cost of living by supplying ourselves with the necessities of life. Perhaps if we eliminated the middleman's profit we could raise our real wages even though we accept the low wage offered by the cotton industry. Why not give it a try? We need capital. Where can we find it? Let's establish a subscription list whereby each of us pledges to invest a minimum of two pence a week. They did. The Rochdale Equitable Pioneers Society was organized.

At the end of one year the Rochdale Pioneers had twenty-eight pounds in capital—all collected by a weekly subscription—owned by 29 consumer investors. They can't be called *capitalists* because they intended to limit the earnings of the capital they invested. Nor can they be called *worker-investors* because they were investing in a business that was going to serve them as consumers. These charter members of the Rochdale cooperative would still have to put in a long day in the cotton mill for their daily bread.

The Rochdale cooperative was opened on Toad Lane, "a street which was as unappetizing as its name", on December 21, 1844. Some of the town's tradesmen and some doffer boys they hired harassed the new enterprise on its first day of business. The store, however, was a success. The entire stock of flour, butter, sugar, and oatmeal was sold on that first day. Less than 100 years later, the society had 30,257 members and over 2 and 1/2 million dollars worth of business a year. More significant, however, the consumers cooperatives that this Toad Lane store nurtured became the largest business in the British Isles.

The important contribution of the Rochdale Pioneers that distinguishes them from the countless other cooperatives organized before their time was the regulations they adopted for their business. Now known as the Rochdale principles, these regulations have been the guidelines for almost all of the successful cooperatives that have developed since that time.

The Rochdale principles are usually divided into two groups. The first three given in the list below are considered inviolable. That is, if these three principles are not adhered to, then the association is not a bonafide cooperative. The other six principles are useful but not indispensable.

The Rochdale Principles

1. Each member shall have exactly one vote.
2. Limited interest on capital. Capital invested in the association shall receive a fixed rate of interest which shall be not more than the

minimum prevailing rate.

3. The savings (profit) made by the association shall be returned to the patrons of the business in proportion to their patronage.

4. No person shall be excluded from membership because of color, religion, or political beliefs.

5. Membership shall be voluntary.

6. All business shall be done for cash.

7. The association shall be neutral in questions involving religion and politics.

8. A fixed percentage of the business receipts shall be used to educate the public about cooperatives.

9. The association shall, when feasible, endeavor to expand its business (or in combination with other cooperative associations) to provide goods the members need and, whenever possible, secure access to raw materials.

The first principle guarantees democracy. Each person shall have only one vote regardless of the number of shares he or she may own. The second principle makes capital a servant of the business. The principle implies that the owners of capital are entitled to a reasonable return on their investment but that the business is not run for the benefit of the shareholders. The third principle ensures that the association is run *for use, not for profit*.

The last principle, the ninth principle, is often called the *continuous expansion principle*. It is the most radical principle in the set. It states that a cooperative association shall endeavor to obtain control of the means of the production and of the natural resources. When the means of production and the natural resources are cooperatively owned we will have, of course, a *cooperative commonwealth*, a society not incompatible with the ideal society envisaged by socialists.

The continuous expansion principle is not an original Rochdale principle. The Ninth Biennial Congress of the Cooperative League of the United States of America (CLUSA), held in 1934, added the continuous expansion concept to the original Rochdale set. This action came at a handy time because at this period the Finnish-American cooperatives—especially the cooperatives in the Middlewest—were moving away from their socialist and labor orientation because of the attempts by the communists to capture control of them. In order to remain independent this cooperative movement had to develop its own philosophy—a purely consumer-oriented philosophy. The continuous expansion principle became part of that newly evolving cooperative philosophy which was labelled *pure cooperation*. Its adherents were called *pure cooperators*.

Pure cooperation was new to the Finnish-American consumers cooperative movement but it wasn't new to the Cooperative League. The league had been founded by the father of pure cooperation, Dr. James Peter Warbasse. A famous medical surgeon and medical educator of the early 1900's, Dr. Warbasse was a former member of the Socialist Party who became disillusioned with socialist philosophy—perhaps because of his strong antipathy to the political state.

Socialism, Warbasse claimed, would merely replace one set of exploiters by another. The political state would not wither away, as Marxist theory claimed, after socialism was established. On the contrary, the socialist state would dominate the lives of its citizens to a far greater extent than the capitalist state does. "What politician ever relinquished his power voluntarily?" he once asked a group of his students in a seminar.*

Dr. Warbasse also rejected the idea of a class struggle. He stated this often and wrote in his book *Cooperative Democracy*:

> There is only one class struggle. This struggle consists of the struggle of the workers to get out of the working class and into the capitalist class.

This statement gained considerable popularity among pure cooperators. They have (and do) quote it often, usually in a much more embellished form. However, the statement, although clever, cannot stand close academic scrutiny. As we shall see, Dr. Warbasses's analysis of the origin and purpose of the political state is quite similar to that of any Marxist socialist. And that analysis (Dr. Warbasse's analysis) implies the existence of a class struggle.

The Finn co-ops (as the Finnish cooperatives were called) joined and supported Dr. Warbasse's Cooperative League as soon as it was founded even though the Finnish cooperatives did not become truly neutral politically until the early part of the 1930's. It should be noted, incidentally, that the Finnish cooperatives and Dr. Warbasse were the Cooperative League's main financial support in the early days.

The Finnish-American cooperatives may have been a little

---

*I was a student in the first session of the Rochdale Institute (1937), a training school for cooperative managers. The school was sponsored by the Cooperative League and the New School for Social Research. Dr. Warbasse was the president of the institute in addition to being a frequent lecturer and seminar leader.

thorn in Dr. Warbasse's side when the League was first organized. But there wasn't much he could do about it because without the American Finns the Cooperative League would have been a tiny reformist sect. The politically conscious American Finns had an attribute Dr. Warbasse should have appreciated, though. They did not try to dominate nor try to capture control of the Cooperative League even though it was something they could easily have done.

Most historians of the Finnish-American experience like to write about the Finnish involvement in consumers cooperation. They usually devote many pages to the co-op movement, sometimes more than to any other topic. I think they do so because the word *cooperation* has such a pleasant connotation. No harsh class struggle concepts—no picket lines and no protest rallies. Things are much more pleasant, much more agreeable. Everyone is banded together. Everyone, all American Finns—Lutherans, Congregationalists, socialists, wobblies, and communists—working together for the common good. Sounds good, doesn't it? It creates a pretty image, an image that I wish were true but isn't.

The Finnish-American cooperative movement was part and parcel of the Finnish-American socialist movement just as the cooperative movement in most Western nations was allied to the socialist movement in each respective country. The slogan, for example, used by the successful Swedish cooperatives in 1908 was: *Don't buy from the capitalists. Buy from the workers' store.* The prevelant point of view among most of the world's cooperators was that the cooperative movement was part of the labor and socialist movement.

It was not until the late 1920's that the Swedish cooperatives began to develop a philosophy distinct from that put forth by the Swedish socialist movement. This is just about the same time that the Finnish-American co-ops began to travel down the road of political neutrality and Dr. Warbasse's concept of pure cooperation began to gain a considerable number of adherents among the administrators of the Finnish co-ops.

Actually the Finn co-ops in the Middlewest had no choice but to accept the *pure cooperation* philosophy. The final schism that destroyed the old Finnish Socialist Federation had ended the long association of the Finns of that region with the Socialist Party. The monolithic Workers (Communist) Party began to lose its lustre and appeal as that party expelled its individualistic Finnish members from its ranks. The communist attempt to capture control of the Central Cooperative Exchange was the last straw. The Finn co-ops had to have some base in order to remain independent and they chose the Cooperative League. These cooperatives, therefore, became firmly committed to the principle of political neutrality and to the doctrine of pure cooperation.

I said the continuous expansion principle was radical. It is. Dr. Warbasse explained in his lectures at the Rochdale Institute (and the same thoughts can be found in his book *Cooperative Democracy*) that under the principle of continuous expansion the cooperatives would displace not only most of private enterprise but the political state itself.

The state, according to Dr. Warbasse's thesis, was created to protect the property and the privileges of a few against the demands of the propertyless and unprivileged. Laws are passed and laws are interpreted in behalf of the privileged group. Officials of the state often break the law in order to perform their main function which is to protect the rights of the privileged. The main purpose of the state is not necessarily related to the concept of justice.

The political state in a cooperative society, however, would have no purpose. It would be obsolete. The state would not be needed because there would be only one class, the consumers. The political state, because it would have no function to perform, would wither away. There would be no need for a physically powerful social organization, the state, to protect the privileged from the unprivileged because there would be no unprivileged. Privilege and property would belong to everyone since everyone is a consumer.

The Finnish socialists, the ones who were active cooperators when I was a boy, had a different opinion about the cooperative movement. They viewed the cooperatives as a useful tool in the struggle to achieve socialism. Look at what happens in a society when the co-ops are weak or nonexistent, they asserted. Whenever the owners of industry, the capitalists, are forced to give a wage increase to their workers, they can recapture their profit (the surplus value) by merely raising the price of their product. When the co-ops are strong they can't do that because they can't raise their prices with impunity. The competition from a strong cooperative movement will force these private entrepreneurs to keep their price increases to a minimum. Thus, they will lose part of their surplus value (profit) with each wage increase.

In fact the competition from the co-ops which will result in lower market prices and the pressure from the unions to increase wages will tend to make all profits disappear. There will be little or no surplus value for the capitalists to enjoy. The capitalists will be ground to bits between the upper and lower millstones. The cooperative commonwealth, or socialism (which is the same thing) will be at hand.

I am going to let Dr. Warbasse have the last word because of my deep admiration for him and his work. He writes:

> In cooperation, the root of things is changed by processes which are evolutionary and, hence, slow. The change brought about by the cooperative movement is peaceful and, in general, permanent. Cooperation is never found taking destructive steps to attain a good end. It makes use of constructive measures. The test of radicalism is not in the amount of noise and chaos, but rather in the substantial quality of the changes which it accomplishes.

A CRITIQUE
OF THE FINNISH COOPERATIVE MOVEMENT

The Finnish-American cooperatives were the most successful consumers cooperatives ever built in the United States. There were in 1920 more than 150 Finnish co-ops whose combined annual business volume exceeded $5,000,000 in 1920 dollars. These co-ops were, as I have indicated, the main support of the Cooperative League. The number of Finnish co-ops was so large that one Finnish-American delegate to the 1920 cooperative convention told Dr. Warbasse, "...with good reason we could demand that Finnish be made a second official language at this convention."

These co-ops, almost always organized by members of the Finnish Socialist Federation, served a real need in the Finnish community. The co-op was a place where the first generation Finn could buy the groceries so important in the Finnish diet of that era: cardamom spiced coffee bread (*pulla*), Finnish rye bread, lingonberries, (*puolukoita*), herring, smoked salmon, and that Christmas staple—*lipeäkala* (dried codfish cured in a solution of lye water). The co-op was also a place where the American Finn could speak his own language. That, incidentally, was no small asset to an early immigrant.

The co-ops, however, could have done more for the first generation Finns than they did. The co-ops could have saved their members money! They didn't do that and because they didn't, these Finnish co-ops started to disappear when the ranks of the first generation began to thin out. The second and later generations of the Finns have had little motivation—neither idealism, language, nor economy—to "shop co-op". In due time, therefore, all the remaining Finnish consumers cooperatives will go out of business.

The cooperative stores when I worked in them in the 1930's, 1940's, and 1950's could not compete, with respect to price, with the large grocery chains. Our grocery prices were hopelessly out of line. An individual who bought in the co-op did so because it was convenient to do so or because he or she was an idealist who was willing to pay a little more, to sacrifice a little, to promote the cooperative movement. These idealists envisaged a society based on the brotherhood and sisterhood of all human beings. Purchasing their groceries in the co-op was just a small contribution to changing our competitive society into one based on love and service.

We cooperators, Finnish and non-Finnish, idealists and non-idealists, imprisoned our minds. We stopped thinking. The Rochdale pioneers had been so successful that we became convinced that it was because their principles were sacrosanct. We thought private business, motivated by profit, had absolutely no chance competing against a business owned and run for the benefit of its customers. The truth was: the large private grocery businesses did a better job than our small co-ops did. But, no matter how often we failed, no matter how meager our growth, we blamed the failures and the lack of growth on ourselves, on our own inadequacies as individuals. We didn't dare let the slightest suggestion that the Rochdale philosophy itself might be the basis of our failures enter our conscious mind.

I recall a seminar at the Rochdale Institute, led by Dr. Warbasse, in which a lady in the audience asked the doctor why Campbell brand tomato soup cost one cent a can more in her co-op than it did in the A&P grocery store. Dr. Warbasse, an idealistic and intellectual leader far removed from the realities of the grocery business, didn't understand her question.

Dr. Warbasse didn't understand the question because he just didn't believe Campbell's tomato soup was priced cheaper in the A&P than the co-op. The lady must be mistaken. Or, he suggested, the co-op manager may have mispriced the item. The A&P, he carefully pointed out, had to make a profit to survive. The co-op didn't. Therefore it was plain as your fingers when you put your hand in front of your face (*ipso facto*) that the co-op should be able to sell the tomato soup at a lower price than any private-profit business.

My mind, excited, almost slipped out of its "obedience to faith" constraint that night because deep within me, pushing hard to get out, was the knowledge why the A&P (or any large grocery chain) had cheaper prices than the co-op. Yes, I knew then and I know now why the A&P was able to sell a can of tomato soup cheaper than the co-op could. Life would have been a lot different had my mind been able to slip out of its well-worn groove. Alas! It didn't. I merely pushed the information I possessed into a seldom used segment of my mind and nodded my agreement with Dr. Warbasse. I continued in the almost impossible task of trying to run and develop a healthy, growing cooperative grocery business.

Yes, I knew why the A&P was a more effective merchandiser than any co-op I managed. The A&P was a volume buyer and a volume seller. The A&P, like the other grocery chains, didn't care one hoot how much profit was made on a single item nor how much profit was made as a percentage of sales. The private grocery chains were interested only in how much profit was made as a percentage of the capital invested.

If ½% profit per dollar of sales gave the grocery chain two dollars a share earnings (profit) when the stock was selling at $15.00 a share, the chain was doing exceedingly well because the stock might very well rise to $20.00 a share. The management of private-profit grocery chains insisted, therefore, on fast turnovers of their inventories. To get fast turnovers, the chains developed highly efficient and highly economical operations. This policy generated high profits with respect to the amount of capital invested.

One-half percent profit per dollar of sales in our co-ops would have allowed us to declare a small patronage refund of less than $2.50 for each $500 of purchases—not much of an enticement to draw crowds into our co-ops. Further, it would have been difficult

The 1930 Central Cooperative Exchange Convention where the delegates insisted on an independent cooperative movement.

for the co-op to earn that ½% on sales with prices as low as those charged by the chain stores.

How come the Rochdale pioneers were so successful? The Rochdale pioneers opened their cooperative long before any efficient system of distributing consumer goods had been developed in England. The Rochdale pioneers didn't compete against such efficient retailers as Sears Roebuck, Safeway, A&P, J.C. Penney, and others. The Rochdale cooperative society competed against small individual entrepreneurs who, generally, had a policy of gouging, if not cheating, their working-class customers. The philosophy of the retail trade in that era was *caveat emptor*—let the buyer beware. The retail customer then had to be alert, as alert as today's customer who intends to purchase an automobile from a used car dealer.

I said we were blinded by our ideals. I don't feel that our blindness resulted in a bad deal for the middle-class doctors, lawyers, school teachers, and ministers who were members of the cooperatives I worked for in the late 1940's and early 1950's*. These middle-class intellectuals were well off. They bought in the co-op because it made them feel good. The psychic return that this middle-class clientele received from shopping in the co-op was well worth the little extra they had to pay.

---

*The rapidly growing cooperative movement, during this time, was a middle-class phenomenon. The working-class was not attracted by the cooperative movement of the 1930's.

It was a darn shame, though, that the Finnish grocery cooperatives did not provide their members with lower grocery prices than the chains charged. I said it was a darn shame because these co-ops could have done that and the Finnish-American workers could have used the increase in their real incomes. It is my opinion that these co-ops could have provided the Finnish worker with a substantial increase in real income. The Finnish co-ops didn't do that because the co-op administrators (and the leaders of the Finnish Socialist Federation) were hypnotized by the Rochdale principles and motivated by a deep desire to evangelize. They put their small co-ops on the main streets instead of keeping them in the sheltered environment of the Finn hall. They forgot the *raison d'etre* of a cooperative association. Provide your members with lower prices than the private sector.

The Finnish co-ops developed a large group of able administrators who gained from their work experience an extraordinary expertise in running marginal businesses, businesses that put forth a brave front in the competitive world on Main Street. What a tremendous waste of talent! These same administrators would have developed a far more important expertise—an ability to discriminate about what to buy and sell in the co-op—if the Finnish co-ops had travelled down a different road. To illustrate I'll use the co-op in Gardner as an example but the example fits many Finnish co-ops organized elsewhere in the United States.

The co-op in Gardner was originally housed in the socialist Ash Street Hall. The socialists should have kept it there. Only members should have been allowed to buy in the co-op. The work in the co-op should have been done, as much as possible, by volunteer (free) labor. Some contribution of labor (or a cash equivalent) should have been expected from everyone who wanted the privilege of buying in the co-op. The membership should have been limited to progressive-minded people of all races, nationalities, and religions. They were the only ones who joined the co-op anyway.

The manager of such a co-op, a co-op which stayed in the shelter of a Finnish socialist hall or some other protective environment, would have had an opportunity to develop a valuable expertise, how to choose the most appropriate merchandise for the co-op to handle. He would have had a chance to build a new type of business that might have provided its members with substantial savings. I believe that if this approach had been followed in Gardner as well as in the other Finnish communities in Massachusetts, the co-ops in Gardner, Fitchburg, Quincy, Worcester, Maynard, and elsewhere would be thriving businesses today.

The Workers Credit Union of Fitchburg is the best example of a cooperative that was developed in a sheltered environment. This credit union, one of the first in Massachusetts, was organized by the board of directors of the Finnish socialist *Raivaaja* in 1914. The Workers Credit Union was housed in the Raivaaja building on 48 Wallace Avenue for about 30 years. It was known among the first generation Finns as the Raivaaja Bank *(Raivaajan Pankki)*. The Workers Credit Union prospered, even though it never hid its socialist affiliation, because it produced real savings for its members.

In fact the Workers Credit Union went out of its way to identify itself as a socialist institution. As late as 1926 the credit union purchased an ad in the *Fifth Anniversary Review* published by the Young Peoples Socialist League of New England. That ad read:

WORKERS CREDIT UNION
Fitchburg, Mass.
To our knowledge the only socialist savings institution
in America. A purely cooperative organization. A deposit
of $5.00 will open an account with us.

I note that the Workers Credit Union is the most successful enterprise, which still exists, built by the first generation Finnish-Americans in the United States and the largest institution of any kind built entirely by Finnish immigrant money.

Chapter Fifteen

EPILOGUE—GOODBYE TO ALL THAT
(with apologies to Robert Graves)

A few years after I left the cooperative movement I went to work for a regional grocery chain in the San Francisco area. I was an excellent grocery clerk—a fast checker and my ability to recall prices, quite an asset in the 1950's, was well above the average. The chain used me as a utility man. I was supposed to go wherever I was needed but my main function was to check the goods that were delivered into the warehouse of the grocery store where I worked.

I was 36 years of age at the time. For some reason, maybe because I was a little restless with my life style, that old Finnish pagan god *Väinämöinen*—old and lusty—stepped into my life again. I must state right here and now that my wife doesn't believe in *Väinämöinen*—but then she's not of a Finno-Ugric background. She insists that she tried to get me to go to school for the entire three years we had been married then. *Väinämöinen*, she claims, had nothing to do with it. The former statement is true but the latter isn't. I believe *Väinämöinen* "bugged" my wife into "bugging" me. It is as simple as that. My wife does admit that the watermelons did play a momentous role in my rash decision to quit my job. And *Väinämöinen* was responsible for the watermelons too. I'm sure of that.

We lived way out in Lagunitas, a little hamlet which is west of San Rafael, San Anselmo, and Woodacre. The house in which we lived was about five miles or so from Point Reyes. I mentioned this because maybe the water I drank had something to do with the medical problems I began to encounter. I understand that some gouty people get attacks when they drink red wine but they can drink white wine with impunity while others get attacks from white wine but red wine merely increases their libido. Was it the water? Maybe, but I believe that *Väinämöinen*—old and lusty—began to work his magic. Väinämöinen, as I said in the Introduction, performs his magic in a rather unusual and sometimes disconcerting manner.

Well, anyway, I began to experience a tremendous amount of pain—not steady pain but sharp quick flashes of pain in my legs, my back, and my groin. The pains hit without warning. The pains didn't last long but they were so intense that I had to stop whatever I was doing because I was left gasping for breath. Once I fell down a long flight of stairs as a severe flash of pain overwhelmed me when I was returning to work from the employees' room on the second floor. A little battered, but unbowed, I went on with the job.

The Kaiser Foundation Health Clinic was unable to find anything organically wrong. They knew I was gouty but these symptoms didn't appear to be caused by gout. The doctor was a little suspicious because I told him the symptoms never ocurred at home. "You're just another malingerer," he told me with a smile. I became convinced, as the flashes of pain intensified, that it was the beginning of the end. It was, however, the beginning of the beginning.

One day, about a week before the Fourth of July, we advertised a gigantic watermelon sale to celebrate the second or third anniversary of the opening of our market. Two huge trailer trucks loaded with watermelons from San Joaquin Valley drove into our parking lot. My spirits, not very high, sank even lower as I realized how stiff I would be after unloading those several hundred watermelons. And, it entered my mind, that although I would survive the ordeal I could look forward to years and years of unloading watermelons, potatoes, cases of canned goods, and sundry other grocery items—provided, of course, that I survived whatever was causing my pains. The ditty of my blueberry childhood popped into my head:

Hail! Hail! Knock those blueberries off the bush!
Hail! Hail! Knock those blueberries off the bush!
Hail! Hail! Knock those goldarn blueberries off the bush!

I rebelled! The hell with those watermelons! I took off my apron, hung it up, put on my coat, and looked around for my easy-going good-natured boss Ray. I had news for him!

"Hey," I told him when I found him in aisle C where he was working hard stocking canned fruit on the shelves. "Those watermelons have got to me. I'm not going to unload them. I'm going to quit my job."

"Oh, you don't have to unload them." Ray replied. "I'll get a couple of kids to do it as soon as I finish here. You just make sure they do it right."

"Thanks a lot, Ray," I replied. "But if I can't do my job, there's no point in my staying here. It'll only be something else next time. I'm going to school. I guess I should have gone to college years ago."

Väinämöinen must have been smiling in the background. *Väinämöinen* had to be close by because I, a hopeless monotone, kept hearing music. And *Väinämöinen* performs most of his magic by music. I even began to hum to myself. Off tune, of course. It didn't matter! I was extremely happy. Goodbye grocery business! Goodbye grocery business! Goodbye to the time-consuming back-breaking grocery business! Goodbye to all that!

Strange. As I walked to my car, my favorite song, *Men of the Soil* popped into my mind. *Men of the Soil* had been the official song of the Massachusetts League of Cooperative Youth Clubs. I hadn't heard that song for at least twenty years but I (or *Väinämöinen*) sang. Why not? It was appropriate. I was going to claim my own.

Men of the soil! We have labored unending.
We have fed the world upon the grain that we have grown.
Now with the dawn of a new day ascending
Giants of the earth, at last we rise to claim our own.
Justice throughout the land, Happiness as God has planned.
Who is there denies our right to reap what we have sown.

There is a lightning in the sky. There's a thunder shouting high.
We will never rest until the sons of men are free.

THE FINNISH GLOSSARY

This glossary is a simple guide to the pronunciation of Finnish words and names. Pronouncing Finnish words is easy if you follow the simple rules given here; speaking the language is, however, another story. Even though its syntax makes Finnish one of the most difficult languages to master, it's fun to learn how to pronounce the words.

The Finnish alphabet has eight vowels. These vowels are listed the normal Finnish alphabetical order in the vowel table with *y*, *ä*, and *ö* at the end. (Note carefully the difference between the short and long vowel sounds.) Since the letters *b*, *c*, *f*, *g*, *x*, and *z* do not appear in words of pure Finnish origin, they have been omitted from the table of consonants. The letter *w* has been omitted, also, since *w*, which appears in some Finnish words, is pronounced as if it were a *v*.

There may be exceptions to the rules that I have given that I don't know about. (After all, aren't there always exceptions to rules?) I suggest that the reader read through all the tables—The Vowel Sounds, The Diphthong Table, The Syllable Rules, and The Consonant Table—before trying to pronounce the words in the word list. Use these five hints:

1. Divide the word into its syllables.
2. Remember *y* is always a vowel.
3. No silent letters. (Every letter must be pronounced. If a word has, for example, two consecutive *k*'s, both must be pronounced.)
4. The sound of each letter, unlike English, is always the same.
5. Always accent the first syllable of each word.

Be sure to try your voice with *Ot-to Huh-ta-nen*. It is my favorite Finnish name.

The Syllable Rules

1. The second of exactly two consecutive consonants in a word begins a new syllable.

   examples: *kyl-lä*, certainly - *kuk-ko*, rooster - *kir-ja*, book - *kok-ko*, bonfire *pom-mi*, bomb - *Man-ni-nen*, a name

2. The last consonant of three consecutive consonants begins a new syllable.

   examples: *Rans-ka*, France - *kort-ti*, card - *kirk-ko*, church - *kink-ku*, ham palk-ka, wages - *herk-ku*, a tidbit

3. A single consonant begins a new syllable.

   examples: *ka-tu*, street - *ta-lo*, house - *poi-ka*, boy - *a-las*, down *Ju-ma-la*, God - *ma-ta-la*, low

4. The second of two vowels which cannot form a dipthong begins a new syllable. (See The Dipthong Table.)

   examples: *lu-en*, I read - *mai-to-a*, milk - *eh-ti-ä*, arrive - *ha-ke-a*, search *a-te-ri-a*, meal - *is-tu-a*, sit

5. Accent the first syllable of each word.

   examples: *kaup-pa*, store - *in-to*, zeal - *Hän-ni-nen*, a name

6. In compound words such as *kirjakauppa* (bookstore), accent the first syllable of the first component and stress, almost as strongly, the first syllable of each succeeding component. Note that there are a lot of compound words.

   examples: *kir-ja/kaup-pa*, bookstore - *vii-kon/lop-pu*, weekend *vii-kon/lop-pu/ma-ja*, weekend cabin, or cottage

The Diphthong Table

The important thing to bear in mind is that a pair of vowels that form a dipthong belong to the same syllable. Pronounce each vowel in the dipthong separately remembering that they are in the same syllable.

The second of two consecutive vowels which cannot form a dipthong begins a new syllable. (See rule #4 in The Syllable Rules for an example.) Note the ordering is important—*ai* is a dipthong but *ia* is not.

ai ai-ka	*ie* pie-ni	*ui* ui-da	*äi* äi-ti
au au-ki	*iu* viu-lu	*uo* Suo-mi	*äy* äy-ri
ei Rei-no	*oi* oi-ke-a	*yi* hyi-nen	*öi* öi-sin
eu neu-la	*ou* Ou-lu	*yö* yö-pöl-lö	*öy* öy-lät-ti

The Vowel Sounds

a   like the *a* in *Cuba*. examples: *a-ho*, meadow - *ham-mas*, tooth

aa   the long Finnish *a*, prolong the sound of the single *a*.
examples: *aa-mu*, morning - *Paap-pa-nen*, a name

e   like the *e* in *end*. examples: *se*, it - *hen-ki*, spirit

ee   The long Finnish *e*, prolong the sound of the single *e*.
examples: *e-teen*, in front of - *ee-den*, Eden (Paradise)

i   like the *i* in *ship*. examples: *ni-mi*, name - *pi-ru*, the devil

ii   the long Finnish *i*, like the sound of *ee* in *knee*.
examples: *pii-ri*, circle - *pii-sa-ta*, enough

o   like the clipped *o* in *forget*. examples: *i-so*, big - *on*, is

oo   the long Finnish *o*, prolong the sound of the single *o*. (rare)
examples: *sa-noo*, he or she says - *oo-piu-mi*, opium

u   like the *u* in *pull*. examples: *pul-la*, coffee bread - *Uk-ko* (a god)

uu   like the *oo* in *moon*. examples: *uu-si*, new - *uu-ni*, oven

y   like the *ü* in the German *über*. examples: *yk-si*, one - *sy-dan*, heart

yy   prolong the sound of the single *y*. examples: *syy*, cause - *syy-vys*, depth

ä   like the *a* in *at*. examples: *äi-ti*, mother - *Ve-nä-jä*, Russia

ää   prolong the sound of the single *ä*. example: *ää-ni*, voice

ö   very close to the *er* in *perk*. examples: *yö*, night - *tyt-tö*, girl

öö   prolong the sound of the single *ö*. (rare)
examples: *Öölanti*, *Öland* - *Töö-lö*, a suburb of Helsinki

The Consonant Table

d   like *d* in *don't*. examples: *sade*, rain - *e-des*, at least

g   rare, usually preceeded by an *n*. *ng* like *ng* in *ringing*.
examples: *ren-gas*, ring - *hen-gäh-tää*, to catch one's breath

h   like *h* in *Henry*. examples: *ha-me*, dress - *nu-ha*, common cold

j   like *y* in *yes*. examples: *Jus-si*, John - *jos*, if

k   like *k* in *nick*. examples: *ku-ka*, who - *kuk-ka*, flower

l   like *l* in *billion*. examples: *Ol-li*, a boy's name - *lem-pi*, favorite

m   like *m* in *mama*. examples: *mies*, man - *lam-mas*, lamb

n   like *n* in *Nevada*. examples: *nel-ja*, four - *nyt*, now

n(k)   *n* followed by *k*, like *n* in *sink*. example: *Hel-sin-ki*

p   like *p* in *part*. examples: *pa-ha*, bad - *pap-pi*, pastor

r   like *r* in *rain*. Roll the *r* but do not blur the sound of succeeding vowels.
examples: *ra-ha*, money - *her-ra*, mister (also Lord)

s   like s in *sissy*. examples: *si-su*, "guts" - *mis-sa*, where
t   like t in *today*. examples: *pa-ta*, pot - *mat-to*, mat or carpet
v   like v in *very*. examples: *vai-mo*, wife - *viik-ko*, week

THE WORD LIST

The compound words are designated by an asterik (*). The components of each compound word are separated by a slash (/) in the pronunciation column. Recall that the first syllable of each word is accented and that an almost equal stress is given to the first syllable of each component of a compound word.

The symbol ** (double asteriks) attached to an English word in the definition column indicates the Finnish word was a temperance society name. Umlauted *a*'s and *o*'s have been dropped from Finnish names in the United States and Canada. I have put the umlaut back in this glossary.

A

Aalto	*Aal-to*	a name, *alto* = wave
aamu	*aa-mu*	morning
Aarnio	*Aar-ni-o*	a name
*aarniopuu**	*aar-ni-o/puu*	an ancient tree
*Aamunkoitto**	*Aa-mun/koit-to*	Day Break**
aapinen	*aa-pi-nen*	a primer or ABC book
Aho	*A-ho*	a name, *aho* = meadow
Ahti	*Ah-ti*	ancient pagan water god
Ahtio	*Ah-ti-o*	a name
aika	*ai-ka*	time, era
aika valhe	*ai-ka val-he*	a big lie—whopper
Aino	*Ai-no*	a girl's name
*akanilma**	*a-kan/il-ma*	a storm (feminine)—slang
*Alajärvi**	*A-la/jär-vi*	a Finnish town—Lower Lake
*Alavieska**	*A-la/vies-ka*	a town in Finland
Amerikan	*A-me-ri-kan*	American
Annala	*An-na-la*	a name
*Armonlähde**	*Ar-mon/läh-de*	Fountain of Grace
Asikainen	*A-si-kai-nen*	a name
Asunmaa	*A-sun-maa*	a name
auki	*au-ki*	open
Auringon Säde	*Au-rin-gon Sä-de*	The Sun's Ray**

E

ei	*ei*	no
Elinan Surma	*E-li-nan Sur-ma*	name of a Finnish tragedy
en	*en*	word used to form negative
en voi	*en voi*	I can't
eno	*e-no*	uncle—mother's brother
ensimmäinen	*en-sim-mäi-nen*	the first
Erämaan Helmi	*E-rä/maan Hel-mi*	Desert Pearl**
Erämaan Tähti	*E-rä/maan Täh-ti*	Desert Star**
Eteenpäin	*E-teen-päin*	a Finnish-American daily
että	*et-tä*	that, in the sense of lest

H

Haapanen	*Haa-pa-nen*	a name, *haapapuu* = aspen (tree)
hajaannus	*ha-jaan-nus*	a schism, a split
Häkkinen	*Häk-ki-nen*	a name
Halonen	*Ha-lo-nen*	a name, from woodcutter?
Hänninen	*Hän-ni-nen*	a name
Hannula	*Han-nu-la*	a name
Hauskaa Joulua	*Haus-kaa Jou-lu-a*	Merry Christmas
heitti	*heit-ti*	he (or she) threw
heitä löylyä	*hei-tä löy-ly-ä*	"create heat in the sauna"
Heikki	*Heik-ki*	a boy's name—Henry
Herra	*Her-ra*	mister, also the Lord
Herrankin Herra	*Her-ran-kin Her-ra*	The Lord of the Lords
herättäjä	*he-rät-tä-jä*	evangelist
Hiisi	*Hii-si*	another name for the devil
Huhtanen	*Huh-ta-nen*	*huhta* = a burnt clearing
hurratkaa	*hur-rat-kaa*	cheer (imperative case)
humalassa	*hu-ma-las-sa*	tipsy (intoxicated)
Hyvä Toivo	*Hy-vä Toivo*	Good Hope**
hyviä	*hy-viä*	good (singular: *hyvä*)
häkä	*hä-kä*	carbon dioxide—used in my area to designate the mixture of smoke and steam in a sauna

I

*ihanneliitto**	*i-han-ne/liit-to*	idealistic club or society
*ikämiesten**	*i-kä/mies-ten*	older men's (section)
*illanviettoja**	*il-lan/viet-to-ja*	evening social events
*Iltahetki**	*Il-ta/het-ki*	Eventide**
into	*in-to*	zeal, eagerness
Into	*In-to*	a Finnish-American club
iso	*i-so*	large
isä	*i-sä*	father

J

ja	*ja*	and
järjestö	*jär-jes-tö*	organization, association
jo	*jo*	already
Joulu	*Jou-lu*	Christmas
Juhannus	*Ju-han-nus*	Midsummer Day, a holiday
juhla	*juh-la*	festival
Jumala	*Ju-ma-la*	God (Christian), also pagan
juoda	*juo-da*	drink
Jussi	*Jus-si*	a name, John

K

kaakku	*kaak-ku*	coffee bun
Kaarila	*Kaa-ri-la*	a name, *kaari* = bend, curve
kahvi	*kah-vi*	coffee
Kaiku	*Kai-ku*	The Echo**

230

kaivosmiesten*	kai-vos/mies-ten	miners (possessive case)
kalja	kal-ja	near-beer (slang for beer)
Kalevala	Ka-le-va-la	Finnish epic poem
kamala	ka-ma-la	ghastly, frightful
Kangas	Kan-gas	a name, kangas = moor, heath
kansa	kan-sa	people, a nation of people
Kansan Onni	Kan-san On-ni	The Peoples' Luck**
kansallis	kan-sal-lis	national, as in kansalliseepos
kansalliseepos*	kan-sal-lis/ee-pos	national epic
kansakoulu*	kan-sa/kou-lu	public school
kansalliskirkkokunta*	kan-sal-lis/kirk-ko/kun-ta	
kirkkokunta = parish, thus—a parish of the national church
kansalliskokouksia*	kan-sal-lis/ko-kouk-sia	
kokouksia = meetings, thus—national (peoples') meetings
kantele	kan-te-le	ancient musical instrument
kapina	ka-pi-na	mutiny
Karhumaa*	Kar-hu/maa	name, karhu = bear, maa = land
Karoliina	Ka-ro-lii-na	a girl's name
Kauppinen	Kaup-pi-nen	a name
kesä	ke-sä	summer
kesäjuhlakulkue*	ke-sä/juh-la/kul-ku-e	
kulkue = parade, thus—summer festival parade
Ketola	Ke-to-la	a name, keto =field of grass
kilpi	kil-pi	shield
kiltti	kilt-ti	well-behaved
kirkko	kirk-ko	church
kirkkomies*	kirk-ko/mies	a man (or woman) on the way to or coming from church
kiuas	kiu-as	small stones on sauna heater
Kivijärvi	Ki-vi/jär-vi	town in Finland—Stone Lake
kokko	kok-ko	Midsummer Day bonfire
koko	ko-ko	entire, whole, all
kokoon	ko-koon	"into a heap"
Kolehmainen	Ko-leh-mai-nen	a name
Koskinen	Kos-ki-nen	a name, koski = rapids
koti	ko-ti	home
kova	ko-va	hard
kovaa Norja	ko-vaa Nor-ja	a card game, hard Norway
Kukoistus	Ku-kois-tus	The Blossoming**
Kultala	Kul-ta-la	The Treasure**
kunta	kun-ta	parish, county
Kupari Russu	Ku-pa-ri Ruu-su	Copper Rose**
Kurikka	Ku-rik-ka	a name, kurikka = club
kyllä	kyl-lä	yes
kypsymäton	kyp-sy-mä-ton	immature, not ripe
kämppä	kämp-pä	camp

L

Laaksonkukka	Laak-son/kuk-ka	Flower of the Valley**
Laitinen	Lai-ti-nen	a name
laitos	lai-tos	establishment

lakko	lak-ko	strike
lapsia	lap-si-a	children
launantai	lau-an-tai	Saturday
lauantaikaakku*	lau-an-tai/kaak-ku	extra-special coffee buns
Leivo	Lei-vo	name of a Gardner choir
liike	lii-ke	business
liitto	liit-to	league, association
limppu	limp-pu	rye bread
lisää	li-sää	some more
loistoaika*	lois-to/ai-ka	golden age—hey day
Luoma-Aho	Lou-ma-A-ho	a little village in Finland
Luoto	Luo-to	a name, Luoto = craggy islets
Luukkonen	Luuk-ko-nen	a name
lännen	län-nen	western
Lännen Rusko	Län-nen Rus-ko	Western Glow*
Lännen Tähti	Län-nen Täh-ti	Western Star*
Lännen Täimi	Län-nen Täi-mi	Western Seed (Sapling)**
löyly	löy-ly	"steam" caused by throwing water on the sauna "kiuas" or, the heat of a sauna
löylyä	löy-ly-ä	accusative case of löyly

M

Manninen	Man-ni-nen	a name
Marjatta	Mar-jat-ta	a girl's name
mehiläinen	me-hi-läi-nen	honeybee
meille	meil-le	me = we, meille = to us
merirosvot*	me-ri/ros-vot	pirates
minkämöinen	min-kä-möi-nen	what kind, of what nature
mustikka	mus-tik-ka	blueberry
mustikkamies*	mus-tik-ka/mies	blueberryman (mies = man)
myrsky	myr-sky	storm
Mäkelä	Mä-ke-lä	a name
Mäki	Mä-ki	a name, mäki = hill

N

nenä	ne-nä	nose
nenästä	ne-näs-tä	from the nose, by the nose
neula	neu-la	needle
Niemi	Nie-mi	a name, niemi = peninsula
Niemen Kukka	Nie-men Kuk-ka	Flower of the Cape**
Niemen Ruusu	Nie-men Ruu-su	Rose of the Cape**
niin	niin	so, is that so
niin ja näin	niin ja näin	so so, fairly well
Norja	Nor-ja	Norway
Nurmi	Nur-mi	a name, nurmi = green lawn
Nylander	Ny-lan-der	a name
näyttämö	naÿt-tä-mö	little theatre

O

oikea	*oi-ke-a*	right, correct, just
oikein	*oi-kein*	in the right way
Oikemus	*Oi-ke-mus*	a name
Oinanen	*Oi-na-nen*	a name
olleet	*ol-leet*	past tense of *olla* = to be
olemme olleet	*o-lem-me ol-leet*	we have been
oletteko olleet	*o-let-te-ko ol-leet*	have you been
oli	*o-li*	it was
on	*on*	it is
Onnen Aika	*On-nen Ai-ka*	Lucky Times*
opisto	*o-pis-to*	school, academy, college
osasto	*o-sas-to*	section, branch
*osuuskauppa**	*o-suus/kaup-pa*	cooperative store
osuusruokala/	*o-suus/ruo-ka-la*	cooperative boardinghouse
Oulu	*Ou-lu*	a large city on Finland

P

Paapanen	*Paa-pa-nen*	a name
paimen	*pai-men*	shepherd
pehmeä	*peh-me-ä*	soft
Pekkonen	*Pek-ko-nen*	a name
Pennanen	*Pen-na-nen*	a name
Penttinen	*Pent-ti-nen*	a name
Perintö	*Pe-rin-tö*	The Legacy**
pesä	*pe-sä*	nest, fire chamber
*Pieksämäki**	*Piek-sä/mä-ki*	a city in Finland
pieni	*pie-ni*	small
*pikkuporvari**	*pik-ku/por-va-ri*	petty bourgeoisie
piru	*pi-ru*	the devil
pirun	*pi-run*	the devil's
pitkä	*pit-kä*	long
pohja	*poh-ja*	bottom, foundation
Pohja	*Poh-ja*	as used in *Kalevala*: north
pohjala	*poh-ja-la*	the North
*pohjoisamerikkalainen**	*poh-jois/a-me-rik-ka-lai-nen*	
North-American		
poika	*poi-ka*	boy
*poikatalo**	*poi-ka/ta-lo*	*a bachelor's home*
Poikonen	*Poi-ko-nen*	a name
pojat	*po-jat*	boys
porvaristo	*por-va-ris-to*	the bourgeoisie
Pöyhönen	*Pöy-hö-nen*	a name
pulla	*pul-la*	coffee twist
Pulliainen	*Pul-li-ai-nen*	a name
Puotinen	*Puo-ti-nen*	a name
puhutko	*pu-hut-ko*	do you speak
Puranen	*Pu-ra-nen*	a name
Puustinen	*Puus-ti-nen*	a name, *puusto* = stand of trees
Pyrintö	*Py-rin-tö*	The Endeavor**

R

raaka	*raa-ka*	raw, immature
*raittiusseura**	*rait-tius/seu-ra*	temperance society
Raivaaja	*Rai-vaa-ja*	Finnish-American daily
Rauhan Aarre	*Rau-han Aar-re*	A Treasure of Peace**
Rauhan Vesa	*Rau-han Ve-sa*	Peaceful Beginning**
reikäleipä	*rei-kä-/lei-pä*	a Finnish rye bread
Riika	*Rii-ka*	a girl's name
runo	*ru-no*	poem
runot	*ru-not*	poems
ruokala	*ruo-ka-la*	boardinghouse

S

Saaren Kukka	*Saa-ren Kuk-ka*	Island Flower**
*saippuakivikauppias** lye merchant	*saip-pu-a/ki-vi/kaup-pi-as*	
Salminen	*Sal-mi-nen*	a name, *salmi* = strait
*Salojärvi**	*Sa-lo/jär-vi*	*salo* = backwoods, *järvi* = lake
Sampo	*Sam-po*	magic mill (Finnish mythology)
sanomia	*sa-no-mi-a*	news, tidings
sauna	*sau-na*	bathhouse
saunaomaan	*sau-na-o-maan*	to take a sauna
savu	*sa-vu*	smoke
*savusauna**	*sa-vu/sau-na*	"smoke" sauna
setä	*se-tä*	father's brother (see *eno*)
sisu	*si-su*	intestinal fortitude, "guts"
Sointula	*Soin-tu-la*	Harmony
*sosiaalidemokraati**	*so-si-aa-li/de-mok-raa-ti*	social democrat
sosialisti	*so-si-a-lis-ti*	socialist
*sosialistijärestö**	*so-si-a-lis-ti/jär-jes-tö*	socialist group
*sosialistipuolue**	*so-si-a-lis-ti/puo-lu-e*	Socialist Party
Sovinto	*So-vin-to*	Harmony**
sovittaja	*so-vit-ta-ja*	conciliator, arbitrator
sumppi	*sump-pi*	"secondhand" coffee
Suominen	*Suo-mi-nen*	a name
suomalainen	*suo-ma-lai-nen*	a Finn
Suomi	*Suo-mi*	Finland
surma	*sur-ma*	forceful death
Suuronen	*Suu-ro-nen*	a name

T

talkoo	*tal-koo*	a work bee
talo	*ta-lo*	house
tiedän	*tie-dän*	I know, from *tietää*
Tissari	*Tis-sa-ri*	a name
tippa	*tip-pa*	a drop
tippaakaan	*tip-paa-kaan*	not even a drop
toiskieliset	*tois-kie-li-set*	foreigners
Toivon Tähti	*Toi-von Täh-ti*	Star of Hope**
Tokoi	*To-koi*	a name

tosisuomalaiset*	to-si/suo-ma-lai-set	true Finns
tosisuomalaisliitto*	to-si-/suo-ma-lais/liit-to	association of trus Finns
toveri	to-ve-ri	friend, comrade
tulkaa	tul-kaa	come; imperative of *tulla*
tunnustanut	tun-nus-ta-nut	recognized
tuska	tus-ka	pain, ache
Tupsunperä*	Tup-sun/pe-rä	End of the tassel
tyttö	tyt-tö	girl
tyttöjä	tyt-tö-jä	girls
Tyven Satama	Ty-ven Sa-ta-ma	Peaceful Harbor**
Tyyne	Tyy-ne	a girl's name
työmies	työ-mies	a workingman
työväen	työ-väen	workingmen's
työväenliitto*	työ-väen/liit-to	workers' association
työväentalo*	työ-väen/ta-lo	labor temple, workers' hall
työväentemppeli*	työ-väen/temp-pe-li	labor temple
työväenyhdistys*	työ-väen/yh-dis-tys	workingmen's association
Tähti	Täh-ti	The Star**
tana vuonna	ta-na vuon-na	this year

U

uida	ui-da	swim
ukko	uk-ko	old man
Ukko	Uk-ko	top god of Finnish mythology
Uljas Koitto	Ul-jas Koit-to	The Valiant Attempt**
uusi	uu-si	new

V

vaan	vaan	but
vaka	va-ka	usually "steadfast," but I think "lusty" is better
vakaa	va-kaa	steadfast
Valkoruusu*	Val-ko/ruu-su	White Rose**
valo	va-lo	light such as given by sun
Valon Kipinä	Va-lon Ki-pi-nä	Glowing Spark**
Valon Leimu	Va-lon Lei-mu	The Glowing Light**
Valon Lähde	Va-lon Läh-de	The Fountain of Light**
Valon Säde	Va-lon Sä-de	A Ray of Light**
vanha	van-ha	old
vasemmistolainen	va-sem-mis-to-lai-nen	a political term which means left-wing sympathizer
vasta	vas-ta	sauna whisk
vesiosakekaupan*	ve-si/o-sa-ke/kau-pan	sale of "watered" stock
vihta	vih-ta	*vihta* = *vasta*, see *vasta*
virolainen	vi-ro-lai-nen	Esthonian
viulu	viu-lu	violin
voi	voi	butter
voi! voi!	voi! voi!	an interjection: alas!
Voiton Lippu	Voi-ton Lip-pu	The Victorious Banner**
vuonna	vuon-na	a form of *vousi* = year
vuori	vou-ri	mountain

235

Vuoriston Ilo	*Vuo-ris-ton I-lo*	A Mountain of Joy**
Vuoriston Ruusu	*Vuo-ris-ton Rus-su*	The Mountain Rose**
Vuoriston Toivo	*Vuo-ris-ton Toi-vo*	A Mountain of Joy**
*Vuorentakana**	*Vuo-ren/ta-ka-na*	The other side of the mountain
Väinämöinen	*Väi-nä-möi-nen*	hero of *Kaelvala*, pagan god
Väinölä	*Väi-nö-lä*	*Väinölä = Kaleva*

W

Walkonen	*Val-ko-nen*	a name, *valkonen* = white

Y

yhdistys	*yh-dis-tys*	association, union
*Yhdysvallat**	*Yh-dys/val-lat*	United States
*Yhdysvaltion**	*Yh-dys/val-tion*	genitive case of United States
*yksimielisyys**	*yk-si/mie-li/syys*	unanimity, harmony
*Yksimielisyys**	*Yk-si/mie-li/syys*	Harmony**
yö	*yö*	night
*yöpöllö**	*yö/pöl-lö*	night owl

Ä

äiti	*äi-ti*	mother
äyri	*äy-ri*	Scandinavian coin

Ö

öisin	*öi-sin*	at night
öylätti	*öy-lät-ti*	consecrated wafer

NOTES, VIEWS AND VIGNETTES

Note A: The basic source materials that provided me with information about Finnish-American history are Sulkanen, Elis, *Amerikan Suomalaisen Työväenliikkeen Historia* (Fitchburg, Mass: The Raivaaja Publishing Co., 1951) and Syrjala, Frans J., *Historia-aiheita Amerikan Suomalaisesta Työväenliikkeesta* (Fitchburg Mass: Finnish Socialist Publishing Co., 1923). Both books are written in Finnish. Their titles in English are, respectively, *History of the Finnish-American Labor Movement* and *Historical Glimpses of the Finnish-American Labor Movement*.

1. *Page 2 Louis Adamic:* See Adamic, Louis, *From Many Lands* (New York: Harper & Brothers, 1940). *From Many Lands* is an excellent study of our various ethnic groups. Mr. Adamic, however, ignored the Finnish-American labor movement and he spent too much time in his Finnish-American section writing about a Finn who Anglicized his name. Not many first generation Finns did that.

2. *Page 2 Finnish-American story:* Three books (in English) about Finnish-Americans that I recommend are: Karni, Michael G., (Editor) *For the Common Good* (Superior, Wisconsin: Tyomies Society, 1977); Niitemaa, Vilho (Editor), *Old Friends, Strong Ties*, (Turku, Finland: Institute for Migration, 1976); Ross, Carl, *The Finn Factor* (New York Mills, Minnesota: Parta Printers, Inc., 1977).

3. *Page 4 Children in Brazil:* See *Brazil's Wasted Generation* in *Time* magazine, September 11, 1978.

4. *Page 4 Socialism:* I have defined the concept of *socialism* by listing 12 attributes of a socialist society in Chapter 11.

5. *Page 6 Karl Kautsky:* Karl Kautsky, who may have been the most widely-read socialist writer in the Finnish-American circles, opposed the granting of war credits to the German Kaiser. This opposition to the First World War endeared him to the Finnish-American socialists who also opposed participation in that war.

   Kautsky (1854-1938), a German historian, was a friend and disciple of Karl Marx. Before the Russian Revolution he was regarded as one of the foremost interpreters of Karl Marx. His refusal to support the Bolshevik Revolution, however, earned him the titles of *revisionist* and *reformer*. His writings were not translated after 1920 by the Finnish-American leftists. He still remained popular, however, in the Finnish Socialist Federation in New England.

   Kautsky, after World War I, directed the activities of the Austrian Socialist Party. He fled Austria when the Nazis invaded the country in 1938 and died in poverty in the Netherlands six months later.

6. *Page 7 dialectical materialism:* My impression of dialectical materialism is given in Chapter 11.

7. *Page 7 Edward Bellamy:* The novel *Looking Backward* by Edward Bellamy stimulated the growth of the Nationalist clubs whose main program was the nationalization of industry. Pages 161-162 have more information about Bellamy and *Looking Backward*. Bellamy, Edward, *Looking Backward* (Boston: Houghton, Mifflin Co., 1926).

8. *Page 7 Kalevala:* Two good English translations of Kalevala are Kirby, W.F., *Kalevala* (New York: Everyman's Library, 1907) and Magoun, Frances Peabody Jr., *Kalevala* (Cambridge, Mass: Harvard University Press, 1963).

Elias Lönnrot, a scholar of purely Finnish origin even though he had a Swedish surname (see discussion about Finnish names in chapter 7) was the compiler of Kalevala. He began to collect old Finnish poetry to save that poetry from oblivion in 1828. His first publication was *Kantele*. Kantele is the name of the Finnish musical instrument used by the *runo* (poem) singers to accompany themselves when they sang their poems.

According to Bjorn Collinder, Elias Lönnrot knew after his fifth trip into Karelia that he had enough material to compose an epic poem. Lönnrot finished the Kalevala preface on February 28, 1835. That date is now *Kalevala Day*, a national holiday, in Finland. See Collinder, Bjorn, *The Kalevala and Its Background* (Stockholm: Almquist & Wiksell, 1964), pages 10 and 11.

9. *Page 8 Robert Ingersoll:* I am quoting the famous turn-of-the-century agnostic. There's more about Robert Ingersoll later.

10. *Page 9 Thomas Paine:* The quote is from Paine, Thomas, *Age of Reason* (New York: Books Inc., Art-Type edition), page 4.

11. *Page 9 Finno-Ugric:*

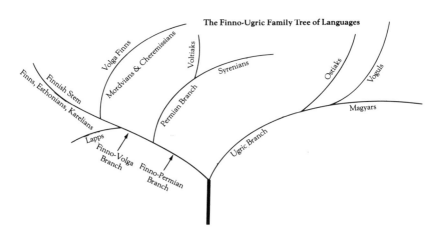

A figure similar to the one above appears in Wargelin, John, *The Americanization of the Finns* (Hancock, Michigan: The Finnish-American Book Concern, 1924), page 25. Mr. Wargelin gave his source as *Tietosanakirja*, Volume IX, page 482 (a Finnish encyclopedia). I have modified the diagram by placing the Magyars on the main stem of the Ugric branch. I have also included the Karelians in the Finnish stem.

1910 Finno-Ugric Population Table

Chermissians	375,400
Esthonians	1,007,400
Finns	3,346,852
Magyars	8,892,300
Karelians	229,800
Lapps	29,800
Livonians	3,000
Mordvians	1,023,900
Ostiaks	18,000

Syrenians	258,300
Vespas	25,500
Voguls	5,000
Votiaks	421,000

This 1910 Finno-Ugric Population Table is from *Tietosanakirja*, Volume IX, pages 286-289 as given by Dr. Wargelin, page 26.

The Encyclopedia Britannica in its 1959 edition has about the same population figures. This encyclopedia states that Mordvians, Cheremiss, Votiaks and Syrenians have been given the right to use their own languages in their schools and in their press.

Dr. Wargelin commented, "Many of these tribes are nearly extinct or are fast disappearing—(especially) the Votes, Livonians, Voguls and Ostiaks. Others are subject to disappearance because of their small numbers (Vespas and Lapps)...Only the Finns, Magyars and Esthonians have become thoroughly civilized...the other tribes are partly nomads, living to some extent on reindeer, agriculture, fishing and hunting." See Wargelin, pages 26 and 27.

I note that the first Finns were converted to Roman Catholicism in 1157 by a crusade led by King Eric IX of Sweden. The Finns, however, relapsed into paganism and had to be compelled to accept Christianity again in 1249.

12. *Page 12 kokko:* The following conversation between a farmer and his hired hand is worth repeating. I leave it to you to interpret. It does make sense.
    farmer: "Kokoo koko kokko kokoon."
    hired man: "Koko kokkoko kokoon?"
    farmer: "Koko kokko kokoon."

13. *Page 14 blueberry soup:* Here is *Äiti's* recipe for blueberry soup.

2 cups water	1 stick cinnamon
3 Tbsp. potato starch	3 Tbsp. sugar
2 cups fresh blueberries	3 Tbsp. cold water

    Be sure to use potato starch, not corn starch. Bring the water to a boil. Add blueberries, cinnamon and sugar. Make a smooth paste with the potato starch and cold water. Add the potato starch paste after the blueberries have cooked about 10 minutes. Add the paste slowly, though; stirring the potato starch paste into the boiling soup. Cook 2 minutes more, or until the soup is thickened. Cool quickly. Serve the soup chilled.

14. *Page 15 blueberry pilgrimage:* My knowledge of the blueberry's role in Finnish-American life was much more limited in the 1920's than it is today. In 1969, quite by accident, I was present at a blueberry festival in Iron River, Wisconsin. The festivities, which I assumed honored or paid homage to the blueberry, included a parade. My biggest disappointment occurred when I discovered that the grand marshall's auto was not occupied by a Big Blue Blueberry.

    Alice, my wife, who is not of Finnish descent, does not believe we were in that locality by chance. Alice claims, when she is in her radical mood, that *Blueberry Power* attracted me to Iron River that day. When Alice is in her religious mood, however, she attributes our presence to the *Finnish Blueberry Mystique.*

239

15. *Page 15 Finnish berries:* An English woman, Mrs. E. Alec Tweedie, traveled through Finland by carts in 1898. She listed in her book the berries she was served fresh, in soups, or in puddings. The list, including the comments, was compiled by Mrs. Tweedie.

Finnish	Latin	Comment
mansikka	*fragraria vesca*	wild strawberries, found everywhere in abundance
mesikka	*rubus arcticus*	red, with splendid aroma, liquer is made from them
vaatukka	*rubus idaeus*	wild raspberry
lakka	*rubus chamaemorus*	black. often made into a kind of black juice, and taken as sweet soup.
mustikka	*vaccinium myrtillus*	(wortleberries) black. often made into a soup of a glorious color.
puolukka	*vaccinium vitis idaea*	(red wortleberry) like a small cranberry, eaten with meat.
herukka	*ribes nigrum*	currant
juolukka	*vaccinium uliginosum*	a common black kind of berry, not very edible.
karpaloja	*vaccinium occycoccus*	...it grows in the autumn under the snow, where it ripens, and is ready to be picked in spring when the snow melts.
suomuurain	(Latin name omitted)	In appearance it is like a yellow raspberry. It is a most delicious fruit, with a pine-tree flavour.

Note that only the blueberry *(mustikka)* grows on a high bush. Thus the evidence is very strong that *Marjatta* was enticed to eat a blueberry.

Mrs. Tweedie's narrative is very exciting because it pictures Finland at the time the first generation Finnish-Americans emigrated. Tweedie, Mrs. E. Alec, *Through Finland in Carts* (New York: The Macmillan Company, 1898), pages 32-33.

16. *Page 16 Gates Hill:* Our pronunciation of Gates Hill was *Gateseas Hill.* Gates Pond was *Gateseas Pond.* Our pronunciation was influenced by our parents who continually converted English words into Finglish. Come to think of it we, the second generation, helped them in the process.

17. *Page 17 Finglish:* Professor Nisonen, a former professor at Suomi College, Hancock (Michigan), is said to have labelled American and Canadian Finnish as *Finglish.* The Finglish language is more than a vocabulary of words borrowed from English. The structure, the syntax used in Finglish is more English than Finnish. See discussion of Finnish and Finglish in Mencken, H.L., *The American Language* (New York: Alfred A. Knopf, 1937), pages 675-680.

The classic Finglish sentence, *"Pussaa peipipoki kitsista petiruumaan"* is there. (Push the baby buggy from the kitchen into the bedroom.)

18. *Page 23 disappointed...Mr. Gates:* If Mr. Gates had known that fifty years later his granddaughter would marry *Isä's* grandson, I'm sure that I would have gotten a glimpse of the "fabulous interior" and *Isä* would have received some good Yankee refreshments. But who has such foresight?

240

19. *Page 26 sweat...blueberries:* Blueberries lose their sheen when handled too much. The loss of the sheen gives them the appearance of being *wet*.

20. *Page 32 La Tourraine:* La Tourraine, the coffee with the French name, was the New England Finns' favorite coffee in the 1920's. La Tourraine was packed as a whole bean coffee in a screw-top tin can. When purchased, the grocer (there was no self-service those days) would set the coffee grinder to the desired grind, pour the whole beans into the grinder hopper, set the empty can under the spout, turn on the grinder, wait, and, finally, screw the top back onto the can which now contained the ground coffee.

21. *Page 42 häkä:* My Finnish-English dictionary translates *häkä* as *carbon monoxide* gas without any particular reference to a sauna. Perhaps the word is not used in Finland in the same sense it was used in the New England Finnish-American community in the 1920's.

22. *Page 48 coffee drinking custom:* Mrs. Alec Tweedie in her 1989 book *Through Finland in Carts* describes a scene in a Finnish play, *Anna Liisa*, that she saw in Sordavala in 1898, "...and like true peasants they poured the coffee in a saucer, and putting a bit of sugar in their mouths drank the beverage through it, supporting the saucer on five fingers..." See **15**.

23. *Page 58 lack of interest in the church:* Wargelin, Raymond W., *Finnish Lutherans in Canada*, an essay in *The Faith if the Finns*, edited by Jalkanen, Ralph J., (Michigan State University Press, 1972), page 131.

24. *Page 59 A more dangerous enemy:* Kohlemainen, John I., *The Finns in America* (New York City: Teachers College Press, Columbia University, 1968), page 21.

25. *Page 59 illiteracy rate:* It is my understanding that the Lutheran Church of Finland would not allow an illiterate person to be married. I have not verified if this excellent prerequisite for matrimony was actually enforced.

26. *Page 59 catapulted into the starless night:* Kolehmainen, John I., *Sow the Golden Seed* (Fitchburg, Mass: The Raivaaja Publishing Co. 1955), page

27. *Page 60 spread like wildfire...Robert Ingersoll's writings:* See Kolehmainen, pages 13-14. See **26**.

28. *Page 60 The Lutheran Church Confiscates the Family Cow:* At least two other second generation Finns have told me that they, too, heard a similar story.

29. *Page 61 Doctrine is pure:* The Rev. Juho Nikander quotation is given in an essay by Ollila, Douglas J., *The Suomi Synod: 1890-1920*. Dr. Ollila's footnotes refers the reader to the November 13, 1899 issue of *Paimen Sanomia*. The essay is in the *Faith of the Finns*. See **23**.

30. *Page 66 Puotinen quote:* Puotinen, Arthur E., *Ameliorative Factors in the Suomi Synod-Socialist Movement Conflict*, an essay in *The Faith of the Finns*, page 230. See **23**.

   I failed to find, in spite of the title of the essay, a single example of an ameliorative factor (in the conflict between Finnish socialists and Lutherans) given in the essay.

31. *Page 67 age of earth:* The scientists today claim the earth is more than 4 billion years old.

32. *Page 68 John Stuart Mill:* The English philosopher John Stuart Mill wrote at least three essays on religion. My quote is from the *Utility of Religion*. See Marshall, Cotten, *The Philosophy of John Stuart Mill* (New York: The

Modern Library, 1961), page 517.

33. *Page 69 Darrow Debate:* I have been unable to verify that Clarence Darrow was the negative protagonist in the debate. The story of the debate is, however, in the Darrow spirit. See Darrow, Clarence Seward, *The Story of My Life* (New York: Grosset & Dunlap, 1957).

34. *Page 71 Havumaki:* Axel Havumaki lived in the little village of Pitcherville in Hubbardston. All the residents of Pitcherville were Finnish. I always thought his wife Dorothy was Finnish, too, because she socialized and mixed so well with the first generation Finns. I even saw Dorothy Havumaki play the coffee game I mentioned in Chapter 3, just as if she was descended from Finnish peasants. Later, however, I discovered she was born Dorothy Greenwood, a descendant of an old Yankee family.

"I learned to speak the Finnish language even before I met Axel because all my neighbors were Finnish," Mrs. Havumaki wrote me. Axel and Dorothy visited Finland in 1960. Axel said his wife had to translate his Finglish into Finnish for him. She had become more proficient in Finnish than he.

35. *Page 72 Polish limppu:* I asked Victor Starzynski for the recipe for his father's *Polish limppu.* Here is his reply:

Dear Reino,

I was very glad to hear from you as it brought back pleasant memories to me about how I found the soda bottle and my fond thoughts of the Hannula boardinghouse where I delivered bread for years.

I would gladly give you the formula for Starzynski's bread but I'm sure it will be hard to understand because basically it's a *one-man* operation. But I'll try and you can use it any way you want to.

#1. We had a *sour* fermenting for the 49 years we ran the bakery. I don't know where it came from originally. The *sour* is the key. You "had to understand it" and feed it 3 times a day with rye flour or it would rot and spoil.

#2. We scalded rye flour in boiling water to make a smooth mixture of pasted consistency which after being cooled was the *food* for the sour.

#3. We now mixed the sour and cooled "food" together in a wooden tub and let it ferment for about 8 hours. You knew it was ready when it started to drop in the wooden bucket.

#4. Now we mixed the fermented mixture with 100 pounds of rye flour plus 1 measure of salt and made the dough.

#5. We let this set for about 3/4 hour and then we moulded it by hand to the desired size and weight.

#6. We let this shaped dough rise until it was double size. We then washed the top with a mixture of rye flour and water. We baked it in a brick oven which had lots of steam. The steam was used so the bread would get wet and not crack until the heat stopped our sour from working.

I hope this helps you. Good luck on your narrative.

As Ever,
Victor Starzynski

36. *Page 73 kalja:* The following appears on pages 31 and 32 in *Through Finland in Carts.* See *15.*

"There are two special drinks in Finland—one for the rich and the other for the poor.

"*Mjod* (the drink for the rich) is one of the most delicious beverages imaginable. It is not champagne, and not a cider, but a sort of effervescing drink of pale yellow color. . .

"The other drink is called in Swedish *Svagdricka*, but as it is really a peasant drink, and the peasants speak Finnish, it is generally known as *kalja*. . .It looks black, and is really small beer. Very small indeed it is, too, with a nasty burnt taste, and the natives up-country all make it for themselves, each farm having half a dozen or twenty hop poles of its own, which flavours the *kalja* for the whole party for a year, so its strength of hop or amount of bubble is not very great."

37. *Page 75 non-religious funeral:* I mentioned *Isä's* non-religious funeral only because there was a tremendous uproar when the first American Finn, Pekka Heikkila was buried (in Worcester, Mass.) "without benefit of clergy." Sulkanen, page 78. See Note **A.**

38. *Page 75 translated works:* Robert Blatchford was an English socialist who claimed environment, not heredity, was the basic cause of criminal behavior. John Spargo was an American socialist writer who wrote popular accounts of socialist doctrines. His books usually went through many editions. There is more about Edward Bellamy later.

39. *Page 76 befuddled by heady material:* Kohlehmainen, page 15. See **26.**

40. *Page 76 Ingersoll:* Colonel Robert G. Ingersoll may have been the greatest orator in the United States. He certainly was the greatest orator in the years 1880 to 1900. My favorite lectures—which, of course, I have read only as essays—are *Some Mistakes of Moses* and *What We Can Do To Be Saved.*

Robert Ingersoll was also the foremost American authority on the Scottish poet Robert Burns. A poem, a tribute to Burns, written by Ingersoll is at the entrance to Robert Burns' birthplace. Ingersoll was also an authority on William Shakespeare, Thomas Paine, and Alexander Humboldt, the German scientist.

Robert Ingersoll was undoubtedly the most widely-read religious writer among the American Finns from 1906 to 1920.

41. *Page 76 Robert LaFollette:* The quote by Senator LaFollette appears on the jacket of Volume II of *The Works of Robert G. Ingersoll* (New York: The Ingersoll League, 1900).

42. *Page 77 Robert Ingersoll. . .tenets:* Ingersoll taught "Happiness is the only good. The time to be happy is now. The way to be happy is to help make others happy."

43. *Page 91 reikäleipä:* Here is a recipe for *reikäleipä,* the Finnish rye bread with a hole in the center. Be sure to punch that hole in the center—like the hole in a doughnut—about 1½ inches in diameter for an eight inch circular loaf. The recipe was sent to me by Carl (Kaarlo) Poikonen who was one of the last master Finnish bakers in New England. Carl, a second generation Finn, a Gates Hill blueberry picker, retired in 1977. (Note: *Reikäleipä* was sometimes called *Republican bread* because it was considered to be good enough for even a Republican.)

Recipe for Reikäleipä

Ingredients
2 tablespoons of sugar (one ounce)
2 tablespoons of salt (one ounce)
2½ ounces of yeast (two cakes)
1 ounce of shortening (oleo, or butter)
1 lb. 2 oz. of rye meal (rye flour)
1 qt. skim milk (warm)
White flour as needed
Note: The dough should be made on the stiff side.
1. Put about ½ cup of warm milk, pinch of sugar, and the yeast in a bowl, set in a warm place.
2. Mix the rye flour and sugar wuth the rest of the milk.
3. When the yeast has begun to rise, add it to the rye flour-sugar milk mixture and set in a warm place covered. Wait until it has doubled in bulk (about 45 minutes).
4. Add the rest of the salt, shortening (oleo or butter). Add white flour (hi-gluten if available) until the mixture is firm enough. Roll out onto a floured board and knead, adding white flour until the dough is elastic (knead at least 15 minutes—you can't knead the dough too much).
5. Place in a lightly oiled bowl. Cover with a towel and let the dough rise in a warm place until it is double in bulk. Punch it down and let it rise until it doubles again.
6. Punch it down again. Form into 2 or 3 loaves of whatever shape you desire. (Finnish *reikäleipä* is always circular with a hole punched out in the center.) Place the loaves on a bake sheet which has been sprinkled with corn meal. Cover the loaves.
7. Let the loaves rise until they are about the size you want. Bake in an oven preheated to 350° for about 50 minutes to one hour.
8. Cool on cooling racks.

44. *Page 95 Wheelwright:* John Brooks Wheelwright is gaining recognition as a part of "great intellectual excitement." There is a book of his poems edited by Rosenfeld, Alvin H., *Collected Poems of John Wheelwright* (New York: New Directions Publishing Corporation, 1972). He is aso discussed in a book by Dr. Warren Austin who labels Wheelwright as a New England Saint. See Austin, Warren, *New England Saints* (Ann Arbor, Michigan: The University of Michigan Press, 1956).

I regret that I was unable to find anyone to give me permission to quote some of Wheelwright's poetry. John Brooks Wheelwright was killed by a speeding truck near Boston Commons in 1940.

45. *Page 97 anti-communist parody:* The communist movement was in the midst of a major policy change at this time, a change almost as extreme as the flip-flop that occurred when the Nazi-Soviet pact was signed. The new line of the communists called for the liberals and even socialists (whom they had labelled as *social-fascists* for years) to join with the communists in a common effort to stop the rise of fascism. The most successful *United Front*, as these common efforts were called, was in France where Leon Blum, a social democrat, was elected prime minister of France.

Browder in the parody is Earl Browder, head of the Communist Party in the 1930's. Ford, a Moscow-educated American black, was the Communist vice-presidential candidate in 1932. Father Devine was at the peak of his religious career at this time. I give the parody from memory

Our Line's Been Changed Again

The Negro masses jilted Ford.
Our Line's been changed again.
Father Devine is now the lord.
Our line's been changed again.
  Chorus:
I knows it, Browder.
I knows it, Browder.
I knows it Browder,
Our line's been changed again.

United fronts are what we love
Our line's been changed again.
From below and from above
Our line's been changed again.
  Chorus:

First we're red, then we're green.
Our line's been changed again.
Kaleidoscopic's what I mean.
Our Line's been changed again.
  Chorus.

46. *Page 97 John Reed:* John Reed was an American journalist and socialist who died of typhoid fever while covering the Russian Revolution. His account of the Bolshevik uprising against the provisonal government is a radical classic. See Reed, John, *Ten Days That Shook The World* (New York: The Modern Library, 1935).

47. *Page 98 Comes the Revolution:* John Brooks Wheelwright was giving the punch line of an old joke dear to the hearts of all socialists in the 1930's. The story goes somewhat as follows:

It seems there was an old socialist soapboxer who spoke each night on a Hester Street street corner in New York City's lower East Side, One night he harangued,

"Comrades, what do the rich eat?...Strawberries mit cream! What do the workers eat? Herring.

"Comes the revolution, the workers will eat strawberries mit cream. And the rich? The rich will eat herring."

A poorly-dressed worker interrupted the speaker. "Mr. Speaker! Mr. Speaker! I don't want to eat strawberries mit cream! I get the hives when I eat strawberries."

The speaker was *not* non-plussed. He replied, "Comes the revolution, comrade, you'll eat strawberries mit cream. The rich will get the hives!"

Note: My only comment is: How times have changed! Only the rich can afford herring today, but all of us can afford strawberries.

48. *Page 103 palindromes:* Here is a Finnish palindrome sentence. *Nisumaa oli Isäsi ilo aamusin.* The sentence makes sense, too. It states: The field of wheat was your father's joy in the morning.

For more information about palindromes see Bergman, Dimitri A.,

245

Language on Vacation (New York: Charles Scribner's Sons, 1965) and his *Beyond Language* (New York:Charles Scribner's Sons, 1965). Another good book is Jacobs, Noah Jonathon, *Naming Day in Eden* (New York: Macmillan, 1958).

49. *Page 104 Alfred Baker Lewis:* Alfred Baker Lewis is one of the most impressive men I have ever known. He always works hard for causes he believes in, contributing his time and money. The last I saw him (in 1940) he was speaking from a soapbox on the corner of 8th Street and 6th Avenue in Greenwich Village (New York City) under the auspices of the *Committee to Defend America by Aiding the Allies.* Mr. Lewis is now over 85 years of age. I asked him to contribute a message via my book. Here it is:

"Every company tries to maximize its profits. To do that they have to cut costs. Usually the largest single item of cost is labor. So they try especially hard to cut their labor costs.

"But labor is not just a cost of production. It is also, taken as a whole, the biggest single source of purchasing power. In exact proportion as they succeed in cutting their labor costs, they reduce the purchasing power of the great mass of people who are workers. That is why capitalism is so inefficient and operates at far less than the capacity for full production which our technological ability makes possible."

Yours for racial and economic justice
Alfred Baker Lewis
National Treasurer Emeritus of the NAACP

50. *Page 110 Sibelius, Topelius:* I have been unable to verify that these names are Latin. My only source of information about their Latin origin is from conversations with some first generation Finnish-American friends of my youth.

51. *Page 125 Solidarity Forever:* This song, which is the unofficial anthem of the American labor movement, was written by Ralph Chaplin, an IWW leader. See Chaplin, Ralph, *Wobbly* (Chicago: 1948). The complete song can be found in Kornbluh, Joyce L., *Rebel Voices—An IWW Anthology* (Ann Arbor: The University of Michigan Press, 1972).

52. *Page 128 What's taking him so long:* The sale of alcoholic beverages was prohibited at this time by the Eighteenth Amendment.

53. *Page 129 anti-picketing injunction:* Cesar Chavez, who organizes farm workers on one of the salients of fiefdom left in the United States, is continually faced with the same dilemma that was faced by the Gardner workers in 1935. Judges, knowing very well that a higher court will overturn their injunctions, still issue orders banning all picketing by his union in many strikes. The strike, however, will be lost before the higher court can act so Chavez has no recourse but to show his contempt for such judges by defying their injunctions. Cesar usually has to go to jail. See Chavez, Cesar, *Cesar Chavez Goes Home Again and Finds Himself Decidedly Unwelcome* (Los Angeles Times, Sunday, June 25, 1978), Part IV, Page 3.

54. *Page 132 first Finns in Gardner:* Sulkanen, pages 384-391. See Note **A**.

55. *Page 136 Saima Labor Society ritual:* Sulkanen, pages 58-60 and Syrjala, pages 35-36. See Note **A**.

56. *Page 138 A Storm hits Rockport:* Sulkanen, pages 61-64 and Syrjala, pages 37-38. See Note **A**.

57. *Page 144 Hendrickson in Florida:* Savele Syrjala supplied me with the information about Hendrickson's real estate career in Florida.

58. *Page 144 Hendrickson's ironic fate:* See Kuusinen, Aino, *The Rings of Destiny* (New York: William Morrow and Company, Inc., 1974), pages 96-97. Aino Kuusinen was the estranged second wife of Otto Kuusinen, the head of Stalin's Terijoki government in the Winter War. Aino Kuusinen spent several years in Soviet prison camps.

59. *Page 145 The Apostle of Kalevala:* Sulkanen, pages 68-72 and Syrjala, pages 43-45. See Note **A.**

   Both Elis Sulkanen and F.J. Syrjala recognized the impact that Matti Kurikka had on the first generation Finns even though both journalists had sharp theoretical disagreements with Kurikka. Both, of course, considered the "Apostle of Kalevala" confused.

   The 1918 *Kalevainen* periodical (a Finnish-American publication for the February 28 celebration of Kalevala Day) shows the influence of Matti Kurikka. The lead article in that issue—*Is Kalevala a Sufficient Faith for the Finns*—could have been written by Matti Kurikka himself.

   A new book (in Finnish) was recently published about Matti Kurikka. See Kalemaa, Kalevi, *Matti Kurikka, Legenda jo Elaessaan* (A Legend While Still Alive) (Porvoo, Finland: WSOY, 1978).

60. *Page 147 Pastors Blomberg and Blomgren:* Arra, Esa, *Finnish Aid Society Imatra,* an essay in *A History of Finnish-American Organizations in Greater New York 1891-1976.* The history was a project of the Greater New York Finnish Bicentennial Planning Committee, Inc. The editors were Katri Ekman, Dr. John A. and Corinne Olli.

   The Blomberg and Blomgren story also appears in Sulkanen, page 56. See Note **A.**

61. *Page 152 free love in Sointula:* Much of my information comes from Anderson, Aili, *History of Sointula* (Sointula: Sointula Centennial Committee, 1969). The quote is on pages 11-12.

62. *Page 156 Social-Darwinism:* The best work on Social-Darwinism is Hofstader, Richard, *Social Darwinism in American Thought 1860-1915* (Philadelphia: University of Pennsylvania Press, 1945). Another good book (with which I find myself in some disagreement) is Bannister, Robert C., *Social Darwinism—Science and Myth in Anglo-American Thought* (Philadelphia: Temple University Press, 1979).

63. *Page 157 American Beauty Rose:* Hofstader, page 6. See **62.**

64. *Page 157 Unknown Soldier:* The Lahtinen quotes are from the English translation of *Unknown Soldier* by Väinö Linna (New York: G.T. Putnam's Sons, 1957), page 66.

65. *Page 158 Alexander Agassiz:* Quoted by Train, Arthur, *Yankee Lawyer— The Autobiography of Ephraim Tutt* (New York: Charles Scribner's Sons, 1944), page 213.

66. *Page 158 income of Carnegie and Rockefeller:* Galbraith, John Kenneth, *The Age of Uncertainty* (Boston: Houghton Mifflin Co., 1977), page 43.

67. *Pages 158-159 Pacific Mills in Lawrence:* Train, Arthur, page 217. See **65.** Kornbluh, page 166, claims that the Pacific Mills paid 148 percent in dividends to its shareholders for ten years. See **51.** Since a lot of those dividends came from the labor of little children, I can't refrain from quoting Sarah Cleghorn:

The factory stands so near the course
That almost every day
The little children at their work
Can see the men at play.

An attitude towards America's factories in the early 1900's is given by another of Vachel Lindsay's poems.

Factory Windows Are Always Broken

Factory windows are always broken.
Somebody's always throwing bricks,
Somebody's always heaving cinders,
Playing ugly yahoo tricks.

Factory windows are always broken.
Other windows are left alone.
No one throws through the chapel window
The bitter, snarling, derisive stone.

Factory windows are always broken.
Something or other is going wrong.
Something is rotten—I think in Denmark
End of the factory-window song.

Lindsay, Vachel, Collected Poems (New York: Macmillan Co., 1912).

68. *Page 159 children's death rate in Lawrence:* Kornbluh, page 169. See **51.**

69. *Page 159 Henry C. Frick:* The information about Henry C. Frick can be found in any good history of the American labor movement.

70. *Page 160 Couer d'Alene:* Sulkanen, page 24. See Note **A.**

71. *Pages 160-161 Ludlow Massacre:* Sulkanen, pages 124-125. See Note **A.** Additional information about the Ludlow Massacre can be found in any good history of the American labor movement.

72. *Page 162 Christian Fellowship:* Quoted by Weinstein, James, *The Decline of Socialism in America 1912-1925* (New York: Monthly Review Press, 1967), page 21.

73. *Page 163 John D. Rockefeller, Jr. in testifying:* Quoted by Ginger, Ray, *The Bending Cross* (New Brunswick, N.J.; Rutgers University Press, 1949), page 327.

74. *Page 164 Debs...larger audiences than President Taft:* The information about the size of Taft's and Deb's audiences is given by Ginger, page 282. See **73.**

75. *Pages 165-166 Socialist Party statistics:* See Weinstein's *The Decline of American Socialism.* See **72.**

76. *Page 166 Will Durant:* Durant, Will and Ariel, *Dual Autobiography* (New York: Simon and Schuster, 1977), page 402. "I am still a socialist, but with some cautions. I do not relish the control of economic lives by vast corporations. To keep the benefits and check the power of these mastadons I would favor public ownership of natural resources, including the land and all its minerals, fuels, and other subsoil wealth; also of transportation, banking, insurance, and medical and hospital care. I recognize that invention, enterprise, competition, and the profit motive are activating forces in any productive economy. I know that we must appeal to the acquisitive instincts if we are to get men and women to toil, invent, save, and invest..."

77. *Page 170 White Rose Temperance Society strike:* Sulkanen, page 125. See

Note **A**. Ross, pages 95-97. See **2**.
78. *Page 171 "Blacklists..."*: The quote is from Ross, pages 113-114. See **2**.
79. *Page 172 Finns are Mongolians:* Wargelin, page 166. See **11**. Ross, page 115. See **2**. Wasastjerna and Rosvall, *History of the Finns in Minnesota* (New York Mills: Finnish-American Historical Society, 1957), pages 476-477. The last named reference has the most complete story.
80. *Page 172 Herrankin Herra:* Syrjala, page 76. See Note **A**.
81. *Page 172 Martin Luther himself says:* (New York: The Century Company, 1911), page 257. McGiffert's biography is a sympathetic study of Luther. Surely every graduate from a Lutheran seminary was acquainted with Luther's attitude toward the peasants.
82. *Page 174 fiery followers of the red flag:* Quoted from a Hibbing newspaper by Ross, page 113. See **2**.
83. *Page 175 True Finn League:* Sulkanen, pages 141-142 and Syrjala, pages 72-78. See Note **A**.
   Syrjala states on page 77 that a leaflet (printed in Finnish) distributed in Hancock and Calumet read:
   > *Työmies* and its editors are agitating for anarchism and nihilism in the guise of socialism. Severi Alanne, the present editor of *Työmies*, was a bomber, robber, and the leader of a gang of murderers in Finland. He was forced to flee to America because he violated the provisions of his probation sentence.
   Severi Alanne was one of the most intellectual first generation Finnish-Americans. Mr. Alanne was the author of a classic book (in English) about cooperatives—*Fundamentals of Consumers Cooperatives.* He is also the author of a very popular Finnish-English dictionary, the one I enjoy using.
   Mr. Alanne was honored by being elected to the Finnish Literature Society and he was made an honorary member of the Eugene C. Fields Memorial Association in St. Louis (Missouri).
84. *Page 175 Christmas Eve Tragedy:* Sulkanen, pages 131-134. See Note **A**. Most Finnish-American writers call the tragedy *The Italian Hall Tragedy.* I think this is wrong. The notoriously newsworthy fact about the tragedy is that it occurred on Christmas Eve, not that it occurred in the Italian Hall. Those strikers' children, incidentally, did not belong in any hall, especially a hall in a commercial district, on Christmas Eve, during the tensions of a bitter strike. They should have been celebrating Christmas in a Christian church.
85. *Page 176 Michigan State militia:* Ross, pages 129-130. See **2**.
85. *Page 177 Mountain Rose Temperance Society victory:* Sulkanen, page 31. See Note **A**.
87. *Page 181 shareholder statistics:* Statistice, such as I have quoted, can be found in any *Value Line* (stock market weekly report. The figures constantly change but seldom does any company listed have more employees than shareholders.
88. *Page184 illanviettoja:* The New York Finnish socialist local held more *illanvietoja* (informal meetings devoted to lectures, debates, poetry reading, and chamber music) and its drama group staged more plays to larger audiences than any other Finnish organization in the United States. This New York branch of the Finnish Socialist Federation also collected and donated more material assistance for Finland in her several times of great need than any other local group or any organization in the United States.

Eugene Victor Debs was named the 1920 Socialist Presidential candidate in this local's Finn Hall—the Fifth Avenue Hall. Debs, although he was in a prison cell during the campaign because he opposed America's participation in the First World War, polled almost a million votes—about 3% of the total cast). See Sulkanen, page 349. See Note **A**.

89.   Page 190 the Finn Hall in Weirton (West Virginia): The raid on Weirton Finn Hall made the front page of the *New York Times* (1919).

RAID FINN REDS
AND FORCE 150
TO KISS THE FLAG

Weirton, W. Va., Oct. 7—More than 150 men, declared by the police authorities to have been members of the Red Guard of Finland, were rounded up here today, marched to the public square of Weirton, forced to kneel and kiss the American flag and were driven out of town by police and deputies.

Seven of the men, suspected of being leaders of the radicals, after kissing the flag, were taken to the county jail at New Cumberland. Later, all but one were released. He is being held for investigation by the Federal authorities.

A big American flag was strung across the street over the heads of the prisoners while another flag was used for the kissing. Most of the captured were Finns and they were told in their native tongue that they must kiss the flag or remain in custody. Protests came from many, but they were in vain. Some voluntarily took hold of the flag and buried their faces in it. The prisoners were then informed that they must leave the town.

Today's raid was the culmination of a series of events occurring since the early days of the war, when each of the men arrested refused to purchase Liberty Bonds. They were also the chief agitators in the present steel strike here.

In the literature seized were 5,000 cards bearing the imprint of the socialist flag and the following inscription: "This flag is clean and so is [sic] our principles. May it wave over the universe."

Emil Makinisla, leader of the party here known as the Finnish Socialist Party of America was tarred and feathered at Woodlawn, Pennsylvania, several months ago.

I was about 15 when I first read about the tribulations of those 150 Weirton Finnish-American socialists who had the "gall" to lend their hall to the striking steel workers. And it resulted in the first and only time I baited *Äiti* about religion.

"*Äiti*," I asked in a taunting voice, "Where was Jesus when those men were taken to the town square? Why did He stand by doing nothing? Surely, He was opposed to the actions of those hoodlums."

"Jesus is love, Reino," *Äiti* replied instantly. "Jesus spreads love. I'm sure He was with those unfortunate men trying to give them courage to withstand their humiliating ordeal."

"Jesus, I'm sure," she continued, "also asked His Father in Heaven to forgive those who sinned. Remember when He suffered His own ordeal, He asked His Father to forgive those who had trespassed against Him because they didn't know what they were doing."

I like *Äiti's* feeling much better than that of Reverend John Wargelin,

250

President of the Lutheran Suomi Synod from 1951-1955 and President of the Lutheran Suomi College Seminary from 1919-1927. He wrote in his book *The Americanization of the Finn* (See **11**):

> ...Here again, as is so often the case, the sensational papers play up the negative activities of foreign groups in a strong light, while they are entirely silent, on the other hand, concerning their positive achievements...We...refer to an incident reported in the *Boston American* in 1920 [sic]. This paper came out with a glaring headline on the front page, "150 Finns Made to Kneel Down and Kiss the Flag"...
>
> We admit that there may have been a group of Finnish socialists in Weirton whose type of Americanism might be suspect by certain other types of Americans. But why cast a reflection on the whole nationality because of the deeds or opinions of a few?"

I think Reverend Wargelin should have protested the treatment of those 150 Finnish-Americans even though he disagreed with their socialist views. The American Flag, after all, symbolizes the spirit of Voltaire: "I may disagree with what you say, but I'll defend to the death your right to say it."

Who understood Americanism best: the Weirton police hoodlums, Reverend Wargelin, or those American Finns who were trying to build a steel workers union?

90. *Page 198 Mother Jones:* See Truman, Margaret, *Women of Courage* (New York: Morrow, 1976) for an excellent short biography of this remarkable woman.

91. *Page 199 strikers' children moved out of Lawrence:* Margaret Sanger, the pioneer birth control advocate, accompanied a group of children to New York City. She testified later, "Out of 119 children [in the group], only four had underwear on..." See Kornbluh, page 161. See **51**. Conlin, Joseph R., *Big Bill Haywood and the Radical Union Movement* (Syracuse: Syracuse University Press, 1969) is an excellent study of the IWW.

92. *Page 201 Samuel Gompers:* Adamic, Louis, *Dynamite* (Gloucester, Mass: Smith Pub., 1934), page 188.

93. *Page 202 Negaunee (Michigan) Finnish Wobblies:* Sulkanen, pages 174-177. See Note **A**. The issue in the power struggle between the Negaunee IWW adherents and the socialists was the way the *ravintola* (cafeteria) was operated. The real issues in a political power struggle are often hidden.

94. *Page 202 Finnish Wobblies:* Sulkanen, pages 189-208 and Syrjala, pages 166-183. See Note **A**. Syrjala's essay is quite partisan and, hence, unfriendly to the IWW. The bicentennial *Old Friends-Strong Ties* has an excellent section on the Finnish wobblies, pages 216-217 and 221-222. See **2**.

95. *Page 205 Land, Peace, and Bread:* My favorite history of the Bolshevik Revolution is Deutscher, Issac, *Stalin, A Political Biography* (New York: Vintage Books, 1949). Mr. Deutscher states that Stalin, in person, delivered the news of Finland's independence to the Finnish Social Democratic Congress. He suggests this act may have been the reason that Russia did not incorporate Finland into the Soviet Union after the Winter War. See page 447 of *Stalin, A Political Biography*.

96. *Page 210 Events between the summer of 1929:* Dr. Michael Karni, a third generation Finnish-American, has made a detailed study of the struggle between the Finnish co-ops and the Communist International. His essay

Struggle on the Cooperative Front: The Separation of Central Cooperative Wholesale From Communism, 1929-30 was published in the *Finnish Experience in the Western Lake Region: New Perspectives* (Turku, Finland: Institute for Migration, 1975). Karni's essay is on pages 186-201.

97. *Page 212 Rochdale pioneers:* My story of the Rochdale pioneers is based on a pamphlet written by Stuart Chase, *The Story of Toad Lane*, published by the Cooperative League of USA in 1930.

98. *Page 215 Cooperative Democracy:* Warbasse, James Peter, *Cooperative Democracy* (New York: Harper & Brothers, 1936). The class statement struggle is on page 85.

99. *Page 216 Finnish cooperatives:* Three examples of Finnish histories which *do not* credit the Finnish-American socialists with nurturing the Finnish-American cooperative movement are Kolehmainen, John I., *A History of the Finns* (New York Mills, Minnesota: Ohio Finnish-American Historical Society, 1977); *Finnish-American Organizations in Greater New York* by Ekman, Olli, and Olli (see **60**); and *Economic Activities of the Finns in the United States* (an essay in *Old Friends-Strong Ties* (see **2**).

   I delivered groceries in a pushcart for the Harlem branch of the Brooklyn-based Finnish Cooperative Trading Association (called Finco by its patrons and members) for about six months in 1937-1938. My pushcart stopped in front of the handsome socialist Finn hall, The Fifth Avenue Hall, at least once a day. Never did I make deliveries to any other Finnish organizations. Almost all the customers, as in the other Finnish co-ops I worked in, were members of or sympathetic to social-democratic organizations.

100. *Page 216 Swedish cooperatives:* Lundberg, W.T., *Consumer Owned: Sweden's Cooperative Democracy* (Palo Alto, California: Consumers Cooperative Publishing Association, 1978), pages 49-50.

101. *Page 218 last word:* Warbasse, page 25. See **98**.

102. *Page 218 Finnish a second language:* Kolehmainen, page 214. See **99**.

252

The Finnish socialist hall in Newport, New Hampshire around 1913. An attempt was made by Dartmouth College to save this hall which was burned down a few years ago.

The Virginia (Minnesota) Finnish socialist opera house. This Finn hall was considered the most beautiful building in Virginia at the time it was built.

The Finnish temperance hall in Rocklin (California). When the Finnish hall was built about 50% of Rocklin's population had a Finnish background.

The Huuhkaja brass band of Quincy (Mass.). The band was sponsored by the Veli Osasto, a branch of the Finnish Socialist Federation.

The Finnish Hall in Conneaut (Ohio) was built in 1899. The hall, now a community center, was called the Kilpi Hall by the Finns.

The Waukegan (Illinois) Finnish Osasto hall (1910)

Finnish Labor Temple, Astoria (1915)

The members of the Mullan (Idaho) Temperance Society in front of their Finn hall (1910). This temperance hall was converted into the Mullan Finnish socialist hall.

The Finnish Socialist Federation hall in Brooklyn (New York) which was built in 1910

The Finn hall in Brainerd, Minnesota

Työmies Building, Hancock, Michigan (1912)

Imatra, the oldest Finn hall, recently celebrated its 90th birthday. The hall is at 740 40th Street in Brooklyn, N.Y.

The Hibbing (Minnesota) Finnish Socialist hall

Finnish hall, Ironwood, Michigan

The Finn hall in Weirton, West Virginia
before the Finns left Weirton.